He Leadeath Me

Elizabeth Boyd

World rights reserved. This book or any portion thereof may not be copied or reproduced in any form or manner whatever, except as provided by law, without the written permission of the publisher, except by a reviewer who may quote brief passages in a review.

The author assumes full responsibility for the accuracy and interpretation of the Ellen White quotations cited in this book. Unless otherwise indicated, all scripture quotations are taken from the King James Version of the Bible.

———————————————

Copyright © 2021 Elizabeth Boyd
Copyright © 2021 TEACH Services, Inc.
ISBN-13: 978-1-4796-1197-3 (Paperback)
ISBN-13: 978-1-4796-1198-0 (ePub)
Library of Congress Control Number: 2020920230

Amplified Bible, Classic Edition (AMPC). Copyright © 1954, 1958, 1962, 1964, 1965, 1987 by The Lockman Foundation.

New King James Version® (NKJV). Copyright © 1982 by Thomas Nelson. Used by permission. All rights reserved.

Table of Contents

Foreword 5
I.   Babe 6
II. Safari Survival Stories..91
III. What's a Nice Girl Like You Doing in a Place Like This? 193
IV. Journey of the Heart 240

Foreword

To my own dear sister,

Your book is not an autobiography as I thought it would be…

It is an exquisite case study in what it means to be a single woman in a world that demands achievement concurrent with a mate and children.

So many churches are not quite sure what to do with a woman, or a man, that is unmarried by choice as though matrimony must be accomplished before anything else.

This book tells about an unmarried woman in a small New England community that is loved and respected without pretense as she lives her life on her own terms.

This is what community really is, what is does, and how to build it.

Study this book.

—*The author's sister*

Babe

Table of Contents

1. Babe 9
2. Babe with Granddaddy and Mama Frankie 12
3. Babe, Meet Your Father 16
4. Neighbor Lady 18
5. Babe's Dollies 19
6. Young Lady in Harm's Way 22
7. Young Lady in School 25
8. Third Grade Mascot 29
9. Music to Her Ears 30
10. Land of the Rising Sun 33
11. Miss Mondy/Mischief and Summer in Japan 35
12. The Teenager in Los Angeles 42
13. Teenager on the Farm 44
14. Long Copper Braids 46
15. College/The Murderer 49
16. From Under the Dark Cloud! 51
17. Volcano Erupts 53
18. Upperclassman 55
19. Senior/She Stumbles 57
20. The Rookie PE Teacher on Her Own 60
21. Sophomore School Teacher 64
22. Ask Your Mother … In Love? 67

23. Loma Linda School of Physical Therapy 70
24. Graduation and Another Pivotal Point 73
25. Where's the Next "Home?" 75
26. The New Grad, New Dreams 78
27. Costly Dream/The Old New England Farmhouse 80
28. Learning to "Neighbor with You!" 83
29. "Costly" at the Old New England Farmhouse 88

1. Babe

Sue

They met their first year at Southern Junior College. Talmadge had already "boot-strapped" his way through nursing and was working his way through premed by doing night duty as a special-duty nurse at the nearby hospital. One evening, he walked by the volleyball court as the college girls were playing. A petite little freshman with long, silky, black hair and bright green eyes caught his eye. *Hmm!* he wondered to himself. *Someday, I will need a woman in my life. But right now I can't afford one! I don't have time for one! But she is so vivacious and energetic! I don't want to lose track of her!*

It was a year later, in July, that Talmadge and Sue made the vow to become a family. Talmadge and his mother, Mama Frankie, drove from Griffin, Georgia, where he grew up, to Florida, where she grew up, to see if Sue would be his bride. He told his mother to bring her best dress just in case. He would borrow a suit from his father-in-law if he needed it!

Honeymoon night:

"When did you stop beating your wife" is not just a joke! That's what the male was to do on the wedding night! It's the way the male was to establish dominance! Show her who's boss!

Sue told the story at all the dinner parties for a few years, but apparently, it became obvious that the story didn't please the rest of the guests! They knew from experience that this is what the fathers told their sons they should do to establish dominance in their relationship! Especially if the male is only two inches taller than the woman!

The honeymoon was in a little treehouse on Daytona Beach, Florida, the beach Sue and her family always visited for their short vacations. The story has it that the first morning after the wedding, Talmadge couldn't find but one sock! He and his little bride searched every place in the tiny treehouse, but no second sock could be found! Finally, he decided to wear another pair! When he took the odd sock off, there was the mate right under it.

Almost immediately, they packed the little Model T and headed for Loma Linda, California, where he had been accepted for medical school. Sue got a job in food service. At least they wouldn't starve. They rented a room in the home of a widow in the village and set up housekeeping. There wasn't much to set up. They bought a little card table from the used furniture shop on Highway 99.

Somehow, God supplied their meager needs with Sue working in Food Service and Talmadge taking some special-duty assignments at night. Becoming a doctor and making the hometown folks proud of their boy could have had some weight in that choice, too.

Then one evening, Sue put a little white tablecloth on the card table and scrambled his eggs just the way he liked them. She even found some wildflowers to put on the table. As they were eating, she smiled at him. How proud she was of his achievements! He was so focused, so determined to be a doctor. Really, nothing else seemed to matter. What would he tell the hometown folks if hometown boy failed?

"Talmadge," she began, "we are now a family of three." She blushed.

"What? Are you pregnant? Oh no! How will I ever get through medical school if there's a baby! Without you working I'll never make it!

Oh, my Father! It's taking every penny I make already! Why didn't you prevent this! Oh! My Father! My Father!" He stood up and paced the floor.

Sue dissolved into a puddle of tears! "Maybe my folks will take the baby," she sobbed.

Talmadge's voice could be heard three houses down! "Your father has never made a decent living! You and your sister would have starved if you were not living next to the orange grove! Oh. My Father!"

"Maybe my own folks would take it. My sister is expecting her first one just three months before this one is due. She and her husband will be living with the folks in my home town in Griffin, Georgia. Maybe Mama could handle twins. Oh, my Father!"

What goes on when a child is conceived, but not wanted? Does the helpless babe feel the pain of rejection or abortion? Only God knows.

There is the story of a twin boy and girl. At birth they were put in separate incubators. The little girl failed to thrive. Her vital signs were critical. One of the neonatal nurses decided to put the little girl in the incubator with her twin brother. The vitals improved, and one of the nurses took a picture of the two sleeping together. The twin brother had his little arm across his twin sister's shoulders—and they slept!

But what happens when tragedy strikes after the child is old enough to be aware? There is a story of a little girl who was hiding behind the couch when the father shot and killed her mother. The father was taken to jail, and the little girl was put into foster care. The foster parents were kind, Christian people and took the child with them to church. When the Sabbath School teacher showed the children the picture of Jesus, she asked if them if they knew who He is. The little girl put up her hand and said, "I know who that is! It's the Man who held me in His arms when my daddy shot my mommy dead!"

Think of that! How kind, how good God is to us! How faithful!

2. Babe with Granddaddy and Mama Frankie

It was a hot, humid day in August when Sue delivered her firstborn at the big hospital in Orlando, Florida. The nurse quickly wrapped the scrawny little girl in a pink receiving blanket and took her to the neonatal nursery. At feeding time they took her to her mother with a bottle of formula. The mother did like all little girls do with their new dollies, she unwrapped the little pink blanket and took all the clothes off the Babe to see if she had all her body parts. The mother was horrified! Instead of the beautiful little doll she was expecting, she saw this scrawny little six-pound, five-ounce girl completely covered with soft black hair! She looked more like a tiny monkey than what the mother was expecting. She was not allowed to nurse because the little 112-pound mother would be leaving for Loma Linda shortly to go back to work in the hospital food service department to help her hubby through school.

Babe went home with her mother for a few days until her father's mother could come on the Greyhound bus and take her to Griffin, Georgia. But nobody in the little one-bedroom house in Maitland, Florida, knew what to feed a baby who wasn't nursing, so they gave her canned milk with honey, not knowing that a child should not have honey until age two! Little Babe had diarrhea. But the show must go on! It was a stressful trip on the Greyhound bus from Maitland, Florida, to Griffin, Georgia. Babe was sick the whole trip with diarrhea, and the whole bus full of people knew it! The stench was terrible, and the little bottom was raw. Nothing was familiar. The Babe wept and could not be comforted all the way to Griffin. Maybe it was well that the bus was filled with tobacco smoke. Does smoke neutralize smelly diapers of a very sick little "throw-away" baby girl?

Poor Mama Frankie.

When they arrived at what would be home for the next three years, the Babe was still sick. Immediately, the grandmother sent the granddaddy to the grocery store for fresh cow's milk. Then they took out an insurance policy on the child because if she died, it would help pay the father's school bill!

The granddaddy was a postal carrier. It made for a more secure meal ticket, for sure. But the aging granddaddy had to walk all day from one house to another. In the cool of the day, he would sit on the big wooden porch swing and rock the Babe. She could smell his scent, feel his body, and hear his strong, gentle voice as they rocked to and fro in the evenings. As they rocked, the Granddaddy would sing to the scrawny little babe. "In the sweet by and by, ... we shall meet on that beautiful shore."

In the cool of the day, he would sit on the big wooden porch swing and rock the Babe

Granddaddy Boyd in San Bernardino, California

The two of them bonded as family.

Who could know that twenty years later, the roles would be reversed? As he lay in the hospital bed, his mind ravaged by dementia, his Scottish-blue eyes would turn toward her and smile as she sang that same hymn to the old man with the fringe of white hair around his bald head. He looked at her with all the love in his aged heart and smiled and said it again, "You ah the sweetest thing"!"

The Babe and the baby cousin would sit on Mama Frankie's lap and play with Mama Frankie's soft, flabby arms. At bath time Mama Frankie would put some warm water in the galvanized washtub in the back yard and let both babies play in it. Both little girls loved playing in the water, but when the breeze came up, their little lips would tum blue, and their teeth would chatter until someone would rescue them.

The little girls loved the pretty colored buttons in the button drawers in Mama Frankie's treadle sewing machine. There was a button drawer on either side of their grandmother. What beautiful moments the grandma had there at the sewing machine making pretty little dresses for her pretty little girls while they played in the pretty little buttons in the button drawer.

Before either of the little girls could talk, the songs Mama would sing while the little girls played at her side were riveted in their young minds. Babe can still hear her sweet soprano voice singing as she lived her life for her family. A favorite is, "'Tis love that makes us happy, 'Tis love that smoothes the way; It helps us mind, it makes us kind to others every day."

Before they could walk, they were chanting, "God is love; we're His little children."

Godly love is another core value the little girls learned at Mama Frankie's knee by the button drawer in the little house in the cotton mill town of Griffin, Georgia. God still molds young minds by songs and stories. The words to a song will find its way into the mind of a demented child of God as they near the journey's end.

The three years spent with Mama Frankie and Granddaddy were a blessing. Mama Frankie would fold their little hands for them, each finger in place, then say to them, "Say blessin'." The little girls would repeat after Mama Frankie each word: "Good Lord, make us thankful for these and all Thy blessings. We ask it in Jesus' name, Amen."

Today thankfulness is a core value of both women. Songs come easily to the two girls as they harmonize together. Life was peaceful there in Georgia, and the little girls were happy together like twins, until …

3. Babe, Meet Your Father

The Babe was about three years old when the front screen door slammed, and there stood a stranger. The little girls were terrified! The stranger called to the Babe, "Come here to me! I'm your father!"

Immediately, the little girls started running to the Granddaddy. But the stranger shouted, "Don't you run away from me!"

"Stand back, old man," he shouted to the Granddaddy as he tried to scoop the Babe into his protective arms.

"Put her down right now! She must learn who is boss!'"

There was no protection! The stranger spanked her little legs so hard she thought she would bleed. "Never run the other way when your father calls you."

The next morning the Father loaded the Babe and the Mother into his 1941 Mercury and left for the Father's new job as a doctor for the army in Tennessee. That first night was terrifying. They stayed in a stuffy little room in a "Tourist Camp.'" But in the middle of the night, a big bear came into the room where the Babe slept at the foot of her mother and father's bed. The bear snorted loudly and rhythmically. Would he eat her? She didn't know. Where was the little cousin, Gwen?

They had always been together. The Babe was afraid to cry. The bear would find her!

Finally, the "bear" turned on his side and stopped snoring!

The Babe slept till the sun came streaming in the little window of the tourist cabin.

What next?

4. Neighbor Lady

It snowed the day the little family moved into the little house on the army base in Tennessee. There wasn't much to move in!

The dining table was only a card table made of cardboard. Everything was strange. But there was a knock at the door. A grandmotherly woman with a blue apron and a big smile asked if the Babe could come next door to her house while the movers brought in what there was of the household goods.

What joy! "Today is February 14," the kind woman smiled. "This is Valentine's day, and we can make some cookies!"

Flour, butter, sugar, egg! Why bother to cook them! The Babe ate her share of the cookie dough! There was enough dough to make fancy shapes with the cookie cutter! But they did improve over cookie dough when they came out of the oven. The nice next-door neighbor let the Babe help decorate the little sugar cookies with red hots.

The kitchen was warm, and there was the smell of cinnamon and molasses. The little girl drew drowsy, and curled up on the rug like a kitten and slept!

May God bless all the neighbors who are sensitive to a little girl's need and bake His cookies for Him! And so life moved on until …

5. Babe's Dollies

June Bug

But life wasn't supposed to keep moving on! Every new house was the place where the little family lived, until a few months later, it was time to pack up and move again. Pets, yes, but the Babe watched as the father put them all to sleep one by one before moving on to the next place.

    The moving from place to place left its mark on the Babe. Some of her values were skewed. Life-long relationships were lost in the shuffle. Did no one understand that there is a bond with a pet that is akin to the bond with family? The little cousin was gone. Granddaddy was gone.

Mama Frankie was gone. Mama Sue was just another one of the mamas. The Babe remembers making friends with one of the father's office nurses, then telling her Mama Sue that the office nurse would be a good choice for the Babe's next mother!

But the little dollies? The Babe put them to sleep one by one in a box and woke them again when the family arrived at the new house. June Bug was the oldest of the dolls. She was the one Aunt Lizzy gave her on the Babe's first birthday. June Bug was allowed to go with the Babe to all the new places. She was a comfort when everything else was strange. But nobody seemed to understand that the dollies were her family!

One of the moves required that all the dollies except June Bug be put to sleep, and the family would be back and pick them up sometime. They never returned. The dollies were sold with the house and all its contents. Could it be that there was something in the Child Growth and Development class in medical school that the father still needed to learn?

Who would know that God had that on the father's curriculum for later? What God does, He does well!

But those first three years with Granddaddy and Mama Frankie and the little cousin, Gwen? The Babe found some security there. Somehow, they kept reappearing in the movie from time to time.

The circle of life brought the Babe back to Georgia again. The family lived in Atlanta, near enough to Griffin to accommodate frequent visits from Mama Frankie and Granddaddy and visits from Gwen with her mom and dad!

The little girls would take their dollies into the bathtub with them and teach them to swim and baptize them, if necessary. Poor June Bug. One day in plain sight of the little girls, June Bug went blind! Her bright blue eyes rolled back into her head. Alas! But June Bug was still lovable. With age and sunshine, June Bug developed a disease called leprosy. Her delicate fingers and toes were the first to disappear. Then the arms and legs crumbled. The last to be eaten away was the rubber back that seemed to be more sensitive than the abdomen. One day June Bug took a tumble, and her fine ceramic head broke to smithereens! Poor June Bug! With only the little rubber abdomen left, the Babe carefully wrapped her in swaddling clothes and put her in a "safe place."

But one day, while the Babe was gone, the mother cleaned out the "safe place," and June Bug was cremated in the incinerator. The Babe wept. June Bug was all she had left that had been hers "forever." Neighbors had to be left behind; Granddaddy and the rocking chair were gone; the little cousin was gone; pets all put to sleep; now June Bug had been sacrificed. Was there nothing sacred? Nothing! But somewhere in the recesses of the Babe's mind was her grandfather's voice singing softly, "Be not dismayed whate'er betide. God will take care of you. Beneath His wings of love abide, God will take care of you."

But where was He that day in the park when …?

6. Young Lady in Harm's Way

One day, there was a knock on the screen door, and looking down, the mother saw the small boy from next door. Buck was his name. His skin was nicely tanned from playing in the Georgia sunshine; his little feet were bare. "Can the Babe come out and play?"

Buck and the Babe trotted off together to the gully, where they could dig in the sand along the bank and make roads for their "dinky toys."

The sun was warm, and they were intent on making their little "town" when they heard a man clear his throat. "I lost my little dog. I need some help finding him. Little boy, I think if you stay here, this little girl and I can go into the woods and drive him back to you, and you can catch him for me."

Of course, they would help.

When they were out of sight, the tall, gray-haired stranger found a dark place deep in the woods. Before the Babe could cry, the old man clamped his hand across her mouth and told her to let him see her private places.

The memory is frightening. He had a knife and told her that if she struggled, he would kill her. Innocence was lost! The little Babe became a woman. His breath smelled of alcohol and stale tobacco. After he raped her, then would he kill her? Time stood still. When he got up, he said, "If you tell anybody, I'll kill you and your mother and your father."

The Babe walked slowly away like a mouse trying to escape a cat. Then, at the top of the rise, she broke into a run.

But, nothing had changed at home on this quiet Sunday afternoon. The mother was still ironing. The father was reading the newspaper. The little Babe ran a tub full of water and tried to get clean. But things had changed... changed forever. The only one who knew her secret was her little cousin, Gwen.

The trusted cousin never said a word to anyone … ever!

Yes, innocence was lost, lost forever. But in its place, there were other priceless gifts that God gives that can only be received when innocence is lost. There are gifts that come only through walking through landmines and booby traps that the adversary thinks up. There is a caution that comes through fear of losing life itself. There is a distrust that God can use to protect His broken children, especially the helpless Babe, who tried to stay under the radar of a cruel and abusive adult. There is a sense of privacy that is a protection to a young lady when entering puberty. Sometimes, a violation of this privacy rushes a young girl into premature adult experiences and promiscuity. Do a grandmother's prayers ever expire? There is no easy road to wisdom! It was years before the young Lady learned to appreciate physical closeness and caressing. Was her reluctance to touch the reason God choose a career path of the medical profession for His young Lady?

God was actually there when the young Lady needed Him? The old man never used his knife!

"God will take care of you," she remembered the granddaddy's song. But where was He when she lay in bed every night trying to get the memory out of her thoughts. Today, she still doesn't really understand.

She lay there alone night after night, wondering if he would find her here and kill her!

But God hadn't gone anywhere! This experience was a sacred trust to be used to empathize with other broken people! It was a most expensive perfume from her Father to be used to glorify His name.

7. Young Lady in School

The young Lady was not surprised to hear her father announce another move. This time it was across the entire United States to a town called Hermiston, Oregon. She had never been out West. Would they have moss on the trees like Florida or cotton fields like Georgia? How could she know there would be desert and sage brush as far as the eye could see. But, at least, it was far away from the frightening memories. There were so many things happening so fast that there was hardly time to think.

The little '41 Mercury followed the old truck that was loaded with household goods all the way across the Great Divide. Hermiston. She liked it! She loved it! She thought the family would stay there forever.

The young Lady was all of age eight that year and started school there. It was in a one-room school house in the basement of the little white church. There were about ten kids. Two of the kids had flunked first grade, so all three of the students did second grade together. Friends! Would they be "forever friends?" Only time would tell.

Mornings were cold there on the edge of the high desert. Having to get up and out of bed and get dressed in time to run the two blocks to school was a new experience for the young Lady. There was no longer time to watch the ants carry tasty morsels to the home underground, or to lie on her back and see faces in the clouds. No! School had started. Now there would always be something chasing her!

Recess was a new kind of fun. They played Red Rover! It's a wonder they didn't all have broken arms. There were two teams lined up opposite each other with their hands clasped to prevent the other team from breaking through.

"Red Rover, Red Rover, let 'Shirley' come over!" The team would send someone to run madly to break through the other line. The big boys were rough. No pity for a young Lady from back East!

There were horses nearby, too. The young Lady knew all about horses, she thought. After all, her uncle Felix, the mid-western farmer, let her sit on Old Doc when the little family stopped at the farm on the way out West. Uncle Felix lifted her into the saddle, tied the reins of the bridle in a knot, and threw them over the saddle horn. Old Doc roved over the massive, unfenced front yard, helping himself to the luscious green grass as he showed the young Lady all the best clover on the farm!

Yes, she knew all about horses! Now, the horses were in the fenced area next to the school. She could pet them and talk to them, but alas, that was all. They belonged to somebody else! Maybe someday she would own her own horse. Just maybe?

The little Boyd family expanded that year. His name was Paul Pai Wong. He was in the playpen when they arrived.

Paul Pai Wong

When he saw the family come in, he held up his little arms and cried, "Mama!" How could they resist the liquid brown eyes with big tears spilling over and onto his plump cheeks! The young Lady knew all about babies, too. Babies came and babies went the same as pets and houses and friends and mamas and granddaddies. The young Lady didn't know this little fellow would be her brother for life! There had been other babies that would come and stay for a while, but like everybody else, they were gone about the time they could say "Mama." Who could know that fifty years later, the young Lady would conduct Paul's funeral?

The young Lady now had a bedroom all to herself in Hermiston! It was a big, empty, attic room in the big white house the family bought when they arrived in Hermiston. But the attic was a scary place all alone at night! There was only a string to pull on for the light bulb in the center of the ceiling. The stairway up from the kitchen was dark. Would the tall, gray-haired stranger find her? Would he hide under the bed?

If the little cousin had been there, they could have faced life together like they did at Mama Frankie's house. But no, there was no one to turn to—or was there? One of the memory verses the little girls learned at Mama Frankie's knee was, "I will never leave thee or forsake thee!"

Nobody knew why the little salty circles were on the white pillowcase every morning. Did anyone even notice? The song says, "He giveth more grace when the burdens grow greater, He sendeth more strength when the labors increase."

There were not many places in a small town in Oregon for a young schoolteacher to rent in 1946. There was a little oneroom apartment on the back of the lot where the big white house was. That was what was available for single women. As teachers came and went, they stayed with the doctor's office nurse in that little room. During the thirteen months that the family lived in Hermiston, five teachers rolled through Hermiston to teach at the little one-room school house that was connected to the church! The teacher and the office nurse would often invite the young Lady to spend the night with them. It was a relief to get away from the heavy-handed father who was already practicing how to beat his two-year-old son. Studies show that when one child in the family is abused, the other children also feel the abuse as if it were their own.

Not realizing the family dysfunction, the young Lady told her Mama Sue that she wanted the kind young office nurse to be her next mother.

Silence!

The hospital in Hermiston was also a wood frame building like the big white house where they lived. There were lots of trees planted around it. The young Lady thought it was beautiful! Once a week the yard would be flooded with water. Water, of course, was to wade in and to float boats!

> *Nobody knew why the little salty circles were on the white pillowcase every morning. Did anyone even notice?*

Sometimes the young Lady would walk to the hospital and watch her father do surgery! The young Lady would circulate in and out of the operating room even while the nurse was dripping ether. There was no other hospital for miles and miles there by the Columbia River in Eastern Oregon. The father was home less and less. The sick continued to come to his office at the hospital more and more, but the people who needed his care were not able to pay! What was a young doctor to do who had school bills to pay and a growing family to feed and clothe and shelter?

A couple months into her third grade school year, the father instructed his little family to pack their belongings yet again. The young Lady had no idea where they were going this time. The father was not with them, but they could stay with Pop and Mama Lucas in their one-bedroom-plus-attic home in California, until they found out where they would be. They would only be able to take one of the dollies. The rest of them must be put to sleep in the boxes until the family could come back later and get them. Yes, of course, they would come back soon and pick them up. They were her friends. They would just sleep for a little while; they would pick them up later. From the time the young Lady went to live with her mother and father, it seemed that there was no returning to pick up anything, even the pretty rocks she would find along the railroad track when they went for a walk had to stay there until they "came back someday." They never came back the same way!

Now the family rolled out of the town again, never to return. Meanwhile, the big white house with the scary attic was sold along with the contents. All the young Lady had left was one dolly and memories of the ones left behind.

8. Third Grade Mascot

Christmas time came and a new school. This time it was San Bernardino, California. The children were preparing for the Christmas program. Every day, they practiced the songs and poems and stories.

But the children in the third grade at the new school looked at the stranger from Oregon as if she were more of a mascot than a person. The older girls locked her out of the bathroom. The walk home was a whole mile. And when she tried to walk home, she got lost! At last, she just melted down into a puddle of tears and pee. Would they never move on to the next place?

Sometimes, one must learn to play opposites. Don't do what you see modeled! Don't do to other kids what your peers did to you. Select your friends. Learn to recognize the traits in others that you would want to copy. Not every person who comes into your life is worth spending your time on! But there are truly some who are "forever friend" material. The Book says, "forsake not your friend or your father's friend!"

But there was a happy song the kids were learning to sing for the Christmas program! And every evening when the star appeared over the top of the neighbors' house, the young Lady took her little brother by the hand and led him into the backyard, and while looking into the night sky, they would sing that little song together as they stood there in the starlight with their arms about each other.

"Star of the East, O Bethlehem's star, Guiding us on to heaven afar.
Sorrow and grief are lull'd by thy light,
Thy hope of each mortal in death's lonely night."

Some songs are like friends. Keep them in the mind to be called from memory when God tickles the brain cells.

"Oh star that leads to God above!
Whose rays are peace and joy and love"
It was a relief to move on to the next place.

9. Music to Her Ears

Mom and Pop Lucas

It was the year 1948. The Second World War was over. The father took a job in Japan. The next place was a very temporary place. It was a little garage apartment where the mother, the little brother, and the young Lady stayed for three months until the father could find a house on the army base in Japan for the little family.

The young Lady had saved her money for a horse. Nickels and dimes began to mount up. There were more than one hundred fifty dollars now!

There was a horse down at the end of the back street! She belonged to the kid in second grade. Wonder? Would they keep another horse in the little pasture and buy hay?

The young Lady's Grandpa Lucas shopped for a horse for the young Lady, and there was an inexpensive one for thirty-five dollars. The army saddle, the halter, and the bridle came with it! Eureka! Finally, she owned her own horse. In her mind she was riding through the sagebrush in the hills behind the school there in Hermiston, Oregon.

But there were problems! The little thing wasn't "broke," but the nice lady that sold her said there would be no problem. Her grandchildren had been sitting on her while the gram led the horse! No problem? The young Lady's mother was terrified of horses. The young Lady knew only that she, at last, owned a horse. What more could one want?

Wake-up call: The little horse had never been taught to stand tied! How was the young Lady going to get the bit in her horse's mouth when she didn't even know how to stand tied! Well, the little horse, Rita, by name, was wearing a halter and had a lead rope. Simple! Just tie the horse to the handle of the car door while you push the bit into the horse's mouth! About three seconds later, the car door was pulled off, the mother was in tears, and the young Lady discovered a very important one of life's lessons. The little horse loved raisins. Raisins were sticky and would stay on the bit while the bit went into her mouth!

Sometimes this reward system works with other than a young Lady and a young horse. Try it sometime!

Does God sometimes answer a young Lady's deepest longings?

There was enough money left to buy the blue and white bicycle she wanted! It had big fat tires and was somewhat cumbersome, but that was what they were selling at Sears at that time. The bicycle made a good "hand-me-down" for the younger siblings and was a friend in the family until, well, what happens to nice loyal bicycles when they get old.

But the last purchase of all was the most precious, lifetime friend. She called him, "Mr. French." Mr. French went everywhere with the young Lady. A second, third, or fourth-hand French horn is a good starter instrument for a ten-year-old! Not! There was no French horn carrying case with it! At length, Mama Lucas saved her money and was able to purchase a shiny new Conn "double horn" from the horn teacher complete with carrying case lined with soft, living blue. When there is an elite instrument, the student practices more, and the music that comes forth is mellow and sweet to the ears. Young Lady was in love again! "Danny Boy" came alive, and in the young Lady's heart, she could hear the music echo "from glen to glen and down the mountainside." It was as though the music of the melancholy French horn expressed the melancholy of her own soul, you know, the part of her soul nobody, but God, knew about!

Mr. French was her soulmate.

10. Land of the Rising Sun

The young Lady's mother loved water! Born and raised in Florida, swimming was second nature. When it was time to choose transportation from the USA to Japan, she said, "We'll go by ship. I can swim, but I can't fly yet!"

But her daughter, the young Lady, was terrified! Often, she would wake up in the night, terrified by a tsunami-type wave crashing over her head. Now, here they were in Seattle, ready to board the ship headed for Japan! In the past she would get nervous when she stepped into a rowboat! What would this big ship be like! She walked up the gangplank and stepped gingerly into the lobby of the huge troopship! It didn't tip or rock. It seemed as steady as though she had stepped into the lobby of a huge hotel!

The passengers stood at the rail on the port side of the ship to wave good-bye to the husbands and wives and children. Each person was handed a coil of paper ribbon. The mother told the children to wait and see what people did as they pulled away from the dock. The deal was that you would throw one end of the coil to your family on shore, they would catch it, and you would hold on to the other end until the ship moved slowly away from land. As it stretched to the limit, it finally broke. Each person had a piece of ribbon to keep for a treasure.

When it was time to choose transportation from the USA to Japan, she said, "We'll go by ship. I can swim, but I can't fly yet!"

Alas, there was no one on shore to catch the ribbon from the fractured little Boyd family! The father left the family at the Fairfield Airfield about six months before. Now, they should be in Japan in a week to ten days. The father should be there to meet them in Yokohama. We'll see!

Over the speaker came the command, "All ashore who are going ashore!"

The ship shuddered and moved slowly away from the fatherland. The army band began to play. "Should auld acquaintance be forgot and never brought to mind …

Should auld acquaintance be forgot and Auld Lang Syne."

What would the future hold for the little Boyd family?

The young Lady helped the little brother tie the blue paper streamer to the railing of the ship and let it go. The mother wept and blew her nose. The young Lady felt a lump in her throat and pulled her three-year-old brother close.

Onboard the ship the young Lady and the little brother were curious about everything. Yes, everything! The spiraling metal staircase went down and down. What an exciting place to play! She and the little brother could ride the banister all the way to the engine room that powered the big propellers that pushed the big ship farther and farther away from home. Home? Where was that, anyway? She wasn't sure, but she knew it was not in a foreign country! Or was it?

In the stateroom there was a double-decker bed with a ladder. For the young Lady, of course! And there was a porthole with thick glass and long metal bolts to keep anyone from opening it!

In the mess hall, all the chairs were tied to the floor! The next morning, they knew why! Everyone was seasick! The mother was sick all except one day, the day they were in the eye of the hurricane! It took twenty-one days to reach land again.

It was noised about that they could possibly see land the next day! There was something there on the horizon in the "Rising Sun."

It looked like a mountain, but was flat on top! Fujiyama! They were in the "Land of the Rising Sun."

11. Miss Mondy/Mischief and Summer in Japan

What is so rare as a lassie in love with life in the summertime in Sendai, Japan! The summer of 1949 was more beautiful than any time in the young Lady's short life. The mother was not burdened with housework and cooking. She enjoyed her volunteer job of teaching English language to Japanese college students. The father would come home after work and enjoy his model railroad hobby. He put together kit after kit of boxcars, cattle cars, and passenger cars for the miniature railroad in the front yard of the little duplex in the housing complex on Kawachi Army Base where the family lived. He would set up a whole town complete with railroad station and electric steam engines. The kids in the neighborhood would all come to put their little "people" in the railroad cars. The stress factor for the doctor daddy was at an all-time low! The young Lady and the little brother would run to meet their father when he came home after work and smother him with kisses. Their only fear was the regular inoculations for cholera! The young Lady and the little brother would hide under the bed, but the father knew what cholera was like in a country where human feces was spread on the rice paddies. The flooded rice paddies was where the rice was planted by hand. The women would wade into the flooded paddy, take the little green rice plants and place them by hand in the muddy muck. But that's what the women did. There were no corners of the rice paddy that hadn't been blessed with bright green rice sets placed there by hand by an old Japanese woman with aching back. Many Japanese men had lost their lives in the war that the Emperor had commanded!

Had life never been as beautiful as those few happy months of summer when the little family was all together and school was out!

The young Lady was able to roam barefoot along the quiet streets of the army base and ride the blue bicycle down the hill into the Japanese city. A young Lady doesn't need to worry about getting lost or being molested by a tall, gray-haired stranger! The dependents were very protected, and the little brother could ride on the back of his sister's bicycle down to the horse stable or to the nearby pond with all the tadpoles.

Time flew by for the young Lady that summer. But alas, it was time for school to start again.

All the students from the fifth grade were excited about being in Miss Mondy's room. They said Miss Mondy was a really good teacher. The young Lady learned to enjoy learning that year.

Fifth through eighth grades also had their own music teacher. She liked happy songs from round the world! The young Lady especially liked the music that had harmony. It flattered the father that the teacher told him about his daughter's ability to harmonize so easily, and that she should enjoy music even as her father did!

And then there were guys. Funny, the young Lady hadn't noticed them before. Boys, you know, had cooties! But they liked to go to the stable with her, and go exploring in the hills with her, and some of them would even sit beside the pond on the grass under the weeping cherry trees with her and tell the young Lady their dreams and their fears.

In Miss Mondy's room, the bell would ring, and all the students would run pellmell down the hill to the gym. Army kids come and go, and about the time you got to be friends with one of them, the whole family would be transferred to another station. But somehow, this year the young Lady's class had lots of guys, and they played freely with the girls and ran down the hill every day to the gym together. The young Lady enjoyed the speed, the exercise, and the camaraderie. Young Ladies that age can usually outrun the male counterpart, and then everything changes when the hormones kick in!

Danny Daniels joined the class a little late that year. Young Lady already knew she could outrun everyone in the class, but that second week of class as she was striding proudly in front of the pack she heard the clump-clump of combat boots behind her. They were gaining on her! She poured on her last ounce of energy as Danny Daniels strode easily by. He had sandy, curly hair and blue eyes. As he passed, he gave her a big grin. The young Lady liked him! Maybe they could be friends. Danny's family were assigned a one-story private house just across the lawn from the little family. His dad was an officer; someone said he was a general! It didn't matter, really. They were all army personnel.

Then one evening, at the supper table, the young Lady's father told the family the commanding general had sent a command that all dependents should pack one suitcase per family and be ready to leave with an hour's notice. The Korean War had started, and there was a threat that Japan would be in harm's way. Korea was only fifty miles from Japan. Anything could happen.

Danny's dad was deployed to Korea. Danny and his mom told the father good-by at the train station and waited for the next move. Danny and his mom were sent back to the States near her mother. The father? Missing in action!

The young girl wrote to her friend, Danny, but the letter was returned. The young Lady felt her heart twist. Where was Danny! Did he cry when he got the news? She wanted to comfort him, but she was not permitted that mournful privilege. The thoughts of grief just got stuffed deeper into the pouch of griefs to be mourned when nobody was around. At night, when all is quiet and the lights are off, a young Lady can let the tears flow and make little salty circles on the pillowcase. They wash out, but the memories don't.

Years later, when the young Lady was in college, the announcer for the baseball team came on the radio while the young Lady was walking through the grocery store in Washington, DC. The crowd was cheering and shouting, "Go, Danny Daniels, go Danny Daniels, Danny Daniels, go!" She listened. She seemed hear again the clomp-clomp of the army boots behind her.

Could this be the same Danny Daniels who strode past her as she ran down the hill to the gym? For a moment, she could see his face and the smile. She'll never know.

At night, when all is quiet and the lights are off, a young Lady can let the tears flow and make little salty circles on the pillowcase. They wash out, but the memories don't

Christmas time came. It was cold. In the back of the barn, where the hay was kept, she noticed that a young mother and her toddler son had arranged some of the hay and moved in. It was warmer there because of the horses, but it was open on one side. They had a hibachi and some charcoal to heat their tea. They were probably wearing all their clothing to keep warm. The young Lady went back to her own warm house and told her mother. "I think the baby could use some of Paul's out-grown clothes." The young Lady's mother was touched. She and the young Lady and the little brother wrapped packages that night with pretty Christmas paper and ribbon and toys and candy and cookies. They even wrapped some sugar cubes and a bar of soap.

The next morning, the whole family took the packages to the back of the stable very early. The young Lady and her brother were excited! They watched as the young mother and the toddler opened the presents! When their eyes met, the young Lady saw tears in the young mother's eyes. That made tears come in the eyes of the young Lady, too. No words were necessary.

It was later that winter when Tony, a classmate, knocked at the back door. The family was eating Sabbath dinner. Tony came in and stood in the kitchen, his little face was grave. "Do you want to see Mischief before he goes?" he asked.

Mischief

"What do you mean? Is he being transferred to Sakanami?"

"'No," Tony answered, his bottom lip trembling. "Mischief is real sick, and I came to get you. They don't know if he'll make it."

The father pushed back from the table and stood. "I'm driving her down. I'll stay there with her."

Miss Mondy/Mischief and Summer in Japan | 39

When they went into the barn, Mischief was there in the center aisle trying to stand, while the Japanese stable boys attempted to put poles under him so the men could lift him back onto his feet. The young Lady watched, horrified! *No! Not my Mischief!* she thought to herself. She went outside and attempted to find something green for him to eat. There were some pope berry leaves that had a good green color. The young Lady picked one and took it back inside the barn and tried to tempt Mischief to eat it. He pretended to be thankful, but could hardly hold his head up. The young Lady knelt down and stroked his neck.

How soft and warm and beautiful! *No, dear Jesus, no! Don't let him die!* She stroked his neck again.

The doctor daddy took charge. "Help him into his stall," he said to the stable boys. They were able to get him into the nearest stall.

"'Now cover him with some rice straw so he won't get cold."

"Now, Daughty, we have done all we can. Let's go." The young Lady obeyed her father, and the two of them rode home together in silence.

Sleep that night was fitful with flashbacks appearing in her dreams. As soon as it was light enough to see, she got up and into her overalls and rode the bike down the hill to the stable. What would she find?

All was quiet when she entered the barn;, too quiet. She parked the bike in front of Mischief's stall. He hadn't moved. She knew it was all over.

She left the barn and blindly went out the back door and toward the river. There was a quiet spot there, and she wanted to be alone. The sun was up now, but she didn't notice. *Mischief, my friend, my only real friend!* She wept aloud as she stood there beside the river. She felt as though her world had fallen apart. Mischief was dead. Never again would she snuggle against his warm body and warm her hands under his long, flowing mane. She could confide all her troubles to Mischief, and he always seemed to understand. He would turn his head around and nuzzle her hair. She looked at the swiftly flowing river just over the edge of the bank. Her body shook with emotion, her cries were loud and deep. Mischief was dead, and she had never been able to talk to a human the way she could talk to Mischief. Now, there was nobody! She felt all alone in the world again! Nobody understands when a little girl gets attached to an animal. It's kind of weird. Where was Jesus? How could she know that He was right there beside her, feeling every teardrop? No, she wouldn't stop the pain by jumping into the swiftly flowing river. No! She turned and walked back into the barn to retrieve the bike, but she didn't look at Mischief again.

It was hard to go back to school the next day. People don't know what to say to someone who is grieving. Their silence seemed awkward.

Overnight, the young Lady became a woman at age eleven. But time goes on.

A woman at age eleven. Yes, although heartbroken and very alone in her grief, her take-home when looking back is the foreknowledge of God. At that time, the eleven-year-old didn't know that the family would be stuck in the gang district of Los Angeles, California, for five years! The backyard was only a concrete slab, fifty by fifty. Although the grief was intense and her little heart was broken, God knew she would not want Mischief imprisoned with her in the cement jungle. She didn't know God had a much more expansive plan for her love of horses. She would need to wait and trust!

Springtime came around again, and with it the cherry blossoms, the green grass, the rice paddies. One evening at the supper table the father made another announcement.

"Up in the mountains, there is a hot spring and the hotel where the emperor used to take his vacations. I have made arrangements to take my family for a vacation."

"Wow! When do we go?" All four of the little Boyd family were excited.

A few days later, the family drove up into the mountains to the most lovely spot in the world! It was now a Japanese resort, but the part where the emperor vacationed was for the Occupation. At the door the little family left their shoes and slipped into zories and a white kimono and were taken to the suite. There were sliding paper doors and elaborate grass mats.

Next, they were taken to the private hot tubs where the hot water was so hot the new Woman thought they would cook. There were three hot tub rooms in a row, separated by a paper wall.

One for the father and his wife, one for the little brother, and one for the New Woman. The little brother and the new Woman cooled their hot tub to a comfortable temperature and proceeded to float their little handmade wooden boats. For the "little people," the young ones used a couple of fingers and let the fingers do the walking.

The mother, being from Florida, stepped out the sliding paper door and onto the lush carpet of hand-manicured spring-green grass where a clump of daffodils bloomed in one corner. In her bare skin, she soaked up the sun and took a nap. She turned onto her back and saw a Japanese man observing from his balcony.

They all forgot they were naked. Later in the day, they took a tour of the rest of the hotel and saw a whole hot tub as big as a swimming pool full of happy Japanese bodies. Nobody gave any thought about naked bodies. It was more like a nudist colony. "Everybody's doing it."

When bedtime came, the housekeepers brought in a pile of feather futons! The children made their own puffy pallet on the rice mats next to their mother and father, and were soon asleep. They didn't see the full moon rising and shining through the open door and onto the puffy pallet where the father and his little bride lay in each other's arms.

The time at the hotel went by all too quickly. Who would know they were now a family of five? The new Woman thought the hotel would be a wonderful place to live the rest of her life. But then she thought of Mischief. Every night, down upon her knees she prayed the Lord for "A horse like Mischief." Would He hear the prayer of the broken little girl who was forced into adulthood prematurely? Would He? Did the little salty circles on the pillow matter to God?

12. The Teenager in Los Angeles

Proud Father with His "Beloved Son"

It was a foggy, drizzly Saturday night not long after they arrived in L.A. The family had gathered at Mama Frankie's house about three blocks away from their own house. As usual, there was no spot to "just be," and the Teenager put on her raincoat and went out the door intending to just walk around the block. But, as she passed a deserted spot beside the parochial school, a group of pot-smoking teenage guys stood laughing and talking in Spanish. By the time the Teenager got to the corner, she was aware that someone was following her. By the time she got to the dark part of the street with a hedge on one side, the potsmoking teen guy stepped up beside her and wanted to see her private parts! She knew from the experience in Atlanta that she was in trouble! Big trouble! With hardly a split-second warning, the guy bumped her against the hedge, intending to knock her to the ground. He then pulled out his switchblade knife!

Immediately, even without thinking, the Teenager broke into a sprint, leaving the assailant wondering what happened! Her legs carried her back to Mama Frankie's house, about a block away.

Apparently, nobody had missed her, and she stepped, breathless, into the living room. Nothing had changed! They were still gossiping and scolding and unaware of what just happened.

Her take-home from the experience was, "You are the Teenager in the gang district of one of the three largest cities in the United States. Look for your way out before you get into a compromised situation. Consult your 'gut' and stay alert."

Yes, take precautions, but remember it is only the presence of God's holy angels that will carry you in a case like that. "The angel of the Lord encamps around those that fear Him, and delivers them." Who knows the times we were unaware of danger and our God stepped in to thwart the evil one's plans.

Remember that sanctification is God's purpose in all His dealings with us. Romans 8:28 states that "All things work together for good to those who love God, to those who are the called according to His purpose"(NKJV). When walking the streets of Sendai, Japan, it was safe and even friendly to make eye contact and to smile at the passers-by, but this was another world, and a thirteen-year-old girl is so fragile!

Someday she would understand why the five-year incarceration in the concrete jungle.

13. Teenager on the Farm

A happy turning point came the next summer when Mama Lucas asked the Teenager to ride cross-country with her to visit the relatives in Missouri and Florida. They crossed the desert and the Great Divide again. Then the Mississippi. The grass was green, and red white-face cattle lay in the shade and chewed the cud contentedly.

From the cement jungle of Los Angeles and the constant tension of always being in a state of alert, the rolling hills, the rivers and streams, the livestock mowing the green, green grass seemed like heaven.

The Aunt Mary and Uncle Felix raised cattle and had a "teensafe" bay gelding to ride! The Teenager begged to stay at the farm while the grandmother took Aunt Mary and little brother with her to visit the relatives in Florida. The Teenager was free at last!

Is there any sound so cheerful as a meadowlark on the fencepost at the start of a day on the farm?

At that time, the farmhouse had only two bedrooms, a living room, and a kitchen. There was an important little freestanding structure about 100 yards down the hill from the house—an outhouse. There was a hand-cranked phone on the wall, a wood cookstove in the kitchen, and lots of windows. The water was what ran off the roof when it rained. It was collected in the cistern and hand-cranked back up to fill the bucket for the kitchen. The Teenager slept on the couch that summer.

The first sound in the morning was the rattle of the milk bucket and a calf bawling for his ma. The uncle and the Teenager would head for the barn together. Together, they would do the chores and head for the hayfield in the old Dodge pick-up truck. Is there any sound so cheerful as a meadowlark on the fencepost at the start of a day on the farm? Is there a smell so sweet as new-mown hay at the close of day? Is there any moment so comforting as the cool of the day looking west into the sunset and thinking the long, long thoughts of youth?

Before the days of baled hay, the farmers stacked their hay in a pile of what they called a hay "rick." They used an apparatus called the ricker to lift the hay to the top of the pile, where a stacker organized it into a structure that would keep through the winter and feed the cattle.

No, they didn't really need the Teenager that didn't know how to harness a horse, but the Teenager was teachable and needed the farm. She even learned to harness a horse! From the hayrick, Uncle Felix would chat comfortably with the Teenager who handled the ricker horse and would and tell stories as he stacked the hay. It was always stories with a point. Wisdom from the hayrick is what the Teenager absorbed that summer, and peace and God and love!

Sabbath came, and the two of them drove together on the red dirt road across the rolling hills to the little white church on the ridge across the valley. After the service, the women would bring out the covered dishes to feed the hungry crowd. After eating, Uncle Felix would start the sing. There was four-part harmony all over the place!

That Sabbath evening, as the Teenager stood alone in the quietness of the sun that was setting over the rolling hills of the farm country, she remembered how God had carried her all her life. She and God had a little chat. "Yes, I have carried you, and someday, all these crazy crises will have a reason. Would you allow Me to be your escort for life?"

There in the cool of the Sabbath day, the Teenager watched the sky turn gold, then pink, then mauve, and the mauve turned to the darkness of night. As she watched the stars come out, she invited her Creator to be her life companion. His answer: "I will never leave you nor forsake you." Could it be that this humble farm is the safe place she could always come back to?

14. Long Copper Braids

Paul, DeWitt, and Susie

It was about the time the little Boyd Family went to Hermiston that the Babe decided to let her hair grow. Said she wanted Mama Frankie to be able to curl it. By now, the Teenager had hair she could sit on! But now, all the teen girls in her group of peers had short curly hair and perms. Every night, they put the hair up in pin curls. Every night, the strange Teenager let her long, thick, copper hair hang loose. It was a time when all the younger siblings would come running into their sister's bedroom and hop up on the bed and snuggle close and let her long copper hair pull them all together. This is the only moment that the baby sister still talks about that was a happy time. By now, there were four siblings in the "Counsel of the Kids!" It was older brother, Paul, that always made the same request. "Tell us a story." So there, snuggled together in the bed, the big sister would let her long, copper hair flow around the little Counsel of the Kids and tell the Bible story.

But to the kids at school, a fourteen-year-old peer with long hair was a misfit. People don't know what to do with someone who is not like themselves. One day the cousin, Gwen, asked the Teenager, "Don't you WANT to be pretty?"

Pretty? Beauty? So one day, the Teenager allowed the cousin, Gwen, to curl her hair with bobby pins! All night the Teen slept on huge pin curls! In the morning, the hair was still slightly damp when Gwen tried to get her cousin's hair ready for school! Disaster! What a frizz! That was the last time Gwen tried to make the Teen beautiful by pin curls!

But, later that year, the cousin coaxed the Teen into allowing her to cut her bangs! Hair grows, right? Not fast enough to catch up with the part that didn't get cut. But not to worry! Braided hair didn't have that problem. Braided hair doesn't get in the way when a Teen is working in the hayfield!

The parents allowed their Teen to return to the farm again the next summer! This was the way life should be! Nobody there was embarrassed by the Teen with long braids! In fact, since there was no running water on the farm, Uncle Felix poured water from the dipper onto the hair while the Teen lathered it as under the faucet in the city. Then Uncle Felix watched as she dried her hair by mounting her horse and galloping away down the East Road with hair flying behind.

Friends? Montgomerys had six. Smiths had four. Uncle Felix and Aunt Mary had only one named Martin. The young ones played wood-tag in the summer twilight and squealed and laughed together.

It didn't seem to worry anybody that in the summer, the Teen slept in the attic now, with just a sheet hung on a wire between Cousin Martin's bed and her own bed. It was an intimate time for the cousins. The younger cousin was more like a sibling and wanted stories after dark, just like the Teenager's siblings in Los Angeles. And in the dark, he could ask questions about life and God and talk things over with the older cousin with long braids.

In the dusk, the whip-poor-wills would start talking to each other about important things. The locust trees were in bloom, and the sweet scent wafted on the evening breeze of early summer. The cicadas humming was comforting. They slept.

Who can calculate the value of those few summers on the farm and away from the predators of the cement jungle?

The whole world was not like the dysfunctional family! After the simple meal of tomato sandwiches on homemade bread, Uncle Felix and Aunt Mary would sit there together with the kids. Uncle Felix would reach over and put his big, strong hand on his wife's gentle, capable one and smile and say, "Have I told you yet today that I love you?"

The aunt would act as though it was all news to her. Her face would light up, and she would look into his sunburned face and blue eyes, and no words were necessary! Here was love. Copper Braids knew this kind of godly affection must be a core value of her own home someday. Home? She was collecting things. They were not things for the hope chest like some girls do. There were no dainty cups and saucers and nighties with lace around the neck. She was collecting values. What were the things that were of real value in life, anyway?

15. College/The Murderer

It was the last day of her senior year and the day before graduation. The Teen stood there looking out over life. Everything was an unknown. Through the years of childhood and youth, the adults are always asking, in their most condescending voice, "What do you want to be when you grow up, dear?" Then, "Where to go to college." "What to take in college." Now, it really was the first day of the rest of her life! What do you really want to be when you grow up? As a child, she didn't have all the options! "When I grow up, I want to be a housewife like my Mama Sue."

For a female teen graduating from high school in 1957, there were only three choices: secretary, schoolteacher, nurse. The best place to start seemed to be nurse. That first summer, the Teen stayed with Mama Frankie in L.A. and did nurse's aid work at the big hospital, where she had once earned $12.50 per day doing messenger service. Now, by the end of the summer, she had saved enough for the first semester of college, plus room rent to Mama Frankie!

The Teen's Escort had kept His promise, "I will never leave you nor forsake you."

The Teen's greatest desire at this point was to move out of the dysfunctional family and make her own mistakes! But no, the father had his own well-thought-out plan for her life. Live with the family that year and take pre-nursing at Pacific Union College near San Francisco. You see, the father made the decision to get another degree to add to his existing medical degree. His real interest was in public health. No night calls, no weekends. He was accepted at the University of California in Berkley, California, just outside San Francisco. He moved his growing family to a tiny rental house about a mile from Pacific Union College. The father would be home on weekends.

The load fell on the mother. It was a new place. One kid in college, one in sixth grade, two in first grade. There was a bed in the living room for the granddaddy who was already diagnosed with dementia! The angry male sixth-grader was hitting puberty. The mother was in her first year of menopause. The little kids went to the first grade at the little public school within walking distance. In the tiny house, there was a narrow hallway with a cot for the Teen. There, this should work out fine. But the family dysfunction didn't go away. It was only exacerbated by circumstances!

One night, the Teen came home from school to find that the angry sixth-grader brother, had destroyed some of her personal property. The explosion came! The teen knocked the brother to the floor and put both hands around his throat and was in the act of choking him. His face was red, his eyes bugged out, he couldn't move, he couldn't breathe!

The mother walked in. "Get off of him," she said in a calm, quiet voice.

The College Girl obeyed, but was visibly shaken to think that another few seconds and she would have killed her brother!

She had come face to face with herself! A murderer! Was there no way out?

The way out was not to run from the revelation but to look it square in the face, call sin by its right name, and bring it to her Escort.

But she didn't. God didn't strike her dead, either.

The school year was almost over. The grass that covered the hills of Central California was living green from the spring rains. The school flower, the bright yellow Diogenes lanterns, were blooming far back in among the green hills. It was as if God had let spring come all at once that year. The Teen explored the hills. There was a massive formation of rock called "The Palisades," overlooking the valley and a quiet lake and blue sky and puffy clouds. One could take a book and walk and study at the same time. Yes, walk away from the clutter of life, the dysfunction, the exhaustion. Far back in the hills, life seemed to come into focus again.

Her Escort came through.

> *The grass that covered the hills of Central California was living green from the spring rains. The school flower, the bright yellow Diogenes lanterns, were blooming far back in among the green hills. It was as if God had let spring come all at once that year*

16. From Under the Dark Cloud!

The College Girl was at a crossroads again. There was something inside her that was screaming, "I DON'T WANT TO TURN OUT TO BE A NURSE!" She was accepted to the Loma Linda School of Nursing. School was to start in two weeks! A med school classmate of the father came for a visit and went for a long walk with the troubled College Girl. The timing was perfect. By the end of the long walk, the father's classmate had encouraged the College Girl to change her major to premed.

College Girl needed time to get this all figured out. The family had returned to the Los Angeles area, where the College Girl returned to her previous job as a nurse's aide in the heart of Los Angeles for the summer. The friend and mentor who owned the Arab stallion still lived in Loma Linda, only an hour's drive from the city. The hills behind the big Loma Linda University Hospital were brown and dusty now, but College Girl borrowed the stallion and rode the familiar trails through the sagebrush and manzanita for hours. The answer came. She would talk to her dad and get his take on whether he thought she could become a doctor! They actually had a long-overdue adult conversation, and he encouraged his daughter to follow in her father's footsteps! This conversation started a pleasant, healing process! He liked her!

College Girl actually wanted to transfer to Andrews University in Michigan, but the timing was not yet. Her classmate from high school decided to go with her to PUC. They could room together. Neither had lived in a dorm before, so it made the way easier for both of them. They both picked a physical education major with Ingrid Johnson as the major professor. How could College Girl know that when time had fled, Ingrid would be on her Board of Advisors when she took another scary risk and started her own traveling physical therapy company?

The network one makes through college years may be more valuable than any impressive university degree awarded. And a lot more fun! Maybe someday there will be a school that offers a major in mentoring, But really, it is only the Holy Spirit of God Himself that can teach such a delicate subject. College Girl was blessed throughout her life with godly mentors. Could Mama Frankie be labeled as the first?

The PE major was a God thing for both girls. There were camping trips far back into the Sierras and tumbling team trips. There was even a band trip in which College Girl was able to enjoy her French horn again!

It's the interaction of mind with mind that needs to happen in a mentoring relationship. The tennis class was over. The sun shone through the high gymnasium windows. The two students sat on the floor with their major professor and talked about life and dreamed about possibilities for the future. It was almost like being in the Counsel of the Kids again and talking to a big sister! Ingrid's excitement was contagious!

"I'm being called to teach PE at Andrews University next year," she told the girls.

They moaned together! ""Oh, no! What about the majors you are leaving here!"

"Well," Ingrid continued, "Is there any chance you could transfer to Andrews University with me? It would be very helpful to have a couple of my majors who have worked with me before."

College Girl was stunned! This teacher thinks outside *all* the boxes! College Girl remembered Andrews University is where she was planning to go her freshman year! The text came to her mind that she had learned long ago. "All things work together for good to them that love God …" Romans 8:28.

We'll see!

17. Volcano Erupts

Dad Talmadge

College Girl wasn't really expecting the volcano to erupt. It had been dormant for several years. But there they stood, toe to toe at Mama Frankie's house when the twenty-one-year-old College Girl announced that she was transferring to Andrews University in Michigan.

The father's face was red, and the veins stood out in his neck. "I THINK YOU'RE CRAZY!" he shouted in the face of his oldest child! His intent was to unsettle her confidence in her own sanity. That had always worked before, even on his wife.

"AND I'M A CHIP OFF THE OLD BLOCK," she fired back.

Suddenly, he realized that she was right. His past rose up before him, and he saw himself as a young man announcing to his parents that their only son was leaving Griffin, Georgia, and heading for a small school of nursing in Murray, Kentucky! The plan was to work his way through medical school when he became a registered nurse and make the family proud. In 1928 people could do that. "Hometown boy makes good" would be plastered on the front page of the weekly hometown paper.

But hometown boy wasn't supposed to leave his poor old parents all alone. Now, he was looking at the generation he had sired and was repeating the drill.

It was an emotionally-charged departure. Granddaddy sniffed, Mama Frankie sobbed, Mama Sue turned her head and let her tears hide on her soft, white blouse, and Mama Lucas wept. Pop Lucas was the only Yankee in the crowd. He smiled. When he became of age, he had joined the army and fought in the SpanishAmerican War! After the war, he went to Florida to find a beautiful Southern belle to be his wife. He married Clora Estridge and never lived in Indiana after that! The bump on his chromosomes became legendary. "The Lucas Gene" is what the cousins called it. About three-quarters of them have that "Lucas Gene." It drives the cousins crazy who didn't get it. But, oh, what fun!

Ride the wave of the Lloyd M. Lucas Gene!

The steam engine began to puff, and College Girl was on her way. The emotions were mixed as she looked out the window and saw the homes of her loved ones disappear among the "puffer-billies." But she was eager to turn the page. What next?

18. Upperclassman

When the puffer-billy puffed into the Niles, Michigan, train depot three days later, two old friends were there to meet her. How exciting! They skipped up the sidewalk to the Women's Residence Hall and ran up to the third floor, which they would call home for the next two years. Their room was small, but it had all night lights! The rest of the residence hall did not!

Lights went off at 10:00 p.m. and came back on at 6:00 a.m.

There was a job waiting for her as night monitor in the dorm from 1:00 a.m. to 4:00 a.m. The rubber met the road! Upper Classman didn't yet understand that a body wasn't meant to split the night shift. She hadn't calculated sleep into her program. But her Escort didn't turn His head and say, "You're on your own with this one!" No way! He had said, "I will never leave you nor forsake you." "The Eternal God is your refuge, and underneath are the everlasting arms."

There was also a second job in the Physical Education Department. This would be good on a resumé. It would also be a healthy thing for her body.

On Friday night, the Upper Classman slipped on her housecoat and joined a small informal group of young ladies in the second-floor lobby for music and worship. What a beautiful thing!

"O the way is long and weary, And our bleeding feet are sore; Is it far to Cana land?"

Music floated throughout the whole residence hall. She and the roommate joined the rest of the young ladies in harmony.

There, in one of the big overstuffed chairs, were two other young ladies relaxing in their housecoats with their "ukes."

Others sat on the floor and on the couch. The Upper Classman asked if she knew the song called "O The Way is Long and Weary." That song was the one they brought to Andrews from Pacific Union College. It had been on all the hiking club trips and carried to the campfires of the camping trips. The song was dear to their hearts.

"O the way is long and weary, And our bleeding feet are sore;
Is it far to Canaan's land? Is it far to Canaan's land?
In the desert we are longing for its shelter more and more.
Is it far, is it far to Canaan's land?"

How could the young girls know that they would still be singing it fifty years later as they drove together from California to Michigan together for the last time?

The days quickly found a routine of their own.

- Up before daylight on the cold winter mornings.
- Run and slide together along the frozen sidewalk to the cafeteria.
- On to zoology as the sky began to lighten.
- On to genetics.
- On to organic chemistry.
- Run across campus to assist with tennis class.
- Run, run, run!

On Sabbath the roommates were in charge of the teens at the big stone church.

- Run some more!
- Do a little homework.
- Sleep? What's that?
- Do the night shift.
- Repeat!

Ah! The snow was melting from the big blue spruce in front of the dorm. The tiny green sprigs of crocus appeared, then the yellow, and the purple! It wasn't dark anymore when they ran to breakfast! The earth smelled like spring! Couples walked arm in arm back from class.

Ah, Spring!

But how long can a student run without rest! We'll see!

19. Senior/She Stumbles

Sometimes, the priorities become skewed. The Senior wanted to graduate with her class. She took Western Civilization by correspondence. Maybe that would help. She took some private tutoring in a couple of her remaining classes that were required for graduation. She took a twenty-four-hour load of classwork. There!

But summer was the time to catch up on the finances! The hospital in Benton Harbor had an opening for an eleven-to-seven nurse's aide in the neonatal nursery. Her roommate took the job in the surgical unit. Roommate had an old car and was driving to and from the night shift also. Transportation. There! Sleep would just have to wait! But!

Well, the body is boss! One morning, after working all night, she willed her body to go to class. As her hand was taking notes, her brain went on hold! A few seconds later, she came to with a start. The writing on the tablet was illegible. Just a bunch of black scribbles on white paper.

Her roommate made an appointment with the counseling department, and the Senior found help from a wise, godly counselor. The first thing the woman said after hearing her story was, "My dear child, YOU NEED SOME SLEEP! Have you told your parents? You have 'Nervous exhaustion!' It's not a 'Nervous Breakdown.' I think we can help you."

Her assignment for the Senior was to write to her parents.

Oh, no, the Senior thought, *'Not them!*

So, she wrote to each parent separately! Each of her parents had a different way of communicating. The father's type was like a text message before texting was invented. The mother's was like a long narrative with lots of juicy detail. A story, maybe.

> *"My dear child, YOU NEED SOME SLEEP!"*

Their plan was for her to pack her bags and come home. But!

God's timing is never off! It is perfect! Ever notice that? When her friends found out she was packing to go home, there was nothing they could do! They felt so helpless! Sometimes, we don't know how much someone else will be affected by the decision we make! For every action there is a reaction.

Stumbling Senior went to the trunk room in the basement of the dorm and lugged her empty trunk to the third floor. She opened it and began to put things in it. Her hands shook as she knelt there all alone on the cold floor of the dorm room, taking things out of the drawers and putting them in the trunk.

There was a tap on the door, and Sandy came in and sat wordlessly on the edge of the lower bunk.

There was another tap, and Barbara came in and sat beside Sandy in silence.

There was another tap. Mary came in and sat at the desk. Nothing was said.

Again there was a tap. Two more of her friends came in and sat on the floor, silently watching. They, too, felt the helplessness of the situation. Three months till college graduation. The trunk was filling slowly.

Again there was a tap. Two more friends sitting on the floor now. Stumbling Senior's eyes were blurry with tears. *No!* she thought! Not home to that dysfunctional mess that she had finally escaped from two years ago! But what were the options? Go to some hospital and get a job giving bed baths and washing tracheotomy tubes again?

Nobody said a word. What could one say when there was nothing to say! Options were poor. She began to take things out of the trunk and put them back into the drawers. Could it be that the silent ones were praying? Nobody said a word. The options were not clear yet, but the one option she thought was the only option was no longer an option at all! When God sends friends to sit with you in silence, He still has a plan. Remember Job!

The major professor was busy thinking outside the box again! "Your roommate is taking a job in Lincoln, Nebraska, teaching PE at Union College there. A call just came through for a woman to teach physical education at Columbia Union College in Washington, DC. How 'bout that!" she said excitedly.

"But I'm not going to be able to graduate this year!" The Senior said sadly.

"Look," Major Professor said, "I think they'll take you for the job and let you finish your classwork there at their college. Teachers for women's physical education are scarce! Go for it, girl! You can do it, Ole Thing!" (Her pet name for all her majors).

And she did! The time spent in Washington, DC, teaching physical education and interacting on an adult level with other professionals was life-changing! She was catapulted into the adult workforce. What a joy! What freedom!

The network solidified during those four years was of God. Some of them were "forever friends." Her Escort planned for her!

20. The Rookie PE Teacher on Her Own

The father loaned her money for a car. Soon it was packed and on the way across country entirely alone except for her Escort. She liked it! Loved it! She would stop over Sabbath and be with Aunt Mary and Uncle Felix at the farm for a few days and take time to love the folks at the Goldsberry Seventh-day Adventist Church. Her heart yearned for the strength and stability of the little white church on the ridge across the rolling hills of Missouri cattle country. Then to Washington, DC, for the first day of the rest of her life.

It was after dark when she arrived at Columbia Union College! This was the city again! Maybe she could stay in the women's residence hall. The assistant dean told her in no uncertain terms that she needed to make other arrangements! Then she looked at the bedraggled girl without any safety net and told her she could stay just one night! Whew! That bought her a little time.

There was a little basement room in someone's house the next night, and then she noticed a white clapboard house across the street from the college and saw that someone was working on it, getting it ready to rent— the world's smallest apartment! When she found out that the school owned it and let it out to faculty and staff, she was overjoyed. The salary for her first year of teaching PE was two hundred dollars per month. Hmm! Fifty dollars a month for the apartment. Fifty a month for the car payment. Tithe: twenty a month. A bag of groceries at the local grocery store was five dollars. The rest would have to fit in! Not anything extra, for sure, but this was a job for the Escort again!

During the two years at Andrews University, she had no time for personal devotions. She thought of the years she set the alarm for 4:00 a.m. and worshiped for half an hour, and then went back to sleep for a couple of more hours before getting ready for school.

But now, she had no idea how her time would be spent! However, she covenanted to make sure nobody or no circumstances would take away her time with God.

The world's tiniest apartment was a sanctuary. There was only one room with a freshly varnished hardwood floor plus a dinky kitchen and the bath facilities shared with another woman.

There were a pull-out sleeper couch and a small desk with two drawers. Pop Lucas had hand-crafted a cedar-lined hope chest for his oldest granddaughter. She had the little maple rocking chair her parents gave her for her sixth birthday. The kitchen had an old-fashioned, white-painted drop-leaf table and two matching chairs. Adequate. Barely adequate. But, for someone who was just out of college and living on her own for the first time, adequate is a good word. Her father's sister, Vivian, gave her two ceramic plates and two place settings of stainless flatware. You know, the kind you get with green stamps. A good thing about the location was that she could walk to work. One had only to walk across the street and be on campus.

But it was the casement windows on three sides of the room that made it her sanctuary. There was a strip of land between the back of one set of apartments and the apartments on the other street. One could sit and watch the sunrise again while worshiping the Lord!

Unlike the city of Los Angeles, she found that the Washington, DC, area is really beautiful. The city planners made parks and waterways ubiquitous. People plant flowers, and in the spring, there is hardly a home without azaleas in bloom. The rookie PE teacher liked it.

She was alone and friendless when she arrived but discovered that there were still people who worked there who knew her parents when they were there in school. But it was up to the Rookie to build a network. The Rookie was attracted to other people who loved nature, music, and God.

Registration was in the gym, and this time, Rookie was on the other side of the desk! Strange. Most of the students were near her own age! Now she was their teacher!

There, in the center of the hubbub of the gym, was a table with a red flower on it and a woman some twenty years her senior orchestrating all the hubbub with a smile! The registrar!

Rookie decided to make friends. Being used to the dorm setting, Rookie marched herself down the street to her home and was invited in. She flopped herself on the floor, as was her habit in the dorm. But this was the capital of the United States of America! It was also the General Conference of the Seventhday Adventist Church. History and culture were everywhere, and here she had flopped down on the floor of the registrar of the college! There, sitting in a comfortable chair on the other side of the room, was a quiet, self-assured woman that the registrar introduced as "my housemate, Carol." What struck the Rookie was the genuineness of these new friends. Would they be forever friends?

When Sabbath came, she found herself sitting alone near the front of the church. Alone, yes, but not for long. The friendly registrar stepped forward and whispered, "Come sit with us." There, sitting with them, was the chairman of the college language department. She would be Rookie's teacher for the class in Elizabethan Masterpieces because there was still a need for one more class in English before graduation.

The woman had black hair pulled back in a bun and piercing, bright blue eyes. Rookie wondered if she should grow long hair and put it up in a bun! Maybe she should invest in a jersey dress, too. But those thoughts quickly faded at the dinner table when they laughed together!

In faculty meeting that Sunday morning, the Rookie was introduced as "Our new women's physical education teacher." Rookie looked around to see who they might be introducing!

In faculty meeting that Sunday morning, the Rookie was introduced as "Our new women's physical education teacher." Rookie looked around to see who they might be introducing!

Everyone was smiling and looking at HER!

These were now her peers! They were all "old people." Could they be trusted? Yes, there were a few young people on the faculty from the nursing department. Some of them offered to set her up with some of the GIs from the Whitecoats unit.

No, that's not what she wanted to do with the rest of her life! But! just what *was* she doing for the rest of her life? Had it not been for her Escort at this pivotal point in her life, she could have made some grave mistakes. At least living alone in the tiny apartment gave her the time she needed to renew her connection with her Escort!

The first class was at 7:00 a.m., and she was the teacher! She needed to get there early to set up. The jump-start for the day was a page or two in the Christ-centered book about the life of Christ. But the promise is that they who hunger and thirst for God will be satisfied! It worked! How kind of God to satisfy her with the tiny apartment and the sunrise out the back window!

What about horses? Well, she wouldn't have enough income to get a horse for a while, but maybe someday.

21. Sophomore School Teacher

It was Sunday, and the Maryland landscape was carpeted with green—her first spring in Washington. There must be a horse around here to help eat all that spring-green grassland! The Sophomore decided to take a drive and see what was going on in the world beyond the college. The landscape was much like what she had enjoyed in the rolling hills of north-central Missouri. Puffy clouds, blue sky, horse pastures, white fences; maybe she would find a horse like Mischief here. At two hundred dollars per month to live on, there wouldn't be much chance to save for a horse. But we'll see!

The sophomore pulled into the barnyard of the place where she saw horses grazing in the morning sunshine. Maybe they would let her touch one. "Are there any Tennessee Walkers in the area?" she asked as she got out of the car and walked toward the man at the barn door?

"Walking horses, you say? These here are gaited horses, but not Walkers. You looking to buy one, young lady? Why a walking horse?" the man asked.

"Oh," she answered, "I used to ride one on my uncle's farm in Missouri. Smooth as silk!"

"Well," he smiled, "there is a family up the road about a mile. It's right there where the road swings to the left. I think you'll like the people."

So the Sophomore drove up the road and spotted a big black mare with a long mane and tail grazing in the pasture. The house wasn't much of anything, but then, she wasn't looking for a house, just a friendly horse and friendly people.

The little black dog came out, wagging her tail. Well, at least the dog was friendly! About that time, a friendly lady about ten years her senior came out of the barn. It didn't take long to get acquainted with other "horse people." She showed the Sophomore the black mare and proceeded to tell her that this mare was a granddaughter of the famous foundation sire named Midnight Sun.

That didn't mean a thing to the Sophomore. All she wanted was to be around horses! When the woman found out the Sophomore worked at "'the college," she perked up and told the girl that her father was once a teacher there.

Dixi

"Want to go riding with me some time? There are trails around here, and Triadelphia Lake is only a short ride through the woods. If you don't mind riding in what you are wearing, we can go now! I have a horse I'm boarding. The owner said I could use him if somebody wanted to ride with me."

It was all Sophomore could do to keep from jumping up and down! The horse was a lanky, green-broke two-year-old sorrel with a wonderful disposition and a very deliberate four-beat gait.

On the way back to the college that evening, the Sophomore looked into the sunset and prayed, "God, You are so good to me! You gave me a place to live, a job to pay the bills, friends that invite me for dinner, friends that invite me to ride through the meadow with them, friends that can keep me out of trouble in the strange world of academia, friends that have been single in a strange city, but survived! Yes, God, You are so good to me! Amen!"

The learning curve was steep. First job in the adult world, new city, strange people, but He guided the Sophomore like He said He would: "I will never leave thee nor forsake thee!"

Could Sophomore have seen the future, she would have seen the little black filly out of this black mare and the bond between the two of them as forever friends? But, the future was known only to God, and He was smiling!

22. Ask Your Mother ... In Love?

Felix and Friends

"Mama Sue, how do you know when you're in love?" the Young Teacher asked.

You see, there was a letter in the mailbox from the guy she used to study with when in college at EMC (Emmanuel Missionary College/ Andrews University). He asked her if she would like to go on a two-week canoe trip into Canada with him and some other friends.

Well, she didn't really expect that, but this was a really nice guy, and they had enjoyed the time studying together. The idea was appealing! Wow! A two-week canoe trip into Canada! Young Teacher knew she couldn't be away that long, but she asked him if he would like to meet her at the farm in Missouri for a few days.

He liked the idea and brought one of his buddies with him. That was the year they were remodeling the farmhouse, and everything was a mess. About four cousins and their friends plus Young Teacher and her two guests! Two-bedroom house plus small, hot attic. Never rattled by company, Aunt Mary let the company stay in the abandoned chicken house. They put cots for everyone and let the guests figure out the arrangements. No problem. Time to dress for bed, and someone would say, "Don't see me!" and everyone would turn toward the wall and do the job!

The Young Teacher and the Young Man took a long horseback ride along the muddy, red-clay road. Fine, but before they made it back to the barn, a thundershower descended! The horses turned toward the barn, and the lead horse spattered red mud all over the number two person! Alas! The Young Teacher was covered with red mud. At the barn they slid from their horses and looked at each other, laughing! The Young Man grinned and said to the mud-spattered Young Lady, "You have never been more beautiful!"

The Young Man got a teaching job at the college in the fall. There were many precious moments to remember. But the Young Teacher felt uneasy and called her mother. "Mama Sue, how do you know when you're in love?" the Young Teacher asked.

"It could be complicated to try to explain," the mother answered, "but if you have to ask, you're not in love."

That was all Young Teacher needed to hear. The relationship ended.

Young Teacher felt all alone. Life lost its zest. She went through a time of grieving. It causes grief on both sides when something like that happens.

But the Young Man soon found another less-complicated woman who became his wife.

Then one evening, while sitting on the floor at the Registrar's home, her housemate, Carol, asked Young Teacher, "What do you like about teaching physical education?"

Her answer catapulted her out of her sadness and on to the next adventure!

"Like about teaching physical education? Mostly, the kids. But I have been thinking that I would go back someday and take physical therapy."

"How old are you?" she asked.

"Ugh. Twenty-five," Young Teacher answered.

"You're not getting any younger!" the housemate stated.

On the way back up the hill to the tiny apartment with a shared bath, Young Teacher thought to herself, *Not getting any younger! 'Not Getting Any Younger! 'NOT GETTING ANY YOUNGER!*

The first introduction to physical therapy was from the days when she was doing call service at the White Memorial Hospital in Los Angeles. The department was in the basement and had no windows. Much of the caseload was rehabilitation on postpolio patients. A diagnosis of Poliomyelitis was almost like a sentence of life in prison. One was trapped in a body that wouldn't work anymore but still contained the same desires and dreams!

But since then, the profession had grown and even offered a degree from Loma Linda University. God is in no hurry! The option wasn't available ten years earlier! The patients were usually young people with a life in front of them. Maybe she could help restore function, relieve pain, and perhaps inspire these incarcerated minds to function and hope again! Physical therapy would fit well with her physical education experience. In her mind she could see a whole new world of opportunities opening up. She was energized and inspired again! Yes, God was smiling and enjoying His young adult.

In her mind she could see a whole new world of opportunities opening up. She was energized and inspired again!

She applied to Loma Linda School of Physical Therapy and was accepted for the fall term. Would there ever be a time in the future when she would find her home? Really?

23. Loma Linda School of Physical Therapy

PT Student was excited about returning to a place where she already knew people! Mama and Papa Lucas were five miles away in San Bernardino; Mama Frankie was sixty miles away in the City of Los Angeles. Surely the ideal arrangement would be to stay with grandparents only five miles away from school.

It was here that PT Student learned an important lesson. They say, "you can never go home again." Yes, once out on their own, living with relatives should "be like fish. After three days they stink!" So PT Student looked for her own space and found a 'room with shared bath and kitchen privileges' with a cheerful, godly, grandmotherly woman that lived only three blocks from the School of Physical Therapy, and the price was right. "Small but adequate" again!

Physical therapy was not a shoe-in for the PE Teacher. The first thing PT Student discovered was the vocabulary. It was like learning a foreign language! Then there was "Gray's Anatomy" and a real cadaver for each foursome. This was not at all like "Cat Lab" when some ten years ago, the father conducted that first anatomy lesson for the cousins on road-kill at the kitchen table! This was the real stuff! PT Student loved it! But, this was still the "same ole same ole" Southern California! How could she stand this for two more years!

But, this time it was different. Her network of friends included a California Native physical therapist who knew all the waterfalls, streams, pine trees, mountains, and beaches and was willing to show PT Student what she had missed on her past incarcerations in California!

Funding was short, so PT Student took a part-time nurse's aide job at a small nursing home. But, second semester PT students were allowed to work in the University Physical Therapy Department. Again her Escort came through with just enough funding for a room, board, tuition, and tithe.

Once a week, PT Student had a standing invitation to Mom and Pop Lucas'. There were several single guys living in the dorm who were more than happy to come with her for a hardy 'Mama Lu soup' and homemade bread. Mama Lucas loved it when the PT Student would bring hungry boys for her to feed. She would get this look of satisfaction on her face and say, as if in awe, "Look at that boy EAT!"

Occasionally, California Native would pack a picnic box and invite PT Student to lunch on the only green, grassy spot available a few blocks from school. It was well-watered, well-manicured, and not many people walking by. The people there had already completed their time on earth and were awaiting God's call! There, the blue jays and ground squirrels discovered that the California Native's car in the cemetery meant lunch for them, too. There were always crackers and unshelled peanuts for the critters, plus crackers and cheese for the two friends. PT Student noticed that her friend seemed to have a natural way of communing with the little wild things. One afternoon, the blue jay followed California Native's car back to the hydrotherapy lab and hopped inside the building unafraid, expecting more peanuts.

By the time summer vacation rolled around, PT Student was eligible for a summer job as a PT student in the local hospital. Many of the things she had learned as a nurse's aide came in handy when working with the sick and wounded population in the physical therapy department.

But, what was she going to do after the internship? Stay and work in Southern California? Find a job back East where there was green grass, rolling hills, and water? Maybe back to Maryland, where things were not so strange. How 'bout Aunt Mary and Uncle Felix there at the farm in Missouri that she had loved all her life. She requested that she be able to take her five months of internships on the east side of the Rockies. Things were looking hopeful again.

One Sunday afternoon, an old friend invited PT Student to go riding in the hills behind the hospital, where she used to ride in fourth grade with that little filly who pulled off the car door! She could ride his two-year-old mare that had been green-broke, then retired for a year while it healed from an injury. Anything to be with horses again. The sun was shining and only minimum smog. It felt good to be in the saddle again. But, there was a busy highway to cross on their return. Suddenly, a little red car came whizzing around the comer. The horse panicked and reared up on his hind legs. PT Student was no stranger to a rearing horse. No problem. You just lean forward and release the tension on the reins, and the horse will come down. Right?

Wrong! The horse was only green-broke! She went up past the point of return. In a flash PT Student realized that they would not be coming down as planned! She leaned forward and pulled the horse's head to one side. Thoughts of horses going over backward filled her mind. Would the saddle horn rupture her spleen? Would her head be crushed on the highway? Would she be under the horse! In a flash the horse fell to the side and crushed her right leg! Would he step on her when he got up?

Would she be laid up for a while and be unable to finish school?

The ambulance came and took her to the ER. There was no apparent fracture. But the entire leg from the hip down turned black as far down as the top of her cowboy boot.

One of the instructors took PT Student to the hydrotherapy lab where there was ice in abundance and packed the entire leg in ice overnight. By morning, the leg was black except for where the ice was. She was impressed with the ice treatment for a crush injury, and later discovered the many other uses of ice in physical therapy practice.

Could it be that her Escort had planned ahead for extra angels? Only a severe crush injury and crutches for a few days, instead of all the things that went through her head as the horse was falling. A more experienced rider would have realized what was happening and leaped away from the animal before hitting the pavement!

Thankful, PT Student returned to class on Monday morning. Again the all-seeing eye of God knew that the experience in home treatments would make for good neighbors when she finally found her home!

24. Graduation and Another Pivotal Point

The senior year was speeding to a close. Finals were over, and the students were picking up caps and gowns for the weekend graduation exercises. Diane and Doug were coming for the weekend with their six-month-old little daughter, Debbie. Arlene and Joe were coming for the weekend with their six-month-old daughter, Angela, too. Plenty of room in the house now. The kindly Christian lady whose room PT Student rented for two years, passed away a couple of months before. Her family allowed PT Student to stay and take care of the house until school was out. But what about furnishings?

There was a call from the old roommate from EMC. She was all excited about a new job she was taking in Loma Linda, California! She needed a place to rent for a while, and needed to move the household goods from Lincoln, Nebraska, before her arrival! But, sadly, her own arrival would not be until autumn.

PT Student was really on a high! That was until she went to pick up her cap and gown! The dean of the school of physical therapy called her into his office. There was a rule that a student must have a B average in all the physical therapy classes! PT Student was three points less than a B! She had an overall average of a B+, but in therapeutic exercise, she had only a high C+! There would be no need of cap and gown! Now what? Would she have to stay another year in California?

It was California Native who came to the rescue. There was a peaceful spot away from the school activities where PT Student and her guests could take a lunch and spend the day with each other. It was far up in the mountains. But so? What were the alternatives? What a good day it was with old friends, new babies, and new friend California Native, under the dome of heaven. Maybe now, PT Student could catch her breath and find Plan C.

Would you believe, there were seven seniors, one-fourth of the class, who missed the B in therapeutic exercise! The instructor offered to do a crash course for all seven. They could do it in two weeks because therapeutic exercise was the only class they had to study for. And everyone was a repeat!

PT Student was now free to leave Southern California and take a vacation riding with California Native to interview for an attractive position she was interested in. It was in the State of Maine! It would be several weeks before time to show up for the first internship east of the Rockies!

Who but God could have taken all the broken pieces of her life and put it all back together to be a blessing!

Who but God could have taken all the broken pieces of her life and put it all back together to be a blessing!

At this point in her life, things looked broken beyond repair. The real picture may not be clear for years to come. But the God we love and adore has the master plan, and even if it requires a leap of faith across a yawning chasm, we can lean our entire weight on Him. for He cares for us affectionately (see 1 Peter 5:7, AMPC). We have only to see where God has led us in the past to appreciate what He is doing with the future. It really WILL be worth it all when we see Jesus!

25. Where's the Next "Home?"

Aunt Mary and Uncle Felix

The miles rolled by as the girls drove peacefully through the Tetons and Canada and around Lake Louise. But it was the rolling hills of cattle country and the thought that she would sit at the round oak table with Aunt Mary and Uncle Felix again that made the trip most welcome. The trip allowed time for the little white church on yonder ridge and the singing and camaraderie. It also refreshed the memory of the first time she asked God to be her Escort. The memory was almost sacred.

She watched the sun sink in the west behind the rolling hills. Again she saw herself sitting on the arm of the overstuffed chair harmonizing with Uncle Felix. Peace!

At Niagara Falls they crossed into Canada again and entered Maine through the north woods. PT Intern thought the whole State of Maine was like the north woods. This could be a real adventure. PT Intern had long ago given up the idea that there would someday be a permanent home where one could pick the wallpaper and make "forever friends" of the neighbors. But sometimes, when she drove through her native land, the little song she made up as a child would surface.

"I want a home, a home to go to. I want a place to call my own,
Where 'there's one to love and love us,' I want a place to call home!"

On Sabbath, they looked up the Brunswick church but found it abandoned. It looked well-cared for, but there was just nobody there! Later, they would learn that the week of the Fourth of July is when they all meet for camp meeting in Freeport, Maine.

Intern was dreaming of horses again. It seemed that everywhere she looked, there was pastureland bordered by the sea! Some of the old farms had huge, white clapboard barns with dates on them like 1794! This was exciting! But, then again, she would have moments of reality. She hadn't even finished the physical therapy internship yet!

The first internship was in Staunton, Virginia. There was a big rehabilitation hospital there. They also rehabilitated criminals! PT Intern noticed that it was a good mix, though, because the physically disabled youth would get someone who was actually physically whole to push their wheelchair up the hill to the cafeteria! Never mind their history with the law!

She liked it there. Virginia was appealing. They asked her if she would consider a permanent position there when internships were over. Maybe this was horse country, too, and since she had no obligation other than to finish the internship … Hmmm!

The next internship was in Maryland near the college where she taught physical education … was that only two-and-a-half years ago?! It was good to be back in the area and spend weekends with old friends. This facility also asked if she would be willing to consider their facility after internship.

There was one particularly sad case. His bright blue eyes stared wildly out from his charred black face with a fringe of red baby hair around the edge. At this point the Intern thought about quitting physical therapy. He was only two years old! His jealous older sister had set the crib on fire!

Every day, aided by the Hubbard tank, PT Intern tried to debride the eschar from the blackened body and face. She learned later that the child had no scaring after he was released from the hospital. No, thank you for the offer of a job at a burn facility!

The position at the children's rehab in Pennsylvania was in the coalfields. There were young people with brain injuries and cerebral palsy. But the area was beautiful, and it was only a day's journey from the State of Maine.

The last internship was at a small hospital in southern Maine. They had invited California Native to take the position as chief therapist and build up the Physical Therapy Department. They were wanting to expand into wellness. PT Intern's experience in physical education would be very useful. The employees at this facility seemed to be of one accord in following their Chief Physician.

The Intern's parents had given her a $100 bill as a graduation gift. The big black Walking Horse mare that the Intern rode in Maryland a few years ago had dropped her foal in May. The little black filly in Maryland should be able to find a new home by the time Intern was ready to start her new job as a staff PT and health educator at the little hospital with big dreams. The chief got wind of this and found a barn, a pasture, and friends with his own parents at an expansive vintage farm near the hospital.

Ever notice that one can never second-guess God? What an exciting adventure to do life with a Friend who already knows what lies ahead, Who loves You as His only child and has the ability to make everything turn out to be for your best good. But it's costly. The decisions you thought were yours to make, really turned out to be His! Will it be costly? Yes, of course, but it's worth it! The cost? Total self-surrender. As one author said, "Self-surrender is giving God the veto power over all your decisions for the rest of your life." Here was a big decision.

What would God really want? Would she give Him veto power? Would she take the job?

What do you think?

26. The New Grad, New Dreams

New Grad had never dreamed of such a beautiful spot in the whole world! California Native had located a rental cottage on the Maine shore until there was a chance to get the feel of the area. She invited New Grad to share the cottage for the winter. Wow! What's not to love about a winterized cottage where the tide rises, and the tide falls, and the place where lobstermen with their chugging lobster boats awakened the village every morning? What's not to love about the smell of the sea and the crying of the seagulls following the draggers at the end of the day? And here, on the end of Harpswell Peninsula, jutting out into the water, one could watch the rising sun in the morning and the rising of the full moon at night! An opportunity like this had never been a dream, much less a real possibility! This living on the shore could be addictive! Cold, yes! Snow, yes!

The Maine native who worked in the PT Department with the two physical therapists "from away" knew all about Maine winters (and spring and summer and autumn). She told them, "January is a long month, but February is a short month. Now in March you can never tell what will happen. It's 'Mud Season!' But APRIL! Ah! Spring! You'll love it!"

New Grad's parents made a $100 contribution to her bank account as a graduation gift. It should be enough to make the 500-mile trip to Maryland and back with the borrowed pickup truck and a borrowed wooden horse crate in the truck bed. New Grad laid her money on the table and went with the little black filly's owner out to the barn to load up. Poor little girl. She had never been out of sight of her mother before. She had never been tied to anything solid before. Life had been good to this little girl. But when they lifted the heavy door and closed her into the crate, she was frantic! Her pathetic little voice pleaded to let her out and be with her mother! When the truck started to move she really panicked! She got tangled in the rope and fell on the floor of the crate. New Grad stopped the truck and looked at the old owner. Old Owner looked at New Grad and simply said, "Now she's YOUR horse!"

New Grad unsnapped the lead rope and let the little girl free inside the crate. She later learned that it was the best thing to do with an inexperienced horse.

By the next morning, they arrived at the farm, which was to be her temporary home. She shared the stall with another filly about the same age. Neither of them had seen snow before! What glee when they were turned out onto the white fluff! New Grad and California Native spent evenings grooming and feeding the little black filly. New Grad had been praying for a horse like Mischief for years. The filly's color was black, not chestnut.

She was a female, not a male. But did it matter? When the little black filly put her soft nose on New Grad's cheek, the color and the sex didn't matter at all. It was the trusting, loving heart that bonded them for life.

California Native had an old black mare named Dixie when she lived in California. This little black furry filly reminded her of a happy past. "Could we name her Dixi?" Of course! Dixi, it was!

Would this be the "horse like Mischief?" Only God knew and smiled.

27. Costly Dream/The Old New England Farmhouse

Tidy Coon

The cottage by the sea was lovely, but it was only a winter rental. Alas! The summer residents would be needing it from May through September! And where would the little black filly stay? There should be a barn and a house and a pasture. The Chief MD came through again. The Old New England Farmhouse was the place where he wanted his parents to retire, but it was not what they were looking for. The Chief MD told California Native about it, and that evening after work, she took her Australian Shepherd pup and drove by. When she let the puppy out, he climbed to the top of the tallest snowbank and flopped down as if to survey his kingdom! He liked it. There was an adequate barn, a pasture, and the "Old New England Farmhouse."

It seems that the early settlers of Maine had it all figured out. The buildings should have their backs to the Northeast, the direction of the infamous "Nor'easter" storms of winter. The barn should be attached to the house to form an "L." leaving the south exposure sheltered for the yard and garden. This house had it all as one might expect from a 1798 farm in Harpswell, Maine.

But wait! California Native had not even been inside! The Old New England Farmhouse had been standing empty for five years. The folks who bought it five years ago had high hopes of moving their company to Maine, and this would be ideal. But their company went belly up before they even had a chance to move in. Five long winters, it stood shivering in the rain and the sleet and the snow and the hail. The raccoons thought they owned it, and maybe they did … but!

California Native got in touch with the real estate company that listed it and picked up the key. It was a cold, sunny day in February, and the wind was quiet when New Dreams and California Native saw the inside for the first time! Cold, yes, but the bright southern sun was shining onto the kitchen floor and smiling at the two girls "from away." The square kitchen tiles that covered the "punkin pine" floor were turning up at the edges. There were flakes of white paint leaving the ceiling and taking up residence on the floor. And, of course, there were dreams. There was an old oil-burning cook stove. But there were dreams! There was a full basement with a dirt/mud floor. Foundation was good. And there were dreams! The barn was connected to the house by a low workshop/walkway. Yes, there were dreams! The roof was in good shape, except for the family of raccoons who had made their own door in the second floor roof. They would, of course, get the eviction notice when the girls "from away" moved in with the dog. Hmm!

Five long winters, it stood shivering in the rain and the sleet and the snow and the hail. The raccoons thought they owned it, and maybe they did

That night, when all was quiet, Dreamer stood alone outside the cottage by the sea. The moon was rising and looking at himself in the quiet waters of Harpswell Sound. When would she wake from this beautiful dream! When something seems too good to be true, it probably is! From the freshwater pond to the north came the welcome sound of the peepers. A fresh sea breeze flicked her copper hair. On Monday, the girls "from away" would sign on the bottom line and take possession of the Old New England Farmhouse. The Dreamer did a reality check with her Escort. "Dear God," she prayed, "I can't see the future. I'm scared. You know this seems so perfect! I want to make my home here. But You are my Escort. I want to make You happy."

Even as she prayed, the answer came. "Yes, you may move ahead as you wish, but it will be costly!"

OOPS! The answer had an unknown addendum! It was unknown! What would she do? The answer had a qualification. YES, but it would be costly! She felt like the two sons of Zebedee, James and John, who asked to be trusted to sit on either side of Jesus in the new kingdom. Jesus asked them if they were "willing to drink the cup He would drink and be baptized with the baptism." The Dreamer thought she was willing, even if it would be costly.

She went to sleep that night wondering about the "costly" clause, but at peace.

Our God promised that He would never leave us nor forsake us. Did that promise have a termination date? Would it be contingent on anything? That same God said through His friend Job, "He knows the way that I take; when He has tested me, I shall come forth as gold,"(Job 23:10, NKJV).

Gold is costly! Yes, that "costly" word showed up again. What are the options?

OK. There are probably some less-frightening options, but God's purpose in all His dealings with us is to lead us to come forth as gold! God is not going to say, "You made that choice; now you're on your own!"

Costly prayed, "Yes, Lord, even if I can't see what's ahead and have all the details of my life clear, I trust you!

28. Learning to "Neighbor with You!"

The snow began to melt, and people started hanging buckets from their maple trees. Maple syrup is a lot of work, but it's worth it. As soon as the trail through the woods to the neighbors was open, Buster showed up with his sidekick, Daryl. They were the eleven-year-old neighbors from down on the main road.

Somehow, when there's a farm, kids show up. "Hi! You need any help?"

"Do we ever! We have a little black horse we want to bring home. Can you help us build a fence?"

Now people from away who try to farm, don't know about Maine ledge yet. The ledge doesn't move. No. It has been there since creation, and it plans to stay! You are the one who alters your plans to accommodate the ledge! So the boys altered their plan, and if the little electric fencepost hit the ledge, the boys just moved over until they found a place where there was enough room to drive the small fencepost. The fence looked like a ski resort where somebody set up for a slalom. What could they do but laugh and use it for the little black filly?

When Black Filly, Dixi, first touched the electric fence, she couldn't believe it! Surely, nobody would be so cruel as to make a fence that would bite a poor little innocent baby horse! She snorted and wheeled away, ran around the pasture once, and came back to check it again! Incredible! Unbelievable! But from that day on, she never challenged the fence again! She even remembered where the fence used to be and would let you go first!

Sunday morning, the boys were at the bedroom window, calling, "What's on the list today?" They did everything from making bread to building a stall for Dixi.

The neighbors at the other end of the dirt road owned a sizable chunk of shore property. No, the Old New England Farmhouse had no waterfront property. The neighbor's little grandson, Tim, was born the year The Girls moved into the Old New England Farmhouse. Their first introduction was when the toddler came running up the dirt road toward the farm. He was toddling as tight as he could leg it, but not fast enough to stay ahead of his mother, who was trying to catch him. "Timmy, Timmy, come here right now!" The little legs went faster and faster. The little tyke tripped and hit his head! Blood! It was California Native Nurse who came to the rescue. 1) calm the frantic mother, 2) clean and dress the wound, 3) make friends with the neighbors! Tim's mother looked at California Native and said, "You know, if you ever want to, you can come swim in our cove!"

Tim was too young to be of much help around the farm yet, but he had an especially sensitive nature and a most lovable disposition! A few years later, when the chicken died, the girls from away found a bouquet of flowers from the pasture on the kitchen table, you know daisies and red clover. Yes, such a sensitive little neighbor!

The neighbor to the north was Tom Skolfield. He had worked in the woods with horses hauling wood in the winter, and in the summer, he dug quahogs and sold them. He even served his time in the Maine legislature for a while, like most of the men in Harpswell, but his first love was horses. He and Mary lived in another Old New England Farmhouse to the north, and Tom had his stories to tell the girls from away. Dixi would demand his attention whenever she walked with New Dreams down to the Skolfield place. Tom always had an apple for her.

Come summer that first year at the farm, the girls from away needed to find hay to put in for the winter. It was George Skolfield and Nana from the next Skolfield place who said, "I'll neighbor with you. You can use my hay if you'll bring enough into my barn for my little granddaughter's horse, Honey."

The morning they were to bring in the hay, the sky was threatening and gray. New Dreams went up alone to start bringing in the bailed hay. There in the gray dawn, she saw a diminutive teen with copper curls walking into the hayfield. She was rubbing the sleepy out of her eyes as she reached the truck. This was the granddaughter George and Nana were telling about. "You gotta meet my granddaughter."

It was years later after the Copper Curls had finished college and joined the human workforce that the two girls were sitting under her apple trees in the orchard, watching the tide come in while eating apples and feasting on Costly's home-made whole wheat bread when the Copper Curls spoke. "We've been friends a long time," she said. "You are more than a neighbor, more than a friend; you are a 'forever friend!"

It was almost as though the two of them, at that moment, had signed a pact. They are friends for life.

Penny and Dan lived in the little yellow house down the hill on the two-lane highway. Their big black Persian tomcat had made friends with California Girl's calico coon cat. One day when Calico Coon Cat was sitting at the big picture window overlooking the horse pasture, she spotted him and began to pace the floor and cry and beg to let the big black Persian come in. The girls from away looked at each other and nodded. A couple of months later, they nodded again when they saw three adorable kittens sleeping with their mother in their box by the stove. One was a big, black baby kitten! When Penny and Dan came up to see the new-born. They nodded. Big Black had a son!

Early one morning, not long after meeting Penny and Dan, the phone rang! It was Dan. "Penny can't wake up! She's gurgling!"

"We'll be right there, Dan," California Native said as she hung up the phone. California Native, RN, took one look at the situation and called the ambulance. They made it to the hospital in time and solidified another neighbor's friendship.

When the snow was deep, and the girls from away had to hitchhike to work, Penny and Dan's was a good place to stop and get warm on the way through the woods to the highway.

George Skolfield called. "You girls doing alright?"

"Not really, the water froze in Dixi's bucket, and the electricity is out. No water pump! What shall I do about it?"

"Bring the bucket in by the fireplace. That should take care of that. But you can bring another bucket in with snow to start melting."

When the Fourth of July came, the phone rang. It was Tom, Dixi's friend with the apples. "Come on up. The peas are ready. You know what the old-timers say, 'plant by Memorial Day, and have peas by the Fourth of July.' Bring a bucket."

Tom Skolfield lived with his wife Mary on the first floor of another old New England farmhouse on the Liberty Farm just up the road. As they picked the peas, they chatted. Tom's brother, Clarence, lived with his wife Annette upstairs in the old house. "You know, Clarence and Annette were lighthouse keepers on Crow Island for years until they shut it down. It was the last manned lighthouse on the coast of Maine." Tom volunteered.

It wasn't long till Annette came out. The girls from away wondered what it was to like to be on a deserted island in a Maine winter. She answered their unasked question. "We liked it there. All we lacked was another woman to talk about." her faded blue eyes twinkled.

The girls went back to the Old New England Farmhouse to shell the peas. Over dinner California Native commented, "I think I understand now what George meant when he said, 'I'll neighbor with you!' We are all in this together. We belong!"

Would it have been as heart-warming to know the neighbors as if they were family if there had not been the years of "separation syndrome" before circumstances brought Costly to the Old New England Farmhouse? We'll never know for sure, but we can know the tenderness and love that bonded the group together with each one trying to out-do the other by neighboring and by solidifying the security of "forever friends."

Who would have dreamed of finding a rhubarb pie from Sally, still hot from the oven smiling on the red-checked tablecloth in the kitchen when the girls came home from work?

The snow covered the ground now, and Costly followed the blood drops through the snow to the back of the barn. Where did they come from? They were not from the cat. She was sleeping on California Native's lap. It wasn't the dog. He was always at Costly's heels. Was it the cow? No, she was resting in the barn, contentedly chewing her cud. Why was Dixi standing in the snow with her head down? But that was where the blood trail ended! She stood quietly with her head down while Costly checked her all over. Yes, there it was! There were a large puncture wound and a tear in her chest! That sweet little Jersey cow, looking so innocent, had horns! When Dixi tried to share the warm spot in the barn, Tiny Cow objected and punctured poor, unsuspecting, gentle, black Dixi!

Costly wondered how long the blood would drip before Dixi died? She called the vet immediately. Whew! That was a large wound!

As he began immediately to stitch the opening, Copper Curls showed up! She had decided to take veterinary medicine when she went away to college, but it seemed that from the time the girls became acquainted that early morning in the hayfield, she had this uncanny sense and would show up time and again when there was an issue with a sick pet! She seemed to have a calming effect on the pets. Maybe they knew they would be all right if Copper Curls were there!

California Native began to make subtle suggestions that they needed to let Dixi have a foal. They took her to a walking horse stallion in southern New England, but she didn't like him!

Hmm! At that point California Native hinted that they should get their own "Little Baby Black Stallion!"

Costly had a concern about that! "No way! Not a stallion!" But the seed had germinated! "Just a little baby black stallion! But don't they grow up?"

The snow covered the ground now, and Costly followed the blood drops through the snow to the back of the barn. Where did they come from?

The people with the stallion in Southern New England encouraged the idea, and the girls followed the lead to Tennessee, where there were lots of walking horses. The leads took them to a modest stable who had a two-year-old baby black stallion they would sell.

Costly asked Copper Curls to go along and help with the project. By now, she had her driver's license and was the first choice of the person to go along!

It worked! The Baby Black Stallion came to meet his wife! About every two years, Dixi the mare and her husband, Jack, would bring a new Baby Black colt or filly to love. Then they found people to love them and take them home for more love!

29. "Costly" at the Old New England Farmhouse

Costly knew when she saw Mama Sue step out of the car that something was wrong. **Terribly wrong**!

Mama Lucas pulled Costly aside as soon as she could, and told her the drive from Erie, Pennsylvania, to Harpswell, Maine, had been a nightmare! "Your mother almost hit every toll booth!"

"Oh no! Let me take her into the physical therapy department and have Dr. Budd check her out. She told you she is having headaches? He's the best diagnostician I have ever known!"

When Mama Sue stepped down from the examination table, she stumbled on the stool.

"You didn't see that, did you!" Doctor Budd asked in his most professional voice.

"No, I didn't." Mama Sue smiled.

"I'm calling the eye doctor immediately to ask him to work you in today! The snow is already beginning to fall, and things may close down early today. We'll see where we go from there."

When the eye doctor came out of the exam room, his face was grave. "Let me speak with you a moment," he said, looking at Costly. "There is pressure in her head, and it is displacing a portion of the occipital lobe. She can't see out of the left half of either eye!"

Costly called her father, seriously doubting that he would trouble himself to come. But, when he grasped the seriousness of the situation, he hopped the next plane flying into Portland, Maine, and before the nor'easter had a chance to shut down airports, they picked him up and brought him to the Old New England Farmhouse.

When he saw Mama Sue lying on the cot at the top of the stairs, he bent, and, with a rare demonstration of affection, kissed her lips. "How's my Little Bride?"

There was an older woman in the church who was discharged from the hospital after a heart attack but whose home was unheated except for the wood cookstove in the kitchen. There was no indoor toilet. When she was released from the hospital, the girls had invited her to stay with them for a while. They put a bed in the living room for the older woman.

Shortly after, bringing her to be with them at the farm, California Native's mother fell and broke her knee. Native flew out to California and brought her mother back to be with the girls until she could care for herself. So "Mama Native" had the downstairs bedroom, near the bathroom. Mama Sue and Daddy Talmadge had the partly-finished bedroom at the head of the stairs, and Mama Lucas needed the bed in the living room. But now, Mama Sue was facing the final crisis of her life. All were unknown, and it was frightening. Who was there to comfort her?

Susie Before Wedding

Her son was in Viet Nam. Susie was too needy with her own issues, and although she loved her mama dearly, Susie didn't know how to comfort. She was newly married to the military man. Paul was married and busy with his own soap opera. Daddy Talmadge was facing the crisis of his own life; he was losing his own Little Bride. Costly slipped into the hard-shelled "medical professional" mode and dealt with this situation as some detached medical professional would. Send flowers. Keep the phone contacts. It was Mama Lucas and Aunt Mary, who went home with her and Daddy Talmadge to help in a practical way with the house. Emotional support was unknown in this dysfunctional family. "Don't talk, don't trust, don't feel." Small talk wears very thin when nobody can talk, trust, or feel.

California Native, RN, PT, was distanced far enough emotionally to be the steady.

Costly had worked on the neurology unit at the big hospital in Los Angeles as a nurse's aide. She read the charts and the surgical procedures. She had also seen the outcomes. Most of the outcomes that walked into the White Memorial were nothing to brag about. This was in the early days of the craniotomy.

Fortunately, Costly could tell her mother, "That was then. This is now!" She was sure they had improved, and the outcomes would be better.

They may have improved outcomes. But people are still mortal! After her funeral at the little white church on yonder ridge, the "Counsel of the Kids" met as a group with their children and spouses on the spacious lawn at Aunt Mary and Uncle Felix's for the last time. As they were sitting there in a huddle, they saw their widowed father walking as close to them as he could. The counsel had never been open to anyone but the four siblings. But today he looked so lost and lonely.

As he passed them and was walking by, Costly looked up and spoke for the rest of the group. "Daddy Talmadge," she said, looking him in the face, "You done good!"

He turned his face away, but not before they noticed that tears came unbidden into his eyes.

Safari Survival Stories

Table of Contents

1. Broken Dreams 93
2. Alone, Alone, All, All Alone 113
3. You Need to Carry a Gun! 127
4. Warm Sands and Warm Arms 155
5. Almost Home 173
6. Florida Again 182
7. "Remember, We Love You, Liz" 191

1. Broken Dreams

Death on Halloween Night

I was jarred from my sleep by the jangling of the phone beside my bed. It was a moment before I realized that this was not a dream. I glanced at the clock. It was 3:10 a.m. Halloween night. Who could be calling at this hour?

"Is this Liz?" It was my neighbor, Dan, down the hill on the main road.

"Yeah, Dan. What's up?" I asked, trying to keep calm.

"There's been a wreck down here. Some horse was hit by a drunk driver. I think it belongs to Linda-Lee down at the next farm, but she's not home. Can you come down?"

"Be right there, Dan," I answered.

I jumped into my flannel-lined denim jeans and flew out of the house and down the hill, putting my coat on as I went. The blue, whirling lights of the sheriff's car cast an eerie light into the woods. I remembered it was Halloween night! *I hope it's not Linda-Lee's horse,* I thought to myself as I ran. *She's so attached to that little buckskin mare. Her grandfather gave it to her when she was only eight. She broke it herself and would have taken it to college with her if she could.*

I was in the beam of the headlights now. The front windshield of the car was smashed and the roof of the car dented. *It must have been a hard hit,* I thought to myself.

Dan came around the back of the car. His blue-striped pajamas were hanging out from below his trouser legs.

"Where's the horse?" I asked.

"It ran off into the woods," he said flatly.

"What color was it?" I asked, my lower jaw chattering. "Black, I think," he answered.

Time stood still. The world began to whirl. I wanted to faint. "No, God! No! I can't faint now! I've gotta find my horse! I wonder which one. They're never apart. They never get out. Surely, it wasn't a black horse!"

I started back up the hill through the woods. I shone my flashlight as far as possible to the right and to the left and straight ahead. The air was cold now, and the smell of autumn leaves was heavy in the woods. The full moon cast eerie shadows among the naked branches of the birch and maple trees.

It was only a few hours ago I had been on the back of my big black stallion enjoying the Friday afternoon ride through the countryside. I had finished treating the last patient earlier than usual and headed home, hoping to have a little time to ride my stallion through the woods to the shore before dark. Darkness comes early on Halloween night in Maine. The red maple and the sugar maple leaves had already fallen off the trees along the lane that led from my big, white New England farmhouse to the rocky shore. The oak leaves had turned burnt orange and would cling to the branches for a while yet. The white arms of the white birch were bare and stood out starkly against the dark green of the spruce and hemlock in the woodlot behind the barn. Yes, I would probably have a couple of hours to ride before sunset.

I changed into my flannel-lined blue jeans, slipped on my boots and jacket, and headed out the back door of the mudroom and into the shed, which led to the barn. It's comforting on cold winter nights to be able to walk directly from the house into the barn to check on the animals. Dixi and Jack nickered when they heard the mudroom door open and my footsteps in the corridor.

This mid-afternoon snack was a treat for the two big, black Tennessee Walking Horses. I took the curry comb and brush from the tack room and brushed Jack's velvet coat. The silky black satin of his summer coat was gone now. He would be needing all the velvet coat he could grow before the first snowfall. I slipped the bit into his mouth, scrambled up onto his back, and headed for the trail along the shore.

Jack's hoofs clattered on the dirt road as I rode past Bud and Ruth's little white house. She waved from the window.

The squirrels were gathering acorns from beneath the big oak tree that stood at the end of the stone wall. One fat fellow scampered up the backside of the tree and sat on the branch, chattering at me with his bushy gray tail curved over his back.

The field on the other side of the stone wall was still green. Old Sam Alexander only had one milk cow left now. He still put up hay every year, though. His wife, Myrtle, came out and stood on the porch and wiped her hands on her blue-checked apron. "Nice day," she called.

I rode closer. "Smells like applesauce in your kitchen today, Myrtle."

"Yes, I put up twelve quarts of Cortlands this morning. They make such pretty pink sauce."

Sam's father had come here from Massachusetts before Sam was born. Their land bordered on Merrucoonegan Sound. How lucky I was to have neighbors that let me ride freely through their farms.

The sunshine shone brightly, but the rays were slanting now out of the south. December 21 would be the shortest day of the year. The sun was in a hurry.

Jack was always such a pleasure to ride. He had an easy running walk and was always eager to see what was around the next corner. His enthusiasm sprang from the fact that he loved lady horses and was sure that there must be another mare or young filly around the next bend in the road. I took advantage of his enthusiasm and moved him into an easy canter as we neared the shore.

The water was quiet. From the point jutting out into the water, I could look across the bay to Crow Island. Johnsons lived over there behind that island. I smiled as I remembered the bitterly cold day that their thirteen-year-old son, Nathan, skied across the frozen water and up the hill to my house. I called his mom to tell her he'd arrived, but she hadn't even missed him yet.

> *The air was cold now, and the smell of autumn leaves was heavy in the woods. The full moon cast eerie shadows among the naked branches of the birch and maple trees.*

The smell of the salt water, and the call of the seagulls were familiar to me. I had moved to this corner of the world immediately after finishing college. It was my home now. I looked up at the clear blue of the October sky and thought to myself, *How blessed I am to have a peaceful home and trails to ride and this gentle enthusiastic stallion to love!* I felt his rippling muscles under his velvet coat as we cantered back up the hill.

My heart was happy as I slid from his back and turned him out in the pasture with his wife, Dixi. The baby she was carrying would be their seventh child. Chances of it's being black were excellent. Dixi had never dropped a foal of any other color. I patted her belly. I couldn't feel the baby move yet. It wasn't due until May.

Dixi nuzzled my cheek with her soft, black lips. I loved this mare. She was more like a family member than an animal. She was the first animal

I brought to the farm after I graduated from college. She was only a six-month-old filly at the time. It's almost as if we grew up together.

Jack and Dixi stood in the light of the rising full moon and munched on fresh hay. I stood between them with my hands on their withers, watching the moon rise. The white stars on their foreheads almost shone in the dark. Dixi stomped her one white hind foot. I thought how black a black horse is in the dark. *Why,* I thought to myself, *if it were not for the white star on Jack's forehead, you wouldn't be able to see him in the dark.*

I stayed a little longer than usual that night, listening to their munching of the hay and an occasional snort. It was so peaceful. The moon moved slowly across the sky. I went inside.

The fire in the Franklin stove in the kitchen felt good. I heated some tomato soup and helped myself to a healthy slice of homemade whole-wheat bread. I sat in front of the fire and enjoyed the peace of the evening.

I wish Roy were here, I thought to myself. *Maybe someday soon, we'll be married and sit here together in front of the fire on a Friday evening.* But he was far away tonight, and I was lonely for him.

Everything is beautiful when you're in love. I laughed as I thought of yesterday when I was riding Dixi through the fields to the neighboring farm. Even the dry October weeds seemed to sparkle! Someday soon, we'll all be together, Jack, Dixi, their baby, Roy, and me!

But now, I was tromping through the dark woods, looking for a black horse. Could this be for real? I shone my flashlight around and up and down. Nothing. This must be some kind of nightmare!

Would I find my horse in a pool of blood, breathing his last? Would he have a broken leg? The blue lights of the sheriff's car still whirled below me, and I could hear voices. What about the person driving the car? He must have been that other man I saw walking around down there. Doesn't anyone care if I'm tramping through the woods all alone in the dark trying to find my horse? I made my way back down the hill.

"Why the !*$! don't you keep your horses locked up at night!" A man yelled. I cringed. His eyes were bloodshot, and his gait unsteady. "You could o' killed somebody!" By now, he was towering above me, shaking his fist.

Suddenly, Dan was at my side. "You leave her alone!" he yelled at the inebriated attacker. "If you hadn't been out boozing it up tonight and driving like a bat out o' the cave, you'd have had enough time to avoid this!"

Dan turned to me, "Where's your horse, Liz?"

By now, I was shaking all over. I felt sick like I wanted to throw up. Surely this couldn't be happening. "It's too dark, and I can't find him in the woods. I don't know what to do."

"Well, he could have made it back home. Sometimes they'll do that. Let's go check the pasture first; then we'll know which horse it is at least," Dan comforted.

He and I drove back up the hill to the farm and parked his van in the moonlit dirt driveway.

He opened the pasture gate, and I whistled. There was no answering nicker. Dan shone his flashlight over the pasture. There were two horses. We made our way to where they stood. Dixi was scratching Jack's neck and back with her lips. Jack's head hung down, and great spasms shook his body. I ran my hand along his body. It was ringing wet with cold sweat.

I turned to Dan. "It's Jack," I said, trying not to cry. "Let's get him into his stall and call the vet."

Jack tried to follow. Every step was a supreme effort. His left hind leg didn't touch the ground. Dixi came too, staying close beside her friend.

Jack entered his clean stall and lay down on the pile of fresh wood shavings, his head stretched out, and his eyes glazed.

"Can you get the vet, Dan?" I asked. "It's under Jefferson in my personal directory on the telephone table. Tell him to come quick." Jack moaned with pain.

Dan came back into the barn a few minutes later. "I got him. It'll take him about an hour to get out here. Will you be all right?"

"I guess there's not a whole lot I can do right now but stay with him and keep him warm. Might as well go check on the rest of the excitement. Penny will wonder where you are."

I heard the van drive away. I was alone.

I sat in the pile of wood shavings at Jack's head. Pinewood shavings make such fine horse bedding. They smell like the woods and are soft and warm. They don't track into the house as easily as sawdust, either.

Marbie crept into the stall with her tail down and lay beside me. Marbie was such a loyal dog. Australian shepherds are bred to love and care for other animals. She was getting old. I thought of the sixty-seven puppies she had delivered. Some were black and white with copper trim like their father. Some were blue merle like their mother. Then there were the two kittens she had raised. She let them nurse and washed their diapers. Such a gentle mother.

The kittens, George Burns and Gracie Allen, had been such an amusement to me. George Burns was a short-haired yellow kitty with a face that would make anyone laugh. His life was short, though. One day, before he was even a year old, he just didn't show up for breakfast.

Just now, Gracie Allen must have known I was thinking about her. She tiptoed into the stall and settled down between Marbie's paws. She had a litter of kittens in the hayloft. I smiled as I thought of the day I found Marbie in the hay nest with the kittens while Gracie Allen was away hunting for mice. I guess Marbie thought she was the grandmother.

My thoughts were brought back to the present by Jack's moans. I put his head in my lap and caressed his forelock. His mane was so thick and heavy. His ears were so perfectly shaped, and his eyebrows always looked like he was asking a question.

Jack had come to the farm as a two-year-old. Linda-Lee and I brought him back from Tennessee. It was a twenty-three-hour trip driving straight through! Jack was tired when we finally took him out of the horse trailer and put him into the new stall in the barn. Linda-Lee was still in high school then, but a good horsewoman and a good driver. I was glad it wasn't her buckskin that was hit by a drunk driver.

A truck door slammed. Dr. Jefferson, I guessed.

He entered the stall and stood there looking at us for a long moment. He looked tired. Must have been having lots of night calls. I noticed that his hair was getting gray at the temples now. It was brown when Linda-Lee and I first brought Jack back from Tennessee. Could it really have been ten years ago?

The sky was beginning to show signs of dawn. Dave Jefferson placed his big hand on Jack's hip. He felt gently. Jack's eyes were still glassy. Another low moan came from deep inside him.

"Better get an x-ray, Liz," he said, standing up. "I brought the equipment. We can do it in the stall. Where's the electrical outlet?"

"Down the hall and on the right as you go out the door," I answered, still holding Jack's head on my lap.

Dr. Jefferson placed the film plate under Jack's hip joint and snapped the x-ray. "I'll have to take it to the hospital to get it developed," he said. "I'll be back as soon as I can."

We waited.

It seemed like hours before Dr. Jefferson returned. The sun was up now, and the world was beginning to awaken.

Dr. Jefferson's face was grave, and he looked even older and more tired than forty-five minutes ago. Something inside me knew this was the beginning of the end.

"It's not good, Liz," he said. The lines in his face seemed to deepen as he spoke. "It's a shattered stifle. He doesn't have a prayer."

"Oh," was all I could manage.

"We'll get someone out here to dig the grave, and I'll just give him a shot, and he won't hurt anymore."

"OK," I answered. "OK."

The shot was quick. Jack's moaning stopped. His breath stopped. We buried him under the pine tree in the pasture.

The truck door slammed, and Dr. Jefferson drove away. "I hope he doesn't have many of these in a week," I thought. "What a way to earn a living. With him it's more than a living, though. He cares."

Marbie and Gracie Allen and I went into Dixi's stall. I put my arms around her big black neck and smelled the friendly scent of horse. "He's dead, Dixi," I sobbed. "He's dead!"

Dixi nuzzled my shoulder with her soft black lips. I wonder. Did she cry, too?

I walked down the lane through the falling leaves to the neighbors' place. "Tina," I said, as I warmed myself by the wood cookstove that served to heat their kitchen. "I can't believe last night! It must have been a nightmare. But I know it wasn't."

Tina's kitchen was a comforting place. LeRoy built their little home with his own hands when they were first married. He was a tall, rugged man of Pennsylvania Dutch ancestry. As a young man, LeRoy had moved to Maine to work with the horses at the Topsham race track. He could do most anything. He met Tina one sunny afternoon when she was walking down Maine Street in Brunswick. She was trying to get a splinter out of her finger.

The sky was beginning to show signs of dawn. Dave Jefferson placed his big hand on Jack's hip. He felt gently. Jack's eyes were still glassy. Another low moan came from deep inside him

"What's the matter?" he asked. "Looks like you need some help."

"I got a splinter, and I can't get it out," she answered, looking up at him with her soft gray eyes. Her curly brown hair fell softly to her shoulders. He was mesmerized.

"Here," he said, reaching in his pocket for his penknife. "Let me help you."

The rest is history.

Katie was born a year after, and Buster a year after that. Kate had finished college now, and Buster was one of the managers at nearby LL Bean.

"Oh, Liz," Tina sympathized, her gray eyes moist. "Jack belonged to all of us. Katie and I would always bring him and Dixi an apple when we walked past the pasture. He was such a gentle stallion.

"Here, I just made whoopee pies. Have one. Do you think the baby will be black like his father?"

"I hope so," I answered. "Maybe he will have a white star in his forehead, too."

I looked around the kitchen. LeRoy had made the knotty pine kitchen cupboards himself. They were darkening with age. Tina kept the hardwood floor uncovered. She and LeRoy had laid it by hand themselves.

"Oh, Tina, you and LeRoy and Katie and Buster mean so much to me. Your kitchen is so comforting. You are more like family than neighbors."

"I'm here for you, Liz," she said. "I know you'd do the same for me."

She's Only a Memory Now

Back home the real world called. Jack was gone. His stall was empty and clean, but there was Marbie, Gracie Allen, Dixi, and maybe a foal come spring.

The stark maple trees sighed and screeched as the cold wind whistled among their bare branches. Marbie's breath was labored, and it had become difficult for her to climb the three steps from the barn into the Old New England farmhouse. Today I was glad for the old-timers who had connected the barn to the house. I could drive the truck inside the barn and stay out of the rain as I lifted Marbie into the cab of the blue Ford pickup and headed for the vet.

Marbie's head rested on her front paws, and her eyes looked up at me from the seat of the truck. What a history we had shared together. I thought of all the puppies that had tumbled over her patient body. There had been sixty-seven of them, plus the two kittens, George Burns and Gracie Allen. She slept on the rug by my bed at night, and in the morning, would study me to see what kind of mood we would be in for the day. But now she just lay there, looking up at me. She trusted me to do what was best.

The stoplights on Maine Street whipped like a flag in the driving rain. I stopped at Dr. Jefferson's. "She's really sick," I told the vet. "Doesn't seem to be able to get enough air. It's been getting worse over the last few weeks."

"It could be heartworm. In this condition the heart fills with worms, and there's no room for blood. I'll check her out."

I waited. Rain beat hard on the windowpane, and the winter wind howled around the corner of the white clapboard building. Marbie reached over and licked my hand. Tears sprang into my eyes. I looked away. She knew.

"The test is positive," the vet sighed as he took Marbie's head in his hands.

"Do what you've got to do, Dave," I said and turned away.

I drove home in a blur of driving rain and tears. Jack was gone and now Marbie. I thought my heart would break.

Dixi was in her stall still munching hay. "She's gone, Dixi," I sobbed as my tears moistened her black mane. "Jack, now Marbie!"

Dixi turned her head and nuzzled her upper lip against the back of my red jacket. "But we still have Gracie Allen and each other. In the spring we'll have Jack's baby." I felt her belly. Well, I couldn't really expect to feel life yet, but there should be a day soon when we could feel the foal kick.

I gave Dixi her scoop of oats and molasses and stood beside her and listened to the steady munch of grain and the driving rain on the north side of the barn. I was glad it wasn't snow. There's something comforting about being inside when the rain and wind blows about. Inside the barn there is the smell of the sweet hay and clean pine shavings and the sound of Dixi's munching. No more would there be the click of Marbie's toenails on the wooden barn floor, or the excited snap-snap of her teeth when I bridled Dixi.

They say tragedy comes in threes. Should I be waiting for the other shoe to fall?

I was just ready to turn off the barn light and go into the mudroom, when I heard footsteps behind me. I turned. There in the semidarkness of the sixty-watt light bulb was my young neighbor, Tim.

His round, youthful face was grave. "I heard about Marbie. I thought maybe these might help." He pulled a bouquet of blue, white, and pink daisies from under his coat. They smelled like grocery store.

"Oh, Tim! You are so thoughtful. You and Marbie are about the same age. I bet you can't remember when she didn't exist. Remember how you both used to roll and play on the green grass in the spring?"

Tim spoke. "I was just thinking. Maybe it's too soon to think about getting another dog, but the whole neighborhood loved Marbie. Maybe we could start looking for another Australian shepherd. But really, I think all our hearts are too tender right now."

Tim looked down at the pine board floor. Gracie rubbed against his leg. He lifted her to his chest as she tried to lick his chin. "Marbie was your mother, wasn't she, Gracie? Maybe Liz will get another dog for you sometime."

"Neow?" Gracie asked.

"Well, not quite yet," Tim said as he stroked her long soft fur.

Daddy Talmadge

Good-Bye, Daddy, Good-Bye

Christmas came and went, and the short days of winter began imperceptibly to lengthen as the sun moved northward. I pinched Dixi's long black velvet coat between my thumb and forefinger. Sure enough! A few hairs were shedding. Winters are so long in Maine that I was glad for any sign of spring. The nor'easter had stopped, and the morning sun shone on the snow and sparkled like the diamonds on an engagement ring. I buckled on my snowshoes and headed for the shore. I must remember to take extra-long steps so as to avoid stepping on the back of one webbed snowshoe with the other foot.

The trail through the woods was a winter wonderland. Puffs of newly-fallen snow sat on the bare twigs of the oak trees and rested on the green pine branches. I petted one downy puff with my cheek. It was soft and cold. Tracks of a squirrel ended under the snow-covered rock wall. I noticed that the color of the maple tree was changing from cold gray to reddish-gray. *I bet Tom Skolfield is tapping his trees*, I thought. I could almost smell the warm maple syrup boiling.

It would soon be mud season. The old folks say, "frost is comin' out o' the ground." I looked through the snow-covered white birch trees to the waterline of the bay. There, under the leaf mulch at the edge of the clearing, the spring beauties were resting. They were special. Their five pinkish-white petals seemed so hopeful. Year after year, they went to sleep in the fall and came to life, blessing the warm black earth again in the spring. With Jack and Marbie resting under the snow now, I needed thoughts of hope and springtime.

The tide was in when I reached the rocky coast. I listened. The ice moaned as it moved with the tide. The cold, green salt water seeped in between the cracks in the chunks of ice and made little puddles. Quite pretty, I thought. The wind was still icy cold as it blew across the frozen bay. I wondered when the ice would go out of the bay. It seemed that every year, the ice would break up and be taken out to sea with a single tide. In its place would be the dark blue water and maybe a seal or two. It would probably be several weeks yet before I would find the eider ducks bobbing along on the whitecaps and making love. It was only early February! I pulled my red cap down over my ears and turned to snowshoe back up the hill. There behind me was not Marbie, but Gracie Allen!

"Gracie, Gracie!" I called. "What on earth are you doing out here in this cold? We should take you home!"

"Neow?" Gracie asked as I scooped her up and held her against my red jacket.

"Yes, Gracie, now!" I answered as she climbed up onto my shoulder for a ride home. Since Marbie died, she had been trying to take the place of a loyal dog. But I hardly expected her to go for a walk in the deep snow with me. As I followed my own snowshoe tracks back up the hill, I noticed there were little kitty tracks among the snowshoe tracks. *Smart cat*, I thought, *Smart*.

The phone was ringing as I entered the house. "Hello, this is Elizabeth," I said, still taking off my jacket.

"Oh, Elizabeth! Oh! Your father has had a terrible heart attack! Oh, he is so sick." It was my father's wife, Miriam, calling from California.

My heart tightened. "Can I talk to him?" I asked.

"Only for a minute," Miriam answered. "I want his three other kids to have a chance to talk to him before he dies."

Oh, no, I thought. Surely, I must be dreaming!

"Dad, do you hurt anywhere?" I asked.

"Oh," he said weakly, "I just ache all over …" His voice trailed off.

"Good-by, Daddy. Good-by." A lump was in my throat as I hung up the phone.

It was only a couple of years ago that Mama died! Six months later, Dad married Miriam. His first heart attack was on their honeymoon.

I closed my eyes and remembered the last time I saw him. He was standing on the other side of the wire fence at the Ontario airport in California with Miriam beside him as my plane pulled away. The hot, dry air was blowing his pant legs. His usually full cheeks seemed hollow. His white shirt was open at the neck, and the sterling silver pen my mother had given him for his fiftieth birthday was peering over the top of his shirt pocket. His black leather shoes were polished, and his dry-clean-only trousers neatly creased. Miriam had put him on a starvation diet immediately after his first heart attack, and he was no longer five foot 4 inches and weighing 200 pounds. But in my mind, I always saw him as being the "short, fat, moon-faced, bald-headed, married man" he always described himself as. We were never much on hugging or kissing, but his clear blue eyes looked into mine, and he was silent. I seemed to know I should remember the moment but didn't want to admit just why.

I slipped my jacket back on and walked out into the barn. Dixi was standing in the door of her stall in the bright sunshine. She nickered softly as I came to her side. I buried my face in her long, black velvet coat. The tears spilled over and ran down my cheeks. I blew my nose. "Not again, Dixi, not again!"

Her comforting black lips nuzzled my red coat again. "I think I need to make a trip, Dixi. I'll fly out to California for the funeral, then stay for a little while and visit with the rest of the family. Your friend, Linda-Lee, the veterinarian can just stay here in our house and take care of you and Gracie Allen till I get back."

Their Baby

Dad's funeral was over, and my brother, DeWitte T. Boyd, Jr., and I turned our attention to the memories. We reviewed my father's slide collection of days that would be no more. There was the happy picture of DeWitte at the age of about one month sitting on our father's lap at the kitchen table.

Our dad had his stethoscope around his neck and his lab coat on. Dad was eating cereal and milk, and the carton and boxes were on the table. It must have been breakfast time, and he must have been on his way to the big White Memorial Hospital, where he was taking his pediatric residency. Being twelve years older than DeWitte, I was the historian for the family. It hit me as I sat there looking at the pictures, that I was now the oldest member of our immediate family.

We fondled the model trains that Dad had cherished. There was the Bangor and Aroostook model boxcar he had put together himself from a kit. There were the model steam engines and a streamliner. We remembered summer nights when he would set up the whole layout on the front lawn, and all the neighborhood kids would vie to place a little HO gauge person on the flatcar as it stopped at the tiny railroad station.

We listened to the old 78-rpm records. There were recordings of *Aida*, *Faust*, *Rigoletto*, and *The Barber of Seville*. Each brought a memory of what was.

The phone rang, and one of the kids answered it. "Aunt Elizabeth, it's for you. It's someone calling long distance. They said something about wanting to talk to you about your horse, Dixi."

My heart went to my throat as I picked up the phone. It was Linda-Lee. "Does Dixi just stand in the pasture in a foot of snow sometimes? Does she sometimes act as if it hurt to put weight on her front feet? Does she refuse to come in even for meals?"

> *"Good-by, Daddy. Good-by." A lump was in my throat as I hung up the phone*

"No," I answered, my heart pounding. I felt a premonition. "What are you thinking, Linda-Lee. You are the vet. Any ideas?"

"It looks like founder to me. But there's no reason. It's usually caused by getting a horse hot and then feeding or watering it too quickly. It's almost like an allergic reaction. But she hasn't even been ridden."

"Could it be stress, Linda-Lee? She lost her husband, Jack, and her dog, Marbie, and she probably thinks I'm gone for good, too! Do what you can to make her comfortable, and I'll be home as soon as I can get a flight."

My stomach felt like it was occupied by a rock, and my throat tightened. I turned to my brother. "I guess I better get home. It's Dixi this time. My gut tells me this is serious. There's the foal to think about. It's not due till May."

My brother put his strong arm around my shoulders. His kids, Wendy and Edward, Laromie and Jon, gave me a family hug. "I guess I've gotta do what I've gotta do," I said. "I think I can get a flight out tomorrow."

Linda-Lee met me at the airport. "She seems to respond to Butozolodine. That cuts the pain down some. But both front feet and her off hind foot are hot and apparently abscessed. We can lance them and give her Epsom Salts soaks twice a day and see how she responds."

Day after day, Dixi stood patiently with three of her feet in big, black rubber buckets of warm water with Epsom Salts. I stood beside her with my arm over her back. I felt it. A little bump from inside Dixi's belly.

"Dixi! I felt it! It's alive! If you can just hold out for a couple more months, you'll be having Jack's baby bobbing along at your side. Maybe this whole thing is something connected with your pregnancy, and you'll be all better after the baby is born."

Dixi didn't answer. She just stood there with her feet in the buckets and her head drooping. She looked so sad. Did she know something I didn't?

Dixi's condition deteriorated as she grew heavier with foal. The abscesses on her feet were like having boils on the soles of the feet. It was terribly painful to walk with three infected feet. Antibiotics hadn't worked. Topical medications were useless. Butozolodine for pain and Epsom Salts soaks were about all we could do while we waited for the birth of her baby.

The April morning dawned crystal clear. The sun was moving rapidly northward now. A couple of months and it would begin its trip on back south again, but in June, one hardly notices as the sun totters for a few days on its northernmost point and moves south. There are gardens to be weeded and lawns to be mowed and hay to be put up. One is too busy to notice.

But today, it was too early in the spring for mowing of lawns and putting in gardens. I put on my red jacket and started on my morning walk to the shore. I checked the striped maple. Had the leaves just burst open today? It seemed that the woods had come alive again. The fiddlehead fern were pushing their way up through the mud by the spring now. I wondered about the lady slippers. Gracie followed me into the woods to where the flowers had been sleeping all winter. Yes, the thick green leaves were pushing up through the brown oak leaves. Where else in the world could I go where I would know every spot where the wildflowers grow? I checked the dogtooth violets. It would take more sunshine for them to open, but by noon their mouths should be wide.

I walked down the trail. *The spring beauties should be near here*, I thought. *There's something special about them. They give me faith that, although hope may fade, that come spring, the world will come alive again. The spring beauties will bloom again like they do every spring.* I touched their pinkish-white petals and picked one for the little vase on the kitchen counter. Gracie rubbed my leg. I picked her up and placed her on my shoulder, and started home. Cold, clear water babbled over the rocks and into the sea. I stopped for a moment. Gracie rubbed her whiskers on my head. The tide seemed to be motionless for a moment before turning out to sea again. The smell was familiar to me. Eider ducks paddled in the cove and talked to each other with sweet cooing sounds. I saw that each black and white male was following a little brown female. It wouldn't be long, and the males would have their own club again, and the brown mothers would have a line of fuzzy brown and yellow little ones in tow.

I remembered two years ago when I had hopped onto Dixi's sleek bare back on a June evening and ridden her to this very spot. Her misty gray foal scampered at her side, sniffing each new thing and feigning fright. The sun was setting in the west when we neared the spot, and I let Dixi's head down to munch the spring green grass that grew in this clearing at the water's edge. The air was cool and clean. A mother eider duck and a half-dozen ducklings slipped into the water from the rocks, not more than fifteen feet in front of us. Life. It is so new and fresh in the springtime. I wondered if I would soon be riding Dixi down this same trail to this same spot with Jack's foal at side. I wondered if that same mother eider duck would be here in the sunset with her babies. I had only a few weeks to wait.

Dixi's udder began to swell along with her belly. I looked forward eagerly to the delivery date in hopes that everything would clear up after the pregnancy. I took the curry comb from the nail in the corridor and began to brush Dixi's body as she stood, soaking three of her feet in the black rubber buckets. The winter coat came off in gobs and floated away on the spring breeze. Perhaps it would furnish soft bedding for the barn swallows who would soon return to build muddy nests on the rafters of the barn.

How sleek and black Dixi's coat was. I had always believed that she was the most beautiful mare I had ever laid eyes on. Even now, as she stood with her feet in the black buckets and ten months pregnant, she was beautiful. Her black flowing tail touched the ground, and her mane hung down two inches below her neck and rippled in the spring breeze.

At last, it was Memorial Day. The rhubarb was hip-high in the garden now, and I knew the baby should be due soon. The smell of freshly-baked rhubarb pie wafted through the kitchen window Wednesday evening when I came home from work. I smiled. It must be my neighbor, Sally, at work again.

Sure enough, there on the kitchen table was a warm rhubarb pie! A note read, "Time for our spring tonic again, Liz. I picked your rhubarb and made a pie for each of us. Love, Sally."

"How lucky," I smiled. "How lucky I am to own the neighborhood rhubarb patch!"

The lilacs were laughing in the light of the full moon as I went out to check my mare. The night was cool, and the scent of the lilacs filled the air. All was still. I could see Dixi's silhouette in the moonlight as she grazed near the gate. I felt her udder. Warm milk was running down her legs. *She's set the table*, I thought. *The baby should be here tonight. They say it's better if your mare can deliver outside. She's always managed to be outside and have her previous six foals without any trouble. I'll check her again in a couple of hours.*

Midnight passed, and the moon was climbing in the sky. Three o'clock passed. The moon was beginning its descent. No signs of distress. No baby. I slept again.

As the sky began to lighten in the east, I made my next trip. The scent of lilacs still filled the air, and the moon was still bright in the west as I opened the pasture gate. Dixi was standing quietly over a little mound of something dark. In the light of the moon, I could see a white star in the middle of a black furry forehead. It reminded me of his father's. Most of the little fellow was still encased in the birthing sac. My heart leaped. What was wrong! The baby lay motionless, his head in an awkward position. My hand instinctively reached for the baby's head. It was cold and wet and lifeless. I felt the blood drain from my head. I wanted to faint.

The Third Grave by the Pine Tree

I started to lead Dixi out the gate and into the barn. She walked painfully. Then her head turned to call for her baby. A loud shriek pierced the air as she cried for her young one. I tried to comfort her, but she wouldn't be comforted. "It's dead, Dixi," I said numbly. "It's dead! You've got to come in the barn and let us bury it."

She shrieked again. Jack's little black baby was cold and still. There would be no little black colt racing alongside its mother this summer. We would only have a memory of what was.

Dixi was frantic to be with her baby. Even grain with molasses wouldn't interest her. She almost forgot her abscessed feet in her anxiety over her baby. All day she cried.

Her feet began to swell, and the heat increased in spite of our treatments. What was I to do? In my heart I knew. There was no more hope.

My eyes were dry, and I felt numb that afternoon as I called the vet. "Come do what you've gotta do, Dave," I said flatly. "I'll be away for a while."

I packed my suitcase and drove the gray-green Firebird out of the yard. I didn't notice the lingering scent of purple lilacs as I left the yard. I didn't notice the lady slippers along the side of the road as I drove down the lane to Tina's. I only noticed the two grassy mounds in the corner of the pasture near the pine trees. This afternoon there would be another.

"Tina," I said dry-eyed. "The vet is burying Dixi as we speak. This all seems like some kind of bad dream.

"I'm here for you, Liz," she said. "I know you'd do the same for me."

Sabbath came, and I slipped alone into my usual church pew. The children were singing in their various departments.

"Jesus loves me, this I know, For the Bible tells me so."

Esther came down and slipped in beside me. "I heard about Dixi," she whispered as she reached over and took my hand. Tears welled up in Esther's warm hazel eyes. She put her arm around my shoulders and was silent. Esther always seemed to know what to do when people were hurting. She knew how to just be there.

The scent of lilacs still filled the air, and the moon was still bright in the west as I opened the pasture gate. Dixi was standing quietly over a little mound of something dark

Remember, We Love You, Liz!"

Monday afternoon, as I was back at work trying to get caught up on the paperwork, my eyes fell on a card that had come in the mail. "TravCorps now has openings for traveling physical therapists as well as nurses." I blinked.

Maybe I should give them a call. Loneliness reached to the depths of my soul. *Things here will never be the same*, I thought to myself. *My dreams lie shattered at my feet. But I am free. Right now, there is really nothing tying me down. I don't have to stay here and put up with this. Surely, there must be the smell of spring, the singing of birds, and smiling faces somewhere.*

In a few days, the information packet arrived. There were pictures of young people walking hand in hand on sandy beaches and skiing on sunny mountainsides. They would pay wages, lodging, and travel expenses. It sounded like a deal! I failed to ask if the male companion pictured in the brochure would be included.

I talked the idea over with my friends, Alex and Esther. "Go for it!" Alex advised. "If I didn't have a private practice here in Maine, Esther and I would think about doing it, too."

It would still take a while, though, before I would be pulling out of the driveway on the way to my first traveling assignment. But the planning was part of the adventure and would help to keep my mind from the loneliness of the present. There were licenses to be obtained. I would need to find a suitable tenant to take care of my big Old New England farmhouse.

Well, the horses and the dog are dead, so I won't have to worry about getting anyone to take care of them, I thought. *I wonder what my dad would think! Here is his little daughter taking off alone across the United States to help the poor little sick boys and girls who need physical therapy. Maybe it's just as well that he doesn't know.*

Poor Gracie Allen, I thought. *She's been my loyal cat, trying to take good care of me since our loyal dog died. She thought that old blue Australian shepherd dog was her mother. After all, it's not every kitten that has been nursed and had its diapers changed by a mother dog!*

By late summer, all my duckies were in a row. Armed with fifteen state physical therapy licenses, I prepared to hit the road.

Sally called to see if I could come for chowder. "Tide's in and the chowdah's on." From their front window, you could watch the lobster boats chugging up the Merrucoonegan Sound and the eider ducks in the cove. Their ducklings were almost grown now.

"Where's your first assignment?" Sam asked, reaching for some of Sally's homemade bread.

"It'll be at a little one-horse town on the Virginia-West Virginia border," I said. "It shouldn't be far from the Appalachian Trail."

"Where will you stay?" Sally asked. "Aren't you scared? You'll be all alone. And who will go sledding with me this winter!"

We laughed. It was sort of a family joke. Their kids were grown, and they had grandchildren, but Sally still liked to go sledding when the ice was on Will Proctor's hill.

That afternoon, I walked down the lane to say goodbye to LeRoy, Tina, and Katie. The goldenrod and Queen Anne's lace were blooming in the field across the road. The apples on the old apple tree wouldn't be ripe for another month. There were puffy clouds and fluffy trees. One branch of the maple tree beside the house was already presenting a few red leaves. It would be four weeks before the leaves would be at their peak. I would miss the autumn foliage. Of all the places in the world, I knew there could never be anything more beautiful in the fall than this little lane leading from my house to my nearest neighbors.

"We're here for you, Liz," Tina said. "When will you be back?"

I wished they hadn't asked. "When will I be back? Well, this assignment is supposed to be for three months. After that …" I shrugged.

Next morning, I put the few remaining items in the car; then went back inside. Gracie Allen wanted to be carried. All was silent now except the ticking of the grandmother clock in the hallway. I walked silently through the house. It was full of memories. The grand piano in the living room remembered the Saturday night hootenannies and the old songs.

> With someone like you, a pal good and true,
> I'd like to leave it all behind and go and find
> Someplace that's known to God alone
> Just a spot to call our own.
> We'll find perfect peace where joys never cease
> Out there beneath the kindly sky
> We'll build a sweet little nest somewhere in the west
> And let the rest of the world go by."

Charlotte used to sit over there in the corner on a kitchen chair and strum her guitar. Alice sat on the floor with her tenor ukulele. The round oak table in the kitchen remembered Friday night suppers with chicken soup and fresh bread and friends. The red rug in the bedroom remembered sunshine streaming in on a spring morning … and Marbie. I walked out the back door and into the barn. It had memories, too. It remembered snowy winter evenings when Jack and Dixi were sheltered safely inside. It remembered the smell of fresh hay and warm horse breath.

I closed the door. Then turned and drove away.

As I drove down the lane, my neighbor, Ruth, stood on her porch and waved. The late summer sunshine shone on her neat little white house with the green shutters and on her white, curly hair. Why! There was a tear on her pale cheek! Why hadn't it occurred to me that my leaving would cause grief to anyone? Was this running away a selfish thing?

I remembered the time little Tim, her grandson, fell and hit his head on a rock. Blood was streaming down his little brown cheek and onto his little blue overalls when she came screaming into my kitchen with the little fellow in her arms.

I remembered the peaceful look on her face in the early spring when I met her on the trail coming out of the woods. Her hand was full of pink lady slippers from deep in the forest. They had been her friends since she was a child! Every spring, she would return to pet them and gather a few for the vase in her kitchen window.

Now, as I drove away, she stood there on her wisteria-covered porch and waved. "Remember, we love you, Liz!" she called as she grew smaller in the rearview mirror.

Suddenly, I realized how much I loved these people. I realized how much this little speck of the world that I called home had come to mean to me. As a child I had moved from place to place with my parents and "pulled up stakes" and friendships several times a year. I was always the one who moved away. Now, here I was, by my own choice pulling away again. But I had let these people on the rocky coast of Maine become attached by a little tender cord that went directly to my heart! It hurts to leave home! Would I ever be able to come home again?

2. Alone, Alone, All, All Alone

The First Day of the Rest of Your Life

The Firebird thought it was going to Washington, DC, to see friends again, but this time I turned south on I-81. The rolling hills of the Pennsylvania Dutch country took the place of the birch trees and stone walls of New England. The future was unknown.

Near Harrisburg I stopped for the night. I was glad I brought my own pillow. Motels are notorious for a strange array of pillows. Sometimes they are so puffy they crimp your neck. Other pillows look like they were purchased from the more expensive motels after all the puff was gone. Towels are the same way. I wondered how all the towels in the less expensive motels could always appear to be the same age and threadbare. There's a lot I don't know about the hospitality industry.

Tonight would be a flat-pillow motel. No need to unpack. I could just wash out my underwear and wear the same clothes in the morning.

Inevitably, there comes a time when you are left alone with your thoughts. I hugged my pillow and wondered what a nice girl like me was doing in a place like this. What if the house burned down at home or something happened to me here in this motel room? Who would know where I was tonight?

One of the songs from the hootenanny at home around the grand piano came to my mind. It was tradition that, as the party was winding to a close, we would all stand in a circle around the living room and join hands. Then Alice would lead us in "The Night Watch." Tonight, all alone in the strange motel, the song went through my head.

I closed my eyes. "God, you know where I am, and You know why I'm here. I'm in Your hands."

I slept.

Other Peoples' Soap Operas

In the morning, when I opened the drapes to check on the weather, I noticed an intriguing cafe across the street. "Dutch Pantry." There was a big Dutch windmill at the entrance. "Wonder what they have?" I thought. I dressed and walked across the street in the early morning drizzle.

Inside was the smell of coffee and apple fritters. The fritters came with spiced applesauce. There's something about a happy breakfast that makes one forget the troubles from the night before. I ordered.

There was no hurry this morning. It should take only a few hours to drive from Harrisburg to Claypool Hill. My eyes swept the room. There at the end was a big black wood-burning cookstove. Pennsylvania Dutch hex symbols hung on the walls. I liked it.

"Traveling far?" the young waitress asked as she set the plate of apple fritters in front of me.

"I don't really know," I answered. "I'm supposed to be going somewhere in western Virginia to work at a hospital that's needing a physical therapist. I think it will take about eight hours to get there. I've never been there before."

"You're doing what?" she asked incredibly. "You're just taking off across country working at any hospital that happens to be needing you? My, but you are brave!"

"Sometimes, there's only a fine line between brave and foolish," I answered. "Last night, I was feeling like it was the latter! This morning with your pleasant encouragement and a good breakfast, I'm beginning to feel brave again."

She smiled. "Good luck!"

There was no interstate highway system to Claypool Hill, Virginia. From Abingdon I turned north, then northeast toward Bluefield, Virginia, on US 19. Goldenrod and Queen Anne's lace lined the highway. The barns along Route 19 looked like they were more interested in open air than winter warmth. I had to smile later. These barns were for drying tobacco, not for keeping the livestock warm in winter!

It was late afternoon when I arrived in Claypool Hill. I stopped at the only restaurant in the small Virginia town, JR's. The locals stopped talking and stared at me when I entered.

"Sit anywhere," the waitress called from across the room.

I could catch drifts of conversation from the men at the big round table in the middle of the room.

"...And that four-wheeler pulled out and put on the brakes right in front o' me. I had a load of coal comin' out o' the mine and couldn't stop."

So this was the caseload I'd be treating! Four-wheelers tangling with loaded coal trucks! What was a nice girl like me doing in a place like this? Well, I'd only be here in this Appalachian coal-mining town for three months. I could do anything for three months. Already the leaves were preening for fall foliage season.

There were only two motels in Claypool Hill. I chose the better one across the street from the restaurant, the Loretta Lynn. It was a flat-pillow motel. The rug was a patterned brown one that was designed not to show dirt or wear. A wainscoting of dark paneling was underneath the orange-flowered wallpaper. The bedspread was a matching orange. There was a stand-up shower with a clean shower curtain. The towels, though thin, were adequate. The walls were thin, and there was no air conditioning. I opened the window and smelled the sweet smell of freshly-mown grass and honeysuckle. I grew up with smells like this. There must be lightning bugs, too. A coon hound howled in the distance. The full moon shone on the floor, and I drifted off to sleep.

The next morning, the two physical therapy aides stared silently at me when I walked into the department. The company had sent a new therapist for them to train every three months. Their faces wore caution. The last therapist let the aides do all the work, while he sat and read the Wall Street Journal and made phone calls to his broker! They wondered what their lot would be for the next three months!

No one told me where to hang my jacket. No one mentioned where to find the ladies' room. At lunchtime Connie and Donna left, and I found my own way to the cafeteria. I could smell collards cooking. The smell of turnips guided my feet to the cafeteria in the basement. I ate alone.

The hospital was an antique. The hardwood floors squeaked as I walked down the hall. The physical therapy department was under the eaves in the attic. There was no fire escape. The elevator had a poor memory.

The townsfolk had grown up with this hospital. Two years ago, one of the hospital corporations had put in a big, modern facility in the town only a half-mile from Mattie Williams. It usually had about 60percent occupancy. Mattie Williams was usually overflowing. There was an area at the end of each hall where portable white cloth screens were kept. By afternoon, I noticed that all the hospital rooms were full, but there were still patients for admission. Out came the flimsy white screens. Patients in hospital beds were placed in the halls and screened off from the traffic by the portable screens. It wouldn't occur to them to go to the other hospital. Most of them had been born in this one. They had seen their grandparents die here, and some could remember Mattie Williams herself and her husband, Dr. Williams. He was the only doctor in town back then. Without him they wouldn't have had a hospital at all. Their lives were bound up with this old building in the middle of town.

The physical therapy aides, Connie and Donna, were both in their early twenties and divorced. Their world was parenting, tending sick mothers, and trying to make ends meet.

By charting time that afternoon, the ladies were curious to know more about this new therapist. I told them what made me decide to travel. Their eyes softened. They seemed to understand.

There's something about a happy breakfast that makes one forget the troubles from the night before

"Yeah," Donna said softly. "Things don't always turn out like you plan, do they? I found out Guy was sleeping with another woman only three weeks after we came back from our honeymoon. I kicked him out that night. My little girl's only a year old. She's never known her father."

"Connie's old man left her when they'd only been married a year."

"It's OK, I guess," Connie said. "My mom needs me, anyway. She's got a brain tumor. But when she dies, I don't want to live there anymore! My old man's been beatin' up on my mom since I can remember. He drinks, you know!"

I pondered. We all have our own soap operas.

The patient load was heavy. We worked hard and did the best we could. But sometimes, at the end of the day, while we were doing our charting, we would have time to share our thoughts.

"Do they have chiggers in Maine?" Donna asked one day.

"They couldn't live there, Donna," I answered. "It's too cold! And they don't have rattlesnakes, either!"

"Well, what do they have? We've lived here at Claypool Hill and Swords Creek all our lives. It's hard to think of a place that doesn't even have chiggers and rattlesnakes!"

"Some people don't have what you've got, Donna," I answered. "You have the security of a place you know. It's home to you. People have known you since you were a baby and maybe even knew your grandma. Sometimes I really envy what you have. You see, my parents moved around a lot when I was a kid. My first year in school, I had three teachers. The second year, I went to three different schools! And now here I am again, on the road.

"I don't know a soul within miles of this place! If I get sick in the middle of the night, there's nobody to call. I don't even know where the Laundromat is. What happens if the car breaks down?"

The girls were silent, each wrapped in thought.

Almost Like Driving an Oil Tanker

A motel room in a small town in Appalachian Virginia loses its glamour quickly! I could envision myself moving every 4–12 weeks from flat-pillow motel to flat-pillow motel all the way across the United States. There would be nothing but a stack of motel receipts to show for the pilgrimage through all the strange towels and pillows.

I unpacked the Firebird and hung my clothes on the rack behind the door. My own pillow with the pink-flowered pillowcase rested at the head of the bed with the orange spread. I took my little white porcelain vase from the suitcase and placed it on the dresser. Ruth had given it to me years ago, so I would have something just the right size to hold a few May flowers in the spring. At home it would be sitting in the kitchen window.

The afternoon sunshine was still warm. From my first-floor motel window, I could see a field with Queen Anne's lace and goldenrod. Maybe these common little flowers would be pretty in the little white vase. I strode outdoors and out into the field. I could hear coal trucks grunting up the hill but was too far away to smell the fumes. The late summer breeze rustled the weeds in the field.

Kids were getting off the school bus. I smiled. Kids all over the country get off the school bus in the same way. The first thing they do is run! They check the mailbox, then make a dash for the refrigerator. School is such a cramp for five- and six-year-olds. They'd be better off to be left free as lambs to romp in the open fields or lie down and take a nap when sleepy.

The small sprigs of the goldenrod and Queen Anne's lace made a perfect bouquet for the little white vase on the dresser. I wondered if Gracie Allen would like them in this motel room.

In a few weeks, I began shopping for a recreational vehicle. The used ones smelled of stale tobacco smoke. The vans were too small. The motorhomes were depressing. You were always in your vehicle. Trailers were hard to pull.

I was almost ready to give up on the idea when I decided to make a trip to Roanoke for the weekend. The eighteen-wheelers whizzed past and blew drizzle and road scum on the car window. It was a raw Sunday morning. Maybe I could find a Shoney's and take in a nice, hot breakfast of hash browns and eggs and grits with butter. I pulled off I-81 onto the parallel US 11 a few miles south of Roanoke. Off to my right was an RV dealer. I could at least look. A gray-haired gentleman with a kindly face met me in the parking lot. "Can I help you?" he asked.

"Yes, I'm a traveling therapist, and I've been thinking of getting an RV so I won't end up at the end of my travels with only a pile of motel receipts."

He showed me the usual new and used campers and motorhomes. Today, they all looked especially depressing with the raw wind and the drizzle. It seemed they all had dark paneling and brown rugs. I may as well live in a cave. I must have looked about as depressed as I felt. "Let me show you one more," the kindly man suggested. "We just took this one to a big RV show in Washington, DC. Everybody really liked it. It's a demo, so we could adjust the price."

He led me to the back of the lot where a forty-foot fifth wheel was parked. I'd never really thought of a fifth wheel. I hardly knew what one was. I knew the moment I entered, though, that this was my new home. Instead of the dark walnut paneling, the walls and closets and cupboards were blond! Even on a drizzly day, the little home was cheerful. There were lots of windows. There was one all the way across the back behind the coral-colored living room couch. There was another above the little drop-leaf wooden table to the right of the couch. To the left was a full-length window next to the front door. Over the dinette in the kitchen, was another window. There was even a window over the double kitchen sink. In the bedroom there was a window all the way across the front of the RV as well as short, wide ones on each side of the queen-sized bed. The bathroom had a little window over the coral-colored countertop. There were two full-length mirrors on the front of the two closets in the bathroom.

I walked up the two steps from the kitchen entryway into the bathroom. This, in itself, was enough to sell me on the unit. On the left there was a light beige tub and shower with the matching commode beside it. The sink and coral-colored vanity were on the right. There were more mirrors over the bathroom lavatory. Most of the RV bathrooms I had seen were choppy and scrunched. This one was open and spacious. The same light-gray rug carpeted the bathroom and bedroom.

From the bathroom I walked up two more steps into the bedroom. The queen-sized bed was spread with a subtle coral and gray covering. I spread myself out on the bed. *Wait till I show this to Gracie Allen! I thought. I know she'll love it. She will even match this coral-pink and gray bedspread. And she can sneak up onto the bed after I fall asleep and purr till morning! I think I'll put up pink ruffled curtains and bring my pink down comforter from home. Gracie will like that.*

The kindly man was watching me out of the corner of his eye. Salesmen are good at that. "Take a look at the kitchen," he said. "It has a full oven and a microwave. See this little cupboard?" He opened a long skinny door and pulled out a narrow cupboard where the canned goods would fit. There was almost as much room in this one little pull-out cupboard as there was in my own canned-good cupboard at home.

"I think you should know," he continued, "that there are two propane furnaces in this unit. There are also two air conditioners."

He stepped back onto the light-gray carpet of the living room. "Over here is a little corner cupboard, where you can keep your little vases and things."

Wow, was this man ever a reader of people!

"It has a TV and stereo speakers in every room, too."

There were lots of things I didn't know to ask, but I don't think they would have made any difference. The three-quarter-ton Ford F-250 at home had only a 360 motor. Would it be able to tow this ten-thousand-pound home? I didn't know there would be one ton of weight on the hitch in the bed of the truck.

"It has four holding tanks, too," the kindly gray-haired man continued.

"Why does it need all that?" I asked.

"You see, there is one for black water ... "

I interrupted, "What color? Black?" I hated to appear too ignorant.

"Sewage, dear. Sewage from the commode."

We laughed together. He continued. "There's one for water storage in case you are out where you can't hook up to the outside utilities. There are two holding tanks for gray water."

He led me to the back of the lot where a forty-foot fifth wheel was parked. I'd never really thought of a fifth wheel. I hardly knew what one was. I knew the moment I entered, though, that this was my new home

I must have looked puzzled again. He walked over to the closet doors that faced the kitchen entryway. I squealed and clapped my hands as he opened the door. "A washer and dryer!" I exclaimed. "What's the bottom line?"

His answer was what you would expect of a top-notch salesperson. "Well, not as much as you might think. It's a demonstration model, so you should be able to get it for under $36,000."

I blinked. "Could we work out some financing? I'll need to see what I would spend on motel bills in a month and let you know. I'll talk it over with my traveling company.

"By the way, what type of vehicle do I need to pull this thing?"

"We recommend a one-ton truck, preferably a dually," he answered. "It's almost as long as an oil tanker if you include the length of your truck."

"I have only a three-quarter-ton with a small engine," I said.

"You should be able to pull it with that on the highway. I wouldn't attempt to pull it over the Rockies, though." He smiled and shook my hand as I hopped back into the Firebird and headed up the road again, looking for Shoney's.

I talked it over with my company and discovered that I could get both the fifth wheel and a new truck for the money they had allotted for travel expenses. I was ecstatic!

The Pink Straw Hat

The forty-foot fifth wheel became home for the little puffy kitty and me for the next four years! Living in a forty-foot fifth wheel with a sweet little buff and gray kitty with white trim is an adventure. Pulling a forty-foot fifth wheel is almost too much adventure. But I pulled it back to the farm in New England to pick up some housekeeping supplies. Bread pans, cookie sheets, crystal goblets, sterling silver, you never know what you might need for entertaining on the road.

I bought a little pink straw hat, so the truck drivers would be nice to me. I didn't really like the idea of being a woman truck driver. But it could be that I may need their help sometime.

I found a comfortable spot on the bed in the fifth wheel for Gracie and headed south on Interstate 95.

"What's the matter, Gracie?" I asked when we made our first rest stop. She was nowhere to be found! "Did you jump ship, Gracie!" I panicked. "Please, let me find you!"

"Neow?" she asked as she poked her head out of the covered litter box that was stored in the bathtub.

She looked worried, so did I. "Oh, Gracie! What if I have a blowout? What if I can't find a campground? What if I drive into a place and can't back out? What if the camping area is unsafe? Oh, Gracie!" I whispered. My eyes began to sting, but I blinked back the tears.

Gracie only purred loudly and snuggled into my lap.

"Is it OK to be scared, Gracie Allen? It's all so unknown out there!" I held Gracie Allen close and listened as the eighteen-wheelers ground their gears and double-clutched their way out of the service area in Kennebunk, Maine.

"I gotta' go, Gracie Allen," I said, scratching her under the chin.

"Neow?" she asked.

I adjusted my pink straw hat in the mirror, then squared my shoulders, and stepped out onto the black pavement. Diesel fumes filled the air at the truck stop. I went inside the building. Maybe I should take advantage of this stop and get a bite to eat. I checked the serving line. Canned string beans, reconstituted mashed potatoes, pot roast, and pies. I gagged. "So this is what professional truckers live on," I thought. "Hardly a glamorous life."

When I thought of stopping at the Dutch Pantry for apple fritters, a new problem presented itself. How on earth was I to pull into that crowded parking lot and get out again without crashing into some four-wheeler! The combined length of the fifth wheel plus the truck was fifty-three feet! That was almost as long as a semi! The fritters were worth a try, though. As I pulled by the flat-pillow motel of a couple of months ago, I noticed that there was plenty of room for all the eighteen-wheelers. I parked my eight-wheeler up beside one and walked across to the Dutch Pantry. *This is doable*, I thought. *You just have to do lots of planning ahead and don't get into something you can't get out of.*

A Southern Country Gentleman

"Well, I just bought this forty-foot fifth wheel, and after one trip decided that a three-quarter-ton just won't do it," I answered and proceeded to fill him in on the details of my beautiful new home.

McCann, the owner, took me out of the mountains to Johnson City, Tennessee. We tried out an overpowering black diesel dually. I found out that they call it dually because it has dual wheels on the rear.

He tossed me the keys, and I stepped up into the high cab. It looked like it would pull anything I could hitch it to. He climbed into the passenger seat, and we pulled out of the car dealer's parking lot onto the four-lane street.

McCann drew a quick breath. Out of the corner of my eye, I could see a little red Corvette aiming for the door on the passenger side. I gunned the motor. Nothing happened! It was as if the powerful black diesel turned to me, laughing, and said, "What's your hurry? You want pick-up, do you, or power? Take your choice."

The red sports car veered to the side and sped around us. My knuckles were white and McCann's face ashen. "I think I found out what I need to know," I said. "Pulling a fifth wheel isn't the only thing this truck will have to do. Where can I turn around? Maybe my friend Jackie will let me have her one-ton Ford F-350 with a 460 gasoline engine. It's used, but low mileage."

On the way back up into the "holler," McCann took me to the Martha Washington in Abingdon. Inside, the waiters carried white towels draped over their arms, and the chandeliers hung low. It was a lovely visit.

His first marriage broke up, leaving him with two wonderful, hard-working sons. "Jerry can sell anything!" McCann said proudly. "He's a lot like me. He likes the business part of the job. He likes to plan and do things. His brother Gary is excellent in the service department. I'm awful lucky!"

"Had a tough time when my second wife left me. I'd let her be the business manager. She took everything."

"Oh, no!" I sympathized. "What did you do?"

"You do what you have to do and start all over!"

Big Bucks

So, the president of the company was actually going to find his way to Claypool Hill, Virginia. There must be something he wanted to check out with the hospital administration in person. I've always had a curiosity about what goes on in smoke-filled back rooms when the thinking heads get together.

I stayed up late that night, baking small loaves of dark whole-wheat bread in the oven of the fifth wheel. I packed a picnic basket with a large red-checked napkin and placed within it a bottle of sparkling white non-alcoholic grape juice and two long-stemmed crystal goblets. I cut up wedges of cabaret and cheddar and Tillamook cheese. I placed a breadboard in the basket and slept until daybreak.

I was glad Dr. Snider was going to check out this hospital. Although it was JCAH accredited and the love of the locals, I trembled at the situation of the PT department. The first room was barely large enough for a desk and a traction table. The traction table could second as a treatment table. The back room was under the eaves of the old building, and I was in constant alert to keep from whacking my head on the ceiling.

That morning I wore my navy blue corporate suit with the lacy white blouse and high heels.

About noon, Dr. Snider appeared in the doorway. His suntanned face and black hair were set off by his navy blue suit and white shirt. He was a slight man, probably only 120 pounds and five foot four. His dark eyes darted here and there about the room. I chuckled to myself as I contemplated the games of the corporate world.

I spread the red-checked napkin on the traction table as a tablecloth.

"Come," I said simply. "A loaf of bread, a bottle of wine, and thou!"

His delight was apparent. A president never refuses presidential honors, even if he is only a large duck in a small puddle.

Dr. Snider presented me with a proposal to be the lead therapist for his growing company. There would be a 50 percent increase in salary plus the already adequate living expenses. I was as flattered by his proposal as he was by the bread and wine! I had my money spent almost before he had finished his offer.

There is a story in Luke about a rich man that thought he had it made. He had too much grain for his barn and decided to build a bigger one. That night he died! Why was I thinking I needed more money when my heavenly Father had already provided all I needed?

There was one catch to Dr. Snider's offer. I would go wherever they needed me and do whatever they needed for as long as they needed me in that location. But, hey, this was exciting!

Connie and Donna stayed out of the way during the picnic, but I caught Connie's eye now and again as they walked past the door. I knew they couldn't wait to giggle with me as soon as he left.

Oh, How I Love Jesus

But there was work to be done. The patients needed to be treated.

There was Grandma Adams. The sun shone onto the wooden floor through the long, curtainless window at the Mattie Williams hospital. Grandma Adams lay silently on the creaky hospital bed that had to be hand-cranked up and down. I opened the window and let the late summer air fill the room. The silver song of the meadowlark came through the open window.

Grandma Adams had brought up her family of five sons and four daughters and should have had time now to tell stories to her grandchildren as she rocked in the porch swing in the summer evening. She should be baking cookies and singing songs.

Her youngest daughter, Louise, sat in the chair at her side, working on some tatting.

"Your mother has such a peaceful face," I remarked.

"Yes," her daughter returned. "Mama has always been such a patient, gentle person. I don't know how she did it with all us children underfoot. She used to clean us all up and take us to Sunday School every week, too."

I picked up Grandma's right arm and began to give her range of motion. First, the fingers, then the wrist; I watched her face. Was this causing any pain? Was there any motion there at all?

As I moved her limbs, I started to sing softly.

"Oh, how I love Jesus, Oh, how I love Jesus …"

Grandma Adams' head turned toward me, and her eyes met mine. Her lips began to move; then, a crackly voice joined mine.

"Oh, how I love Jesus because He first loved me!"

I glanced at her daughter. A tear was on her cheek.

A president never refuses presidential honors, even if he is only a large duck in a small puddle

I could almost picture the sympathizing angels in this stark hospital room with us. Her guardian angel that had been with her all her life was there at her side now as we were singing. I wondered if this angel felt sad, seeing life slipping away.

A tear came to my own eye. How thankful I was that I hadn't just relegated her to the un-rehabilitable pile! I bent and planted a little kiss on her forehead.

Black Earth and Overalls

It was almost winter. Dr. Snider needed me in Minnesota. How would the fifth wheel fare in a Minnesota winter! The fertile acres of plowed black earth would soon be covered with snow. But the Midwestern people felt comfortable to me. As I drove across the flat landscape of western Minnesota, I remembered summers on my uncle's farm as a youth.

In my memory it was summertime. The Sabbath dinner was over. The dishes were done, and the dishtowels hung across the dishrack to dry. The men were in the living room, talking about cattle and hay, and the women talked of quilts and canning tomatoes.

I made my way outdoors. The screen door slammed a little. It was "discretionary time" for a thirteen-year-old. All week we had worked in the hayfield, but today was the "Day of Rest and Gladness."

The drizzle hit my cheeks and stood in little beads on my long, brown braids. The younger kids were playing underfoot in the house. What was this thirteen-year-old from the city to do on a drizzly Sabbath afternoon on a Midwestern farm?

The city was always clamoring. Our house was only three doors from the emergency room of the large hospital in downtown Los Angeles. It was haunted constantly by the wail of emergency vehicles. Gangs roamed the streets, and a thirteen-year-old girl wasn't even safe on a bicycle in broad daylight.

But here it was safe. The doors remained unlocked day and night. The pretentiousness of the city was put aside, and I was free.

I wandered toward the barn. Swallows! They had a nest in the hayloft. I wondered if the eggs had hatched yet?

I climbed the ladder to the hayloft and peeked into the nest. Happily, the eggs nestled in the nest. The sweet smell of hay was comfortable. The pounding of rain on the tin roof of the barn told me there was no use to venture outside.

I lifted one little egg into my hand. To my delight I saw that it was cracking. The tiny creature inside was trying to find his way out. I was entranced! I held the fragile egg in my hand and seated myself in the hay to watch.

Slowly at first, the little creature began to peck and push his way out of the shell. I watched. At last, the little naked bird lay vulnerable in my hand.

Singing from the nearby house floated softly to the loft. It was peaceful. "I sing because I'm happy. I sing because I'm free. His eye is on the sparrow, and I know He watches me!"

I placed the baby bird back into the nest and climbed back down the ladder. The rain had stopped, and the slant of the sun peeking through the clouds beckoned the near close of the Sabbath. I went back into the house and sat on the arm of the big chair and joined my voice with my uncle. "He's got the whole world in His hands!"

With memories like that, I felt more like I was coming home than going to a new assignment.

Monday morning, a tall, suntanned man with brown hair and bib overalls was waiting for a treatment. "My knee just hasn't been right since I broke it," the tall man spoke. He pulled up his blue denim overalls and pulled his socks down to the top of his boots. The knee area was swollen, and he winced when I pressed the area of the medial meniscus.

"How'd you break it?" I asked.

"Well, we were bringing in that last load of hay. You know how it is. Albert had been stackin' it, but I climbed up to ride back to the barn on top of the load. It was good hay. Timothy and clover. It was a good crop this year. The Timothy was up to the buttonhole on my overalls' bib. Good year! I don't know what happened, but the load started slipping. Albert must have tried to get those last two bales on so we wouldn't have to make another trip. Anyhow, it started slippin', and I jumped to get clear, but I didn't make it." He was silent a moment. "I guess I was lucky I didn't break my neck. I could hear them calling, but I was buried under the hay, and they couldn't find me. You pray a lot in a fix like that!"

I loved these people. The smell of well-cured hay, the black earth, the blue overalls reminded me of those long days in the hayfield with my uncle. I could speak the language of horses and hay and corn. There's something strong and courageous, yet gentle and tender about the Midwestern farmland.

I reminisced to Gracie about the good old days as she crunched her Meow Mix that night. She didn't care what I said as long as I was talking. Hers had been a long silent day with lots of cat naps.

3. You Need to Carry a Gun!

Everybody Else Does!

When the snowflakes began to fly, I knew I must move on. Dr. Snider needed me back in the "holler" on the Kentucky side of the Appalachian Trail. The road sign read, "McDonald's, 26 miles." That was my first clue. It was almost that far from everything else, too. There wasn't even a Walmart! At the drug store on the corner, you could sit at a counter and sip a milkshake. They sold knickknacks, too. There were little figurines about 3–5 inches high made out of coal. You know, the figurines of little girls and boys playing on teeter-totters, or picking flowers, or saying their prayers. I picked up one to bring back to Ruth.

"It'll only be for a couple of weeks," they told me. "We have someone in mind to come and take your place, but they don't have a Kentucky physical therapy license yet."

I was pleasantly surprised at the modern, well-equipped hospital. The physical therapy department was about forty feet by forty feet and had all the equipment a lone therapist and one aide could use. The hospital was on a hillside, so there weren't any windows in the department. The lack of windows made it an ideal place in which to hide patients in the event of a tornado.

There were plenty of young, enthusiastic physicians eager to use the most modern medicine for their clients. The therapy department was affiliated with Cardinal Hill Rehabilitation Hospital in Lexington, Kentucky. Physicians from teaching hospitals held clinics at our Mary Breckenridge Hospital, and specialists were sent for some of the difficult cases.

There was a school for midwives and family nurse practitioners. There was a host of teenaged youth brightening the hallways and running errands.

This place could be fun! Every morning, representatives from each discipline met with the team to talk over the status of each patient and plan an aggressive treatment program. Imagine sitting at the feet of all these learned young doctors and discussing each case on an individual basis! I was "psyched!"

There were four or five of the young doctors who had taken government money for tuition and were paying it off by offering service at this hospital back in the holler. The director of nursing was there as were representatives from dietary, respiratory, social service, and physical therapy departments.

"Mrs. Jones in room 101A had a shift to the left last night. I plan to start her on digitalis today to see if she will stabilize." The young, bewhiskered doctor with an open-neck, short-sleeved yellow shirt continued speaking.

"Mrs. Smith in bed B should be going home today. What are the plans for home care, Dorothy?" He looked at the representative from social service.

"No problem. Her children and grandchildren have organized round-the-clock coverage for her in her own home," Dorothy answered.

Wow! I thought to myself. *I like the way they do things back here!*

I wondered how such a facility came into being so far back in the holler.

When the snowflakes began to fly, I knew I must move on

At lunchtime I made my way to the spacious cafeteria that overlooked the valley. I was reminded that I was still back in the holler, though, by the smell of okra, breaded tomatoes, and turnips. The cooks were great, yet had the wisdom to know that sick people are going to eat best if they have food that is familiar to them.

I spotted a group of young people sitting together at one of the long tables in the dining room. Maybe I could learn something if they would let me sit with them.

"What's the deal?" I asked. "How is it that there are so many bright, enthusiastic, young people here so far from everywhere?"

"Oh," said the slender, young blond sitting across the table. "You don't know the story?"

"No," I answered. "I'm just the traveling therapist that came to serve here for a couple of weeks until our contract company can find a suitable therapist to locate here permanently. What's this story?"

"Take it away, Mary," said the tall, family nurse practitioner. "Tell her your story!"

The solidly-built lady with the gray hair and deep blue eyes smiled. This was her moment of glory!

"Long years before, a nurse by the name of Mary Breckenridge had hit a major crisis in her life. Her husband and children were all killed, and her life was down to the bare bones. When she finally got over the shock, she decided that she wanted to do something meaningful. She wanted to give what was left of her own life to put sparkle in the lives of others.

"She came from England to this place back here. It was really wild then back in the Appalachian mountains of Kentucky. The people lived so far back into the holler that there was no reaching them in an emergency except by horseback. It was the days of bootleg whiskey, and strangers could face a gun unless they could prove they had come to help and not to spy.

"Today we don't go by horseback anymore. We've advanced to nurses with four-wheelers!"

"Are you Mary Breckenridge?" I asked.

Mary looked at the young people with a twinkle of mischief in her bright blue eyes. "No," she said with a little laugh that tinkled like a bell. "Mine is a different story."

"I was living in England and had just graduated from nursing when I heard about the nurses on horseback. I had always wanted a horse of my own and a dog. This sounded like adventure! I pooled my funds and took the ship to the United States. I got my horse, all right, and my dog."

The young people hung on her every word. They always liked to hear the story repeated.

"And you stayed here?" I asked, not wanting to sound too surprised.

"Of course! This is my home! I love these people!" she said as her blue eyes swept the room. "They are my family now."

"Yes, I know!" My thoughts were far away as I looked out the big picture window to the snow-covered mountains across the valley. The words of my neighbor were ringing in my ears. "Remember, we love you, Liz!"

I thought of the songs we sang at home when we all gathered with the neighbors around the warm fireplace in the living room on a winter evening. We'd have hot spiced cider from Linda-Lee's cider mill. We'd have do-your-own open-faced sandwiches on "dark bread" made by Mary and Geneva. Charlotte would bring her guitar and Cy his spoons. The music was ringing in my ears.

"I wonder how the old folks are at home. I wonder if they miss me while I roam. I can almost hear them sigh As they bid their boy goodbye, Oh, I wonder how the old folks are at home."

I glanced at my watch and pushed back my chair. I would have to join her for dinner again!

Poor Little Rich Kids

The campground was an hour and fifteen minutes from the hospital. One had to travel the two-lane Boon Turnpike up the creek to Hazard. It was coal-mining country again like Claypool Hill. Huge dump trucks filled with fist-sized black coal ground their way out of the mines and roared down the mountain. Four-wheelers, beware!

"They don't do much else back here, but what takes care of the miners," Letha told me.

It was a long day at home alone for Gracie Allen. She looked forward to evenings when she could coax me into playing a game of ball from one end of the fifth wheel to the other. She liked the little two-inch mesh plastic kind with a tinkly bell inside. But she still gained weight! Oh well, all a cat needs to do for a living is to purr and play ball and maybe make "dough bread" and sleep on the puffy pink comforter.

It was cold back in the mountains of eastern Kentucky that winter. "Why aren't you in school, anyway," I asked one of the clean-cut young men as he took off his new down-filled LL Bean parka. "I thought you kids would be out of here by now! There's not much going on here for you, is there?"

"We're living over at Windover," he told me. "My dad wanted me to be able to volunteer here at this hospital for a few months. He thinks it's a better education than Colby College in Maine, where I've been taking a psych major. He may be right! There are enough of us couriers at Windover to hang out and make our own fun. Want to come over sometime?"

"Windover?" I asked. "Is that a town?"

He laughed, "No, that's the original log cabin that Mary Breckenridge had built when she first got to this area and started the nurses on horseback. It's kind of like a dorm. We have a cook that feeds us. Come on over Saturday night. We're going to learn 'clogging'."

It sounded like a plan. They gave me a room upstairs in the fifteen-room, two-story log cabin. There was a cot, chest for clothing, and a towel on the rack on the back of the door. The bathroom and showers were down the hall. I looked out the window. The trees were bare and stark on the western side of the mountain on this the shortest day of the year. The log barn up the hill in back of the cabin was empty now. I wondered what stories it could tell.

The dinner bell rang, and I made my way down to the kitchen. The picnic tables had a blue oilcloth table cover, and there was only a bowl and knife and spoon. In the center of the table was a large kettle of tomato soup. The warm home-made bread steamed on the other end of the table.

I think I could live on this! I thought as I helped myself to the butter.

"What brought you here?" I asked a young lady with long, blond hair still smelling of shampoo.

"You see, we're couriers. You've noticed we do almost anything they let us do around the hospital and the school. It really helps the midwifery and family nurse practitioner students to have us here. We run errands, transport patients, help with the filing, you name it. I didn't think I'd like it way back here in the holler, but what an experience!"

"My mom and dad live in Palm Beach, Florida. He owns a national newspaper. I was getting burned out on school, so they let me come here for a semester."

So that's where all these bright-looking, clean-cut young people came from! How'd the "moneyed" people find out about the place?

"I noticed this is really a well-equipped facility, Joan. How do helpful people find out about what the needs are back here?" I asked.

"Oh," she answered, "Mary Breckenridge knew people. She had a lot of her influential friends in the old country, and they spread the word to their friends. Some of them started a newsletter. You know, there are lots of people willing to give to a project like this that really helps people."

We were interrupted by the sound of music and clogging feet. "Let's go!" she said. "You gotta make your own fun around here."

That night, as I lay under the handmade quilt on the narrow cot and looked out the curtainless window at the rising moon, I wondered. "Maybe everyone needs to simplify life sometimes, even poor little rich kids."

You'll Know If You're Being Followed

The women of the hospital pulled me aside after about two weeks back in the holler at Mary Breckenridge hospital to tell me the facts of life.

" 'Lizbeth, you better carry a gun!" Wanda told me. "All the other women do. It's either in the purse or in the glove compartment." She pulled a pearl-handled pistol out of her purse and laid it on the desk.

"I can't do that," I protested. "I don't know anything about guns! They'd just take it from me and use it on me!"

"My husband can take you to the edge of the woods tomorrow and teach you how," Wanda volunteered.

"I just can't do that! I'd be scared to death!"

"Well, then," Letha cautioned, "Don't take the same road home every night. Get out of here before nightfall, and if you are being followed, don't stop for anything! You'll know when you are being followed!"

"Yeah, they buried a whole school bus loaded with kids over there in the gravel pit! There was just enough air so they could breathe! The driver had all the kids praying, and that kept them calm. Yep, you'll know when you're being followed!" Letha's eyes widened.

> *"Lizbeth, you better carry a gun!" Wanda told me. "All the other women do. It's either in the purse or in the glove compartment." She pulled a pearl-handled pistol out of her purse and laid it on the desk*

With that introduction I really wanted to bolt and run. I called the traveling physical therapy company. They had never been anywhere near Appalachia! They promised again to get me out in yet another couple of weeks.

"Gracie Allen," I said to my kitty that night as she crunched her Meow Mix. "These people are afraid. They are afraid of each other. If one person starts to carry a gun, then everyone else has to carry one, too. Probably started during prohibition when everyone had a bootleg still. If they didn't know you, they'd assume you were a law officer coming to make an arrest.

"Remember back home, Gracie, when Sally would walk into our unlocked house and leave a hot rhubarb pie on the kitchen table? Someday, we'll go home."

"Neow?" Gracie asked. "Neow?"

Where Will Home Be This Christmas?

The campground in Corbin, Kentucky, was almost empty. This was no place to be for Christmas. The holiday was on Tuesday this year, so there wouldn't be any time to go home. There was already a light snow on the Boon Turnpike Friday afternoon as I made my way out of the mountains and back to the fifth wheel. It was depressing to think of spending Christmas all alone. I don't know why it's so much worse over the holidays, but it is.

I thought of last year. Jack had died in October, Marbie, in November, and I was in no mood to do the traditional Christmas thing. But I was stuck. Every year since I had moved to Maine, my class of teens from the church had come over to help me celebrate. They climbed into the attic and pulled out the Christmas decorations. They brought out the electric candles with the orange bulbs and put them in every window in the Old New England farmhouse. Extension cords were all over the floor, but you couldn't see that from the road, so that was OK. They cut pine boughs and holly and decorated the mantle. They took the tiny sparkling Christmas tree lights and decorated the ficus tree in the living room.

Next, they made a huge batch of "See's" chocolate candy. You know, the kind of candy where you pour the boiling sugar and milk mixture over the chocolate chips and marshmallows. Next, the little girls would add nuts and spoon the candy onto waxed paper-covered trays. The whole house would be smelling of pine boughs and Christmas chocolate.

I don't know why, but after all that activity, they would get into my clothes closet and dress up in my clothes. They would set the table with the crystal and sterling and pretend that they were at some elegant, queenly party. Oh, all they had was homemade bread and soup, but was ever anything more delightful? They even sang Christmas carols by candlelight

Would they miss me this year? Maybe, but they'd find other ways to entertain themselves. By the time I finished my tour as a traveling therapist, they wouldn't need me anymore. They'd soon outgrow the desire to play like this anyway. But there was something inside me that was missing them.

They say the best cure for loneliness is to find one lonelier still.

Arthur and Jean hadn't pulled out of the campground yet. They were RV lifers and hadn't left for the visit to the grandchildren. Thought they'd let the in-laws have them for Christmas, and they'd be there for New Year's. Jean was kind of strange. Sometimes, she would drift away and not finish her sentence. Sometimes, she would wander around the campground as if she didn't really know where she was. She had a metal plate in her head where one of her cranial bones used to be. She had to wear a metal riding helmet all the time. There had been an auto accident, and removing one of the cranial bones and replacing it with a metal plate was the only alternative. Arthur was good to her, but I think he missed his soulmate.

I knocked on the door of their Airstream trailer. "Come on in out of the cold," Arthur called. "Got all your Christmas shopping done? We just made our last trip to K-Mart to get a few more things for the grandkids. The crowds are worse than ever this year."

"Well, I don't have to worry about grandkids," I answered. "All I have to worry about this year is being lonely. What do you say we make our own fun around here this Christmas?"

I told them about the teens back home and our tradition. Then I asked if they'd come over and keep me from being lonely on Christmas day.

"Sure. Can we bring anything?" Jean asked.

"Well, do you have any favorite recipes that wouldn't be too hard to cook in the RV?" I asked.

"Jean makes really good cranberry relish," Arthur volunteered. "Do you feel like putting some together for the holiday, Jean?"

She thought that would be a splendid idea, so we planned our menu.

Christmas day came, and we sat around the little table in the living room of the fifth wheel. We put on a white linen tablecloth and set the table with china and sterling. We lit the pink candle and said the blessing. No, it wasn't like having the little girls giggling and pretending and putting up lights, but I felt content that I had these neighbors to keep my Christmas from being so lonely.

You Make Me Feel Like a Man

Life in a forty-foot fifth wheel is an adventure in the summer, but winter in Appalachian Kentucky leaves much to be desired. The pipes had to be drained and filled with antifreeze to keep them from freezing. That meant carrying water for cooking food. It meant trudging across the cold campground for showers and potty breaks. The winter dragged on. The company I worked for kept saying, "We have someone in mind who can start in a couple of weeks." The weeks dragged on into months. The hour-and-fifteen-minute drive into the Appalachian mountains and back out every day didn't leave much time for recreation. I had to remind myself that the reason I was there was to treat patients.

Oh, no! I thought as I read the chart on the new patient in ward four. *Not only is this guy a forty-five-year-old quadriplegic, but he's been burned. It says here that he fell into the open fire in the fireplace, hoping to commit suicide. There'll be some underlying problems here.*

"Wanda, what do you know about this fellow, Lofton? The chart says that this is his fifth admission in the last twelve months. You know everybody around here. What's going on?"

"Oh, Lofton," Wanda sighed. "Sad story. He got into a fight with one of his neighbors over a boundary dispute. They had a shoot-out, and Lofton won. Well, that is, he managed to do away with the other guy. Lofton was rendered quadriplegic in the fight, though. He is paralyzed from his neck down. They didn't even bother to take him to jail or have a trial or anything. Guess they figured he was already in jail inside a paralyzed body. He lives back in the holler with his parents. They're getting kind of old, though. I don't know what will finally happen to him."

You mean I'm going to have to treat a murderer! I thought.

"What's the problem this time?" Wanda asked.

"Looks like a suicide attempt from the chart," I answered. "He managed to fall out of his wheelchair and into the fireplace. That would take some doing for a quadriplegic! Let's go take a look at him."

Lofton's face was to the wall when we entered. The food on his breakfast tray was untouched.

"Lofton," I said, touching his shoulder gently. "I'm your therapist, Elizabeth, and this is my associate, Wanda. I think you know her from before. Here, let us crank the head of your hospital bed up so you can get a chance at your breakfast."

Lofton's blue eyes were vacant. The crew-cut blond hair made him look even more like a convict.

"Wanda, let's get him sitting up here so he can get at his breakfast. Opening a milk carton is pretty difficult for a man in a situation like this. How do you open your straw when your fingers won't move?"

We made the breakfast doable and left.

We treated the burns. We treated Lofton. Most of the day, he lay on the bed with his blue eyes staring at the ceiling. At least, the whirlpool treatments in physical therapy made a change of scenery for him.

We talked about life in the world outside the holler.

"What brought you to a place like this. It must seem like it's way back at the end of nowhere?" he asked one day. "Don't you have a family or anything?"

"Oh, I don't talk about it much, Lofton, but I guess you'd say my life fell apart, and I ran away for a while. My dog died, my horses died, my dad died, and the man I was in love with married somebody else. I don't think I really realized, though, until I drove out of the driveway, how much the people in my hometown meant to me. We looked after each other. My neighbor, Ruth, had a tear on her cheek as she waved goodbye from her front porch. Sometimes, I get sad when I think about it."

"Yeah," Lofton offered, "Sometimes, you think there isn't much to live for. But, maybe you hang around for the people that still love you and would be hurt if you left them."

I hooked my arm gently under the back of his neck and brought him to a sitting position. "Think the two of us could get you to a standing position if you lock your arms around my neck, and I block your knees and brace you at the hips?"

"Lofton!" I said aghast, as he came to a full standing position. "Lofton! You're a very tall man, aren't you! How tall are you, anyway!"

His gentle blue eyes met mine as he towered above me. "About six foot four," he answered. Then he added, "You make me feel like a man!"

A Wretch Like Me

Elmer was a pitiful case. He was a quadriplegic who had been injured in a mining accident. He was in his early fifties, single, and lived with his sister. Life was hard. Being unable to move about, he had developed open wounds on the pressure areas of his body. To top it all off, he had inoperable lung cancer.

Day after day, we hoisted him in and out of the whirlpool with a hand-cranked hydraulic lift. His wounds began to improve, but the cancer was taking its toll.

I guess you'd say my life fell apart, and I ran away for a while. My dog died, my horses died, my dad died, and the man I was in love with married somebody else

"Did you have a good night last night, Elmer?" I asked one morning as I examined his wounds.

"Not really," he answered. "I been thinkin'."

"Yes? You been thinkin'?"

"I want to be baptized," he continued. "I want to be baptized by immersion. That means you have to be dunked all the way under the water. Most folks do it in a lake or somethin', but ..."

I was a little surprised, but I shouldn't have been. Some of the folks from the local church had befriended Elmer. Pudgy, dumpling-soft women with hair piled high up on their heads came by every day and read the Bible to him, did errands, and took care of his washing.

How was a paralyzed man to be baptized by immersion? He was like the paralyzed man in the Bible who got his friends to let him down through the roof to see Jesus.

Elmer had it all figured out, though. "If we fill this whirlpool plumb full, I could go all the way under! You get me in and out of here every day with this lift anyway. What do you think?"

The next day, the minister and some of the folks from the local church pushed Elmer into the department on the stretcher. Wanda and I covered him with a clean, white gown that tied behind his neck. Then we slid the canvas seat of the Hoyer lift under him and cranked him into a sitting position. Elmer had no use of his hands but was able to hook his elbows around the chains that held the seat in place. Elmer's limp legs dangled from the seat. Wanda lifted his lifeless legs into the whirlpool and gradually lowered the lift. Elmer sank shoulder-deep into the warm water.

"Do you have a favorite song, Elmer?" I asked as I reached for my autoharp.

"Yep," he answered, "I like that one about, He saved a wretch like me."

The church members joined, and we sang:
"Amazing grace, how sweet the sound,
That saved a wretch like me!
I once was lost, but now I'm found,
Was blind, but now I see."

The pastor raised his hand over Elmer's head and prayed. "Elmer, because you love Jesus, I now baptize you in the name of the Father, the Son, and the Holy Spirit."

The pastor lowered the rest of Elmer's body under the water, and he was baptized.

When we cranked Elmer out of the tank, I noticed that the careworn, anxious lines on his face changed to a look of peace. I'm glad.

A week later, he was dead.

And They Carried Him Away in Handcuffs

Dr. Snider's company secured a contract at a second hospital back in the holler. This Red Bud Hospital was the smallest ever! It was only twenty-seven beds. But three afternoons a week, I would swing by to treat the outpatients. The hospital was clean and friendly, and I was proud to serve with these dedicated people. I wanted to tell the world how wonderful they were.

They had only two doctors on the staff. The older gentleman, Dr. Wheeler, had started the hospital years ago. His kids were all grown now, and he was recognized as the patriarch of the Red Bud Hospital.

Dr. Smith* would have reminded me of a younger version of my own father. He was short and round-faced. His light brown hair was thinning to the point of baldness. He always seemed genuinely concerned about his patients. His practice was basically obstetrics, so I rarely got to treat them. In a small hospital, though, with only two doctors, anything could show up.

Dr. Smith was a single man and had a great sense of humor. One afternoon, after we finished talking over his patient, I asked him about his family.

"Oh, my kids are all in college. You know how it is," he said, taking off his lab coat.

As I spread a clean white sheet on the treatment table, I asked, "You probably don't get a chance to get out of the mountains very often, but I'd like for you to come to Corbin this Sunday for dinner. My fifth wheel is almost as good as an apartment, and I love to entertain. Could you make it about 2:00 p.m.?"

"That would be great!" he answered enthusiastically. "See you then."

Sunday came, and I spread the little wooden table in the living room with a pink linen tablecloth. I got out the Lenox china and stemware and set the table for two.

At 2:00 p.m. the cheese pie was ready to come out of the oven, and the fresh tossed salad waited in the refrigerator.

At 2:15 the cheese pie could no longer wait to come out of the oven! I placed it on the countertop and looked out the window toward the entrance of the campground. Sam was walking his black lab in the bright sunshine, but there were no strange cars anywhere.

The cheese pie sat on the countertop, losing its puffiness by the moment. *Guess I shouldn't have planned a cheese pie*, I thought to myself. *You can never tell what emergency might come up for a doctor.* My soul knew better. Doctors use the excuse that "something came up" whenever they think it's to their benefit. My mother never really expected my dad to be on time for supper. He was only one of seven. The family went on without him.

By 3:00 p.m. the overdone cheese pie was flat and cold. The salad was wilting in the refrigerator.

By 4:00 p.m. I put the Lenox and crystal back in the corner cupboard and put the pink table cloth in the drawer. The cheese pie sat silently. I really had wanted to get better acquainted with this cheerful, charming man with the quick wit.

At 5:00 p.m. I cut a slice of cold cheese pie and put it in the microwave. I helped myself to the wilted salad and seated myself in the breakfast nook to eat. Still, there was no knock on the door. Gracie Allen hopped into my lap and asked for a pinch of the cheese pie. *Oh, well*, I thought, *what goes around comes around. I'll see what Dr. Smith's excuse is on Monday afternoon.*

Wouldn't you know, he was in surgery on Monday, and there were no outpatients on Wednesday.

You can imagine my delight when I came back on Friday afternoon to find the national news media with cameras and crew filming this unique facility!

"Did you hear the news?" Larry, the administrator, asked as I was putting my key in the lock of the office door.

"It really does look like news," I said. "I've always thought this was such a remarkable hospital; I've wished we could get some national attention here."

"No, no!" Larry's voice was agitated. "These people aren't here to tell the world how wonderful we are! It's Dr. Smith!* They handcuffed him and carried him away in the paddy wagon!"

"What!" I exclaimed. "He's fifty percent of your medical staff! How's Dr. Wheeler going to get along, being the only physician here at Red Bud! What happened?"

"Well, Dr. Smith isn't really a doctor," Larry continued. "His name isn't even Smith! When the real Dr. Smith expired, this Mr. Jones* had appropriated Dr. Smith's name and credentials."

I interrupted aghast. "You mean he isn't even who he is? That sounds funny, but you know what I mean."

"Yep," Larry continued. "He just took the dead doctor's credentials and disappeared into the hollers of Kentucky to practice medicine."

"But this is such a lovely, unassuming facility. It's my favorite. Didn't they check his license? Nancy Brinley, the physical therapist in charge of Kentucky physical therapy licenses, knows each one of her therapists personally and who they are and what they are doing." I pulled out my purse and produced not only my Kentucky license but also fourteen other wallet-sized licenses.

"How would he even know enough to play doctor? Did we ever have any lawsuits or anything? How could he do this?" I exclaimed.

"I guess he was a laboratory technician or something. I know he used to call the specialists over at Mary Breckenridge quite often for consultation."

"What will happen now?" I asked.

"That's a good question. To top it all off, he had a heart attack as they were transporting him to the jail in Lexington!" Larry shrugged his shoulders and walked on down the hall.

The pieces of the puzzle began to fit together. Why would a man on the run want to spend the afternoon with a woman who wanted to get better acquainted?

"That's scary!" I told Gracie Allen that night over her Meow Mix. "Here we are all alone out here, and we can't even be sure that the people we are dealing with are really who they say they are!

"You know, Gracie Allen, we are blessed to have a home where people really are who they say they are. They are solid New Englanders and the kind of people who let you know exactly what they think, but we can deal with that! At least we know where they stand!

* Not his real name

There's Somethin' Awful Wrong!

A few months after the trip to look at the truck, McCann tracked me down on the assignment in Kentucky for some professional advice. Little twin girls had come to brighten the lives of his youngest son, Jerry.

"'Lizabeth," he said when he called, "I guess there's something awful wrong with Tiffany and Brittany. Marie took them to the doctor yesterday, and he says they're not right. Brittany can't even sit up yet, and Tiffany's not much better. The doc says they were both born with cerebral palsy. Know anybody that specializes in this kind of stuff? We could fly them anywhere. Bluefield has an airport now, and Jerry could take my plane." Sadness was in his voice as he told me the story.

Through some professional contacts, I was able to direct the family to a facility in South Carolina that was able to follow the cases of these tiny twins.

It's Dr. Smith!* They handcuffed him and carried him away in the paddy wagon!"

A year later, I stopped by Tazewell to visit McCann and his little family.

"Jerry wants you to come by this evenin' and see the girls," he said.

When I arrived, the girls were "swimming" in their pool in the front of the house up the side of the mountain. Little Brittany still had to be transported, but her eyes had the same sparkle as her grandpa McCann's.

Their mother, Marie, and her maid were in the kitchen, putting the finishing touches on a sumptuous meal. It appeared that they must be having special guests for dinner. The table was set with real sterling silver trimmed in gold. The table was spread with a real linen tablecloth. The crystal stemware sparkled with pure, cold water, and a bouquet of pink roses smiled under the chandelier.

I played with the girls for a while. Tiffany showed me how she could kick and float in the water. Brittany sat in a little seat that supported her back. After about twenty minutes, I thought I should excuse myself so as not to interrupt their plans.

"No way!" Jerry exclaimed. "We're planning for you to be our comp'ny for the evenin'!"

McCann's brown eyes met mine. There was courage there now, and peace. He smiled. There was no need for words.

Who Called Di in the Middle of the Night!

As the daffodils began to push their way through the earth, and the buds on the dogwood and mountain laurel began to swell, I began to look for a campground closer to Mary Breckinridge and Red Bud hospitals. The Methodists owned a campground on the Red Bud Hospital property and agreed to let me stay there.

It was a lovely spot right down beside the stream. Oak and ash trees were on the back side of the campground, and the view from the living room window of the fifth wheel would look out over the mountain stream and the valley below. I was a little worried because I would be all alone there, and I remembered what the women at Mary Breckinridge had said about guns and about being followed. But I put my fears aside and decided it would be worth the risk. I prepared to move the fifth wheel to this new campground come Sunday morning.

Before moving I decided to give a quick birthday call to my close friend, Diane, in California.

"Lizzy!" she said when she heard my voice. "Are you all right! I've been terribly worried about you since you called last night."

"I didn't call last night, Di. I'm sure I didn't. I would have had to call from the phone booth across the campground since there's no phone in the fifth."

"Yes, you did," she argued. "You sounded far away and in trouble. Then we were disconnected. Doug was in bed with me and knows you called. Are you all right? I called your other friends, Mary and Ingrid, and we have been praying for you all night."

I didn't move the fifth wheel that day, nor did I the next week.

Then it happened.

The rain had been heavy all night and still reminded me more of a cloudburst than a spring shower. It was 11:00 a.m. when Lile came into the physical therapy department with a concerned look on his face. "What are you doing still here, 'Lizabeth! Don't you know the water is only a couple feet from the bottom of the bridge between here and Hazard?"

"So?" I said.

"Yeah, the water is rolling off the mountain in a torrent, and you may get stranded here for several days!"

Oh, no, I thought, *What about Gracie Allen! She won't have any food and water, and who would play ball with her!*

"You're kidding!" I exclaimed. "What about you, Wanda? You live on the other side of Greasy!"

"I'm out o' here!" Wanda answered as she reached for her jacket.

"I don't think there'll be anyone keeping outpatient appointments today. You and I need to get out of here!"

"Go ahead," Lile offered, "and keep an eye on the news. The bridge may go!"

On the way off of the mountain, I passed the turnoff to the Red Bud Hospital. *Oh, no!* I thought. *I wonder if they'll have to evacuate any patients. That place isn't far from the …* My mind snapped to attention. *The stream! If the little stream in Hazard is almost over the bridge, I wonder where my fifth wheel would be if I had moved it to that peaceful little campground with the mountain laurel on the east side?*

When I came into the parking lot two days later, Lile met me. "Do you know where your fifth wheel would have been, 'Lizabeth, if you had moved it to Red Bud? The quiet little campground near the Red Bud Hospital was submerged in six feet of raging torrent!"

I pondered. Who called Di in the middle of the night?

Comp'ny Comin'

"How did you manage, Mommie Lone, to feed all those kids?"

"It was hard," she answered. "I had to work three jobs. I scrubbed floors for rich people, and took in washin', and did some waitressing at the Lonesome Pine. The kids, they worked, too. We had a garden, and I raised some chickens."

"All your kids have good jobs now, Mommie Lone. Your oldest, Jean, teaches high school, doesn't she?"

"Yes!" Mommie Lone said proudly, "And my grandson, George, is in college in Lexington. Says he wants to be a lawyer."

"You must be proud! Do all the kids get home sometimes so you can have a reunion?" I asked.

"It takes some doin' now, 'cause the grandkids are so spread out, but all my six are around here!"

There was a lot I didn't know about the local culture. I arrived late one morning. The little house was in a secluded spot about forty-five minutes from town. The turn was sharp and steep onto the mud road. *I wonder if I'll ever get out of here*! I thought.

There, nestled on the flat land by the edge of the stream, was the small wooden-shingled house and the large garden. The site was beautiful. The garden was beginning to come on, and there were fresh peas and lima beans. I could see that there would be lots of canning for Mommie Lone's daughters that summer.

The "young'uns" were playing cars and building roads in the dirt at the foot of the long, low porch, while Mommie Lone and two of her grown daughters rocked and chatted. When I arrived, they asked, "You're gonna stay the night, aren't ya?"

Dinner was not ready. The potatoes had not been dug nor the chicken killed. This visit from the therapist was a historic occasion, and Mommie Lone was in no hurry.

What about the patients I had scheduled for the afternoon? Mommie Lone had no telephone! I needed to get back!

A barefoot boy in blue denim overalls and no shirt came shyly to the side of my rocking chair on the porch. "Wanta' come see my baby kitties?" he pleaded with his big gray eyes. "Sugar's hiding 'um under the shed, but I can crawl under and drag 'um out!"

"Sure," I said and took his grubby little hand. He led me to the shed out back.

"Father calls me William. Mother calls me Will. Sister calls me Willie, but the fellas call me Bill," the little guy recited.

"OK, if I call you Bill, too?" I asked.

"Sure can! I named the biggest kitty Bill, after me!" he boasted. "I'll get him out first."

The other kids followed. "Let me! Let me!" they shouted and danced around me, laughing.

We petted each little, sightless kitten, then went on to the henhouse.

"We got biddies in here," said a little three-year-old with pigtails.

I laughed. How blessed Mommie Lone was to have these lively young ones!

"Come see my tadpoles. They're gettin' hind legs now. I caught 'um myself with my bare hands!" Billy urged.

> Twenty froggies went to school
> Down beside a rushing pool,
> Twenty little coats of green,
> Twenty vests all white and clean.
> "We must be on time," said they.
> "First, we study, then we play;
> That is how we keep the rule
> When we froggies go to school."
> Master Bullfrog, brave and stern,
> Called the classes in their turn;
> Taught them how to nobly strive,

Also how to leap and dive.
From his seat upon a log
Showed them how to say "Kerchog,"
Taught them how to dodge the blow
From the stick that bad boys throw.
Twenty froggies grew up fast,
Bullfrogs they became at last.
Polished to a high degree,
As each froggie ought to be,
Now they sit on other logs
Teaching other little frogs!"

By the time I had finished the song, Susie was in my lap, her tousled golden curls against my heart. The sunshine was warm there on the bank by the stream, and she nodded and slept. At length the smell of fried chicken wafted on the air, and berry pie came out of the oven.

> *"Father calls me William. Mother calls me Will. Sister calls me Willie, but the fellas call me Bill," the little guy recited*

We all scrunched in around the big oak table in the kitchen. Mommie Lone plopped a fluffy, white mound of mashed potatoes onto my plate and smiled. What was my hurry anyway? Life is made of moments like these. I trusted my assistant to handle the patients at the hospital, and I enjoyed this bright sunny day beside the stream with Mommie Lone and her grown children and her grandchildren.

The sun was setting when I finally arrived back at the hospital. On my desk was a note from my assistant with a little smiley face. "I knew you wouldn't be back for your two o'clock patients. I had everyone canceled for the rest of the day! Do you realize how significant this was? We invite only family and close friends home for dinner. "

Her Father's Daughter

Dreama was a beautiful girl. Her dark blue eyes and her dark brown curls dramatized her suntanned features. She carried herself like a queen.

It took only a few treatments to clear up the few problems she had from her accident on the side of the mountain with her four-wheeler.

"Dreama," I asked, "What are you planning to do with the rest of your life? You are finished with high school now, and you haven't a job yet. You are bright and beautiful and have so much potential."

"Oh, I s'pose I'll get married and have some kids," she answered flatly. "That's what most people do."

"How would you like to work here in the physical therapy department with Wanda and me? We've been needing some help, and you know your way around by now. I know, it's a bit of a hike from Greasy to Hazard, but you could get a car if you had a job."

She took me up on the offer and became an indispensable addition to the therapy department. She was especially useful on the first of the month when all the unemployed received their unemployment checks! Patients who had not kept their appointments during the month came out of the holler to cash their checks and to lay in groceries. While they were in town, they would just stop in and get a treatment! This would have been no problem had there been only one or two, but –there were ten to fifteen! There was no way they were going to make a special trip out of the holler for a treatment, so we did what we could within the framework of what existed.

One day Dreama asked, "Can you come out to our place for dinner?"

By now, I had learned that come for dinner meant come for the day … and maybe the night! So I cleared the slate for the day and followed Dreama.

"Where do you live?" I asked her.

"Well, I'll show you if you follow me. We live on past Greasy. My dad owns a coal mine up there. You gotta' be careful on the mud road, though. Just hope there are no coal trucks coming out of the mine. It's only a one-lane road, and there is hardly any room for two cars to pass, much less a coal truck. Bring your bathing suit, too. We can go swimming!"

"Greasy?" I asked. "How did a town get the name Greasy?"

Dreama smiled. "My grampa said it's 'cause somebody killed a bear up the creek and skinned it there by the water, and all the greasy blubber messed up the water."

The paved road ended past Greasy, all right, and the trees pressed close on each side. I thought about what Dreama said about the coal trucks! After several miles of untamed road, we arrived at a pleasant clearing bordered on the east by a good-sized stream.

Dreama's father was tall and rugged. Behind him stood Dreama's five tall, rugged brothers! It was almost intimidating! What seemed so striking was their dark blue eyes and their dark brown curls dramatizing the suntanned features of the men. They carried themselves like princes.

Her mother came out of the house and stood on the long, low porch wiping her hands on her apron. I could tell she was really anticipating the visit. Her mother was soft and gentle, but her face wore lines of care.

Dreama and I followed her inside. The kitchen table was set with brown stoneware dishes atop a bright yellow linen tablecloth.

There was a white propane cookstove at the end of the room, and a bright blue and gray braided throw rug on the floor.

"Did your mother make this herself?" I asked Dreama.

"You can call my mom, Ida. She and I made the rug a couple years ago. It's not hard. You just have to have it flat when you get ready to sew it all together, else it will bunch up."

"How'd you learn to do this, Ida?" I asked.

"Oh, it's like I just grew up knowing it. My mother did it, and her mother did it. Of course, back in my grandmother's day, there wasn't any choice. When something wore out, you just cut it into strips and sewed and braided it. It's like quilts, you know.

"Dreama, take her in your bedroom and show her that quilt my mama made for you."

Dreama took me upstairs to her attic room under the eaves. It had a window on one end, looking out over the field and down to the stream. The bed was a simple four-poster with the old-fashioned open springs and a mattress on top. There was a chest of drawers under the eaves on the north side and a dresser with a big mirror by the door as we entered. The bedcover was a handmade quilt with a pieced, dark blue and light blue background and red and white stars. "This blue material was from some worn-out shirts that belonged to my grandpa and my uncles. You know, it's just made of those blue work shirts. The dark blue is from their overalls and the red from their worn-out red bandannas. I think she had to buy the white cloth. I love the way she used her imagination to put things together like this. I want to pass it on to my daughter someday. See here in the corner she embroidered the date, 1967."

I laughed. "I've got one at home that my great-grandmother made for my mother. It used to be red and green on white, but now the green is all faded out, and it looks like bright red on cream. It has 1923 embroidered in the corner.

"Does the full moon shine in your window at night, Dreama?" I asked. "It's such a peaceful view from this window. My window at home looks out on the woods with the red maples and the birch and the oak. I love watching the seasons from my bedroom window. There would be green leaves now, with blue jays flitting from branch to branch and chick-a-dees going, 'dee-dee-dee' in the holly bushes."

"Think we should go see if we can help your mom?"

We went back down the steep stairs.

I was a little better prepared on this visit for a whole day with the family back at the end of nowhere. I brought my autoharp.

"You know 'Country Roads'?" asked the younger brother.

"Sure," I said, "You guys sing along!"

Over dinner they told stories of life back in the coal mines. The men knew what it was to have part of the mine shaft give way and wonder if anyone would be able to get them out. "It's a high-risk job," Butch said with an intense look on his face.

"It looks like you men are up to it, though," I commented.

"I've been really proud of Dreama. She's doing a great job in at the hospital."

"Aw, she won't ever amount to much," her father commented cruelly. "Her mother jumped the fence nine months before Dreama was born!"

I looked around the table. Her mother was looking at her plate, and the red of her cheeks was not from the heat of the oven. Dreama's lips were drawn in a tight line, and her face was bright red. The father's face showed that this wasn't the first time he had enjoyed the glee of crushing people!

I looked at the six strong, handsome men and the conclusive resemblance of the beautiful, queenly daughter. Words came. "I'd claim her if I were you. She looks just like you and your handsome sons. And besides, she's quick and clever!"

My eyes met Dreama's. She could still carry herself like the queen she really was, and be proud to belong to her family. She was her father's daughter.

Does Everybody Really Carry a Gun?

The two weeks in the mountains of Appalachia were wearing away into nine months. It was summer, and the leaves of the huge oak trees sheltered Gracie Allen and the big fifth wheel from the Kentucky sun. Cicadas in the locust trees sang us to sleep at night. The campground began to blossom with people. John and Mary Curtis pulled their twenty-eight-foot trailer into their usual seasonal spot with their backside against the woods. They spread out the little green-grass-colored carpet and rolled out the awning. They put out their flower boxes with bright red geraniums and were set up to spend their fourteenth summer in the shade away from the city traffic.

Other seasonal campers moved in. They walked by slowly and gawked at the huge expanse of the forty-foot fifth wheel and the demure white, gray, and buff kitty sitting daily in the window, waiting. Every recreational vehicle owner, and most others who don't own them, want to know what it looks like in everybody else's camper. They peeked in past the pink ruffled curtains and passed judgment on the layout as compared to their own.

"I see you are away all day except for weekends. You must be working."

"Yes," I answered. "I'm doing a traveling physical therapy assignment at the Mary Breckenridge Hospital up in the mountains near Hazard."

"They say everybody up there carries a gun!"

"Aw, Mary, a gun wouldn't do me much good!" I smiled. "Everybody has them, though. Want a good story?"

"Sure," she said. "Let me get you some lemonade. You look tired. Sit down here and tell me about it."

"Well, Mary, you know about the family nurse practitioner program they have back up there. There's this one guy, Bill, that's really good at what he does. He's six foot seven inches tall and has steel-gray hair. He's about thirty-eight years old, and they always call him doctor. He's very gentle and professional. He would probably make a good doctor. He's already an engineer, but he burned out on that and wanted to do something to make a difference to humanity. I could be really attracted to him."

"Early this week, he hurried down to the Physical Therapy Department with a very agitated patient and the wife following. The man's face was contorted in agony, and his brown hair rumpled. It looked like he hadn't changed his clothes for a month. Anger flashed out of his green eyes."

Mary stopped her crocheting and listened.

"I looked at Bill, towering behind this middle-aged couple, trying to catch my eye. 'I think Elizabeth can help you,' Bill said to the patient. 'She has this little machine that has done wonders for lots of other people in severe pain. Give her fifteen minutes, and then I'll check you again. See what you can do,' he said to me, giving me the eye that said, 'this is a desperate situation. I'll be close by'."

"'Where do you hurt?' I asked Jack. 'What happened!'

"His wife, Sarah, didn't wait for him to answer. 'Three months ago, he came home drunk. He came staggerin' in and wanted to "jump on me" and make love. I wouldn't put up with that, so I just pulled my gun and shot him in the leg! That ought to teach him! Wouldn't you think!'

"'Hey, cut the ___ ___ talkin' and get doin' something! I haven't slept for three months. If you can't do something about this pain right now, I'll fill you full of holes!'

"I could see that Jack was a desperate man! Sarah looked tired, too, but was at least rational at this point."

A mosquito buzzed around my ear. I swatted and missed, took another sip of lemonade, and continued.

"I had Jack drop his drawers and put on a patient gown so I could examine the leg. It was apparent that the gunshot had irritated the nerve, and it was giving him terrible nerve pain down his leg and into his foot.

"Fortunately, I had a gadget called a 'Transcutaneous Electrical Nerve Stimulator' that works on this kind of pain.

"'Give me five minutes, Jack,' I said, 'and we'll take care of this problem for you. Let me feel your leg.'

"The little machine worked! In five minutes his face began to relax, and I asked him, 'Where do you hurt now?'

"'Nowhere, really, all I can feel is that gadget!'

"'Fine,' I said. 'This gadget will help you get some sleep tonight. You and Sarah come see me in the morning. You'll be better!'

"As soon as they left, I looked for Bill. There he was, just out of sight around the corner."

It was summer, and the leaves of the huge oak trees sheltered Gracie Allen and the big fifth wheel from the Kentucky sun. Cicadas in the locust trees sang us to sleep at night

Mary breathed a sigh of relief.

"'That was close!' Bill said. 'Jack threatened to pull a gun on me if I couldn't do something immediately! I thought of that TENS machine you used on that woman with severe post-herpes pain, and hoped you'd be able to do something about this one.' He brushed his high forehead with the back of his hand."

"So that was this week's episode, Mary. What did you say about guns?"

Gracie Allen was waiting when I unlocked the door. She purred and rubbed against my leg. "Ready for something to eat, Gracie?" I asked.

"Neow!" she demanded. "Neow!"

Freight Train Through the Campground

It was Friday afternoon in mid-July. The sky began to cloud over about dusk. I thought of the Boy Scout troop that had set up tents near the pine trees just inside the campground. *What a messy night to have a bunch of Boy Scouts out on a camping trip!* I thought. *Well, at least it'll cool things off. I haven't been able to sleep under even a sheet for a couple of weeks.*

It had been a wearing week, and I was tired. The Bible at my bedside was a comfort to me. When lonely and afraid, I liked to read the psalms by David. I turned to Psalm 34:7 and read, "The Angel of the Lord encamps around those who worship Him and each of them He delivers" (AMPC). I drifted off to sleep with the patter of rain on the RV roof.

Suddenly, I was jolted from a sound sleep with the wind whistling around the corner of the rig, and the whole trailer shaking. Amid flashes of lightning, I could see the young couple with little pop-up camper trying desperately to collapse the unit so as not to be blown away. "This is no ordinary storm!" I called to Gracie Allen. "Where are you!"

Then I thought of the little Boy Scouts and the tents near the pine trees. "Oh, no! Whatever will happen to them!" I said, pulling Gracie Allen close. She stuck her face under my armpit and stopped purring.

"Gracie, what's that noise!" I whispered. "It sounds like a freight train! Are we near a train track?"

"Neow!" she answered. I knew she was right! We were not near a train track at all!

A mighty gust hit the trailer. There were no lights in the campground, but I could see John and Mary's trailer as the lightning flashed. There were huge trees just behind their unit. I wondered if they would be a windbreak, or if they would just blow over and crush them. The trailer shook violently for what seemed like hours. Time stood still. Then the roar subsided.

Gracie Allen was just lifting her head from under my armpit when the "freight train" returned from the other direction! "Oh, no! Not again, Gracie! Those little boys don't have a chance! Maybe we don't either!"

Again the trailer shook violently. Lightning flashed. Thunder rolled, and so did the "freight train."

Then all was quiet. Very quiet!

I must have slept. The next thing I remember is the sunlight streaming in on the bed and Gracie Allen demanding breakfast.

The refrigerator was off. There was no electricity anywhere! I dressed and went outside. One of the huge oaks in back of John and Mary's trailer lay flat on the ground with its mighty roots in the air. It fell away from their little trailer!

"You all right?" I called through the open window.

"Yeah, how are you and Gracie Allen? That was some storm! We were just listening to the radio, and they are telling us not to go out on the roads. There's major flooding, and there's no power anywhere. None of the stoplights are working, so stay put."

"They say what the damages are?" I asked.

"Yeah, I guess we were pretty lucky here," John answered. "Three people were killed in this tornado a few blocks from here!"

I thought of the little Boy Scouts near the entrance of the campground. What about the trees that were in back of their camp?

I jogged across the campground to where they had set up camp. There was the smell of wood smoke and bacon. There was even playful laughter. Whatever damage may have been incurred must have been repairable. The pine trees on the back of their camping area were down. Just like the big oak in back of John and Mary's, these pine trees had crashed away from the campground!

A Healing Time

"Orthopedic clinic tonight," Wanda reminded me as I previewed the schedule for the day.

"How much do we have on that schedule?" I asked. "We have that kid with scoliosis that wears a brace, and we have a whole slew of people with severe neck pain. Here are some with low back pain. There's that baby with club feet, too."

"It looks like a full day before we even start the ortho clinic," Wanda groaned. "I'm glad we only have clinic once a month."

"Clinic starts at 5:00 p.m. Makes me tired to look at it. We won't get out of here till midnight anyway. There are twenty-three patients, and some of them are complicated. Poor Doctor George. He has to drive all the way back to Lexington after this is over."

"Yeah, and the hour and fifteen minutes down the mountain to the campground in London gets longer every night," I answered.

There was a steady flow of patients all day with hardly a chance to grab a bite. Wanda brought a ham sandwich with pickles for Dr. George and a tossed green salad for me about 8:00 p.m. We tried to get a few bites between patients. The Physical Therapy Department had grown over the last nine months, and although I was proud of the growth, I was getting exhausted. Patients were lined up on the benches in the hall in front of the PT department. They had been there all evening, too. No matter what the schedule said, patients from this area came whenever they could get a ride in and out of their own part of the mountain.

A little tow-headed fellow with club feet, who looked to be about eighteen months old, was squalling on his mother's lap. He wouldn't be comforted by the breast. He wanted to go to bed!

Behind the curtain in the booth to the right was a pleasant young lady with light brown hair and a red babushka around her head. "My neck still hurts, Doc," she said to Dr. George. "It's been five months since I got rear-ended by the coal truck, and whenever I try to do anything around the house, the right side of my neck goes into spasms. Can you help me?"

"I think we can help you," Dr. George replied in his characteristic manner. "We'll have Wanda set you up for some physical therapy treatments, and you can come see me at the clinic next month."

The list went on and on.

"How many more do we have, Wanda?" I asked. "You were right. It's almost midnight!"

"Just a couple easy ones," she answered. Her eyes had dark circles. She had been pouring out the energy, too.

The fireflies were out, and the full moon was overhead as we locked the door behind us about 1:00 a.m. I stepped into the truck to head back down the mountain to Gracie Allen and the pink and gray fifth wheel.

It should have been a lovely drive. The fragrance of honeysuckle and new-mown hay filled the air.

But I was exhausted.

"What's a nice girl like you doing in a place like this?" I asked myself for the hundredth time.

I began to think out loud. "My dog died! All three horses died! My dad died. The man I was in love with married someone else, and now, here I am, wandering so far from home." Tears began to well up in my eyes and roll down my cheeks and onto my navy blue skirt. All the hurts of the past years came out of their hiding place in my heart. Some grieving needed to be done over each one. I reached for the Kleenex®.

I didn't feel the warm night air that blew through the open window of the truck and flicked my hair, nor did I hear the whippoorwill that whistled far away. I took out each painful episode and allowed myself the luxury of tears. I drove slowly, not really in a hurry to get back to the campground.

I talked out loud to nobody. I wished I could just see my dad one more time. There were some things we never dealt with.

I could only imagine what it must have been like for my mother to find out she was pregnant and to have to tell my father. It was his second year in medical school. There was no income other than what my mother could make working in the hospital kitchen. How would they ever make it with a baby!

"Oh, Sue! Not pregnant! Oh, my Father! I'll have to quit medical school and get a job. Why didn't you prevent this!" I could almost see my father's red, round face and balding head as he stormed about the room.

My mother's reaction would be to dissolve into tears. I can imagine her long raven-black hair falling around her shoulders and her bright green eyes brimming with tears.

"Maybe my folks will take the baby," Sue offered.

"No, your dad never was able to hold a job, and the kid will starve to death. Maybe my folks could take on another mouth. My sister Vivian and her husband, Mercer, had to move in with them a few months ago. Vivian is expecting her first child in May. Oh, my Father! What will we do!"

"Just take me home!" Sue sobbed. "I want to be with Mama. I'm so scared!

So in July, about two weeks before the baby was due, my father drove her home. They drove almost nonstop across the desert in an old Model T Ford without air conditioning from California to Florida.

Tonight, as I drove down the mountain in the white light of the full moon, forgiveness swept over me. I wished I could tell him I loved him. He was no more capable of giving me what I needed at the time than he was of giving me a million dollars. He just didn't have it.

Soggy Kleenex began to pile up on the floor of the truck on the passenger side. My nose was red and my eyes swollen as I pulled off the Boon Turnpike and headed for the campground.

A great weight seemed to roll from my heart, and I felt at peace. The full moon was almost touching the tops of the tall, still pines west of the river when I pulled into the silent, sleeping campground.

I didn't feel the warm night air that blew through the open window of the truck and flicked my hair, nor did I hear the whippoorwill that whistled far away. I took out each painful episode and allowed myself the luxury of tears

I took Gracie Allen in my arms and whispered, "It's been a long day, Gracie, but tonight there's peace. Tomorrow will be a new beginning."

"Here, let's give you a little kitty food and go on to bed."

"Neow?" Gracie asked and kissed my chin.

Rich Memories

The time came to leave Kentucky and move on to another assignment. I rolled up my awning, folded and put away the grass-green carpet that served as a lawn, and hitched up. I stopped over at John and Mary's for a goodbye hug. There were tears in Mary's eyes. She knew, and I knew that we'd never see each other again. I didn't leave anything there in Kentucky. I will probably never go back. But I took a rich store of memories and peace.

4. Warm Sands and Warm Arms

I'll Meet You in Heaven and Live Next Door to You!

Muscle Shoals, Alabama, was sweltering hot when I pulled the big 5th wheel into the crowded campground. It was August. Spanish moss hung on the trees, and it was muggy. Gracie Allen and I were thankful for the air conditioning.

The company said it would only be for two weeks again. "I wonder if two weeks always means nine months to this company. We'll see. At least they have a Walmart! The campground is only ten minutes from the office. But it's a home health assignment! I wonder how many miles a day I'll have to drive?"

The second day on this home health assignment, I met Lucy. Lucy reminded me of my first doll. The doll's name was June Bug and she was made of rubber except for her head. She had eyes that opened and closed. I don't even remember when my aunt gave her to me. It was my first birthday, I think. By and by June Bug's eyes rolled back into her head and she was blind. Her rubber arms and legs began to slough away and disappear. So it was with Lucy.

"Be prepared," the supervisor told me. "She is a lovely little black lady of about fifty-five. She is a widow and lives in the little cabin on the other side of the tracks with her daughter and grandchildren. And, well, she can't see. She's blind. And, well, last year her left leg was amputated above the knee. And, well, she just got her right leg amputated above the knee. See what you can do."

That afternoon, I found my way across town to the unpainted, wooden frame house. The low front porch stretched the whole length of the little house. The dirt yard was swept clean and there were a few red geraniums growing to the left of the porch.

A young black lady in a cotton dress came to the door. "You lookin' for my ma?" she asked as she opened the screen door and invited me in.

She took me through the living room to the bedroom. Lucy's sightless eyes stared at nothing as she lay on the clean white sheets. A wooden chair in the corner was piled with folded handmade quilts. Lucy's medications and a half-full glass of water were on the dark wooden table beside her bed.

Upon hearing our voices, Lucy turned her face toward us with a wide grin showing a few white teeth and red gums. "You the nurse that come to take care of me?" she asked.

"Yes, I'm the physical therapist they sent to see if we could help you be more independent," I responded.

"Come on over here, and let me see who you are," she said reaching up both of her arms.

I took both of her hands, and she pulled my cheek down to her lips and gave me a kiss. "You have such soft hands."

"Well, Lucy," I answered with a smile in my voice, "if you kept your hands in baby oil about five hours a day like I do, your hands would get parboiled, too."

Lucy giggled.

I felt so helpless. We did bed exercises and activities of daily living, but she knew, and I knew that the prognosis was poor.

I wondered what this woman had to be thankful for. Her eyes were always sparkling, even though she couldn't see. Her face wore a peaceful look, and it was a joy to work with Lucy.

"OK, Lucy," I said as I turned her onto her side. "Let's exercise your hips. This will give you more strength when you need sitting balance. Let's do it to rhythm. You name the song."

I joined Lucy as she started to sing. Her stump moved up and down to the beat.

> When the roll is called up yonder,
> When the roll is called up yonder,
> When the roll is called up yonder,
> When the roll is called up yonder, I'll be there.

I was glad Lucy couldn't see my misty eyes. "Turn on your other side now, Lucy. That was great."

Again our voices blended in harmony. Her voice was sweet and I knew that when she sang "When the Roll is Called Up Yonder I'll Be There," that she was really planning to be there!

Happily, the company did have another therapist ready to move into the position at Muscle Shoals in two weeks.

"Lucy," I said as I was leaving that last day in Muscle Shoals, "I know that when the roll is called up yonder we'll both be there. Remember that little song the kids sing sometime? It goes like this:

"Be happy, be kind, Be loving, be true. I'll meet you in heaven And live next door to you."

I gave her both of my hands, and she pulled my cheek down to her lips again. Tears spilled out of her sightless eyes and onto the clean white pillow case. "I'll meet you in heaven and live next door to you, too," she echoed. "And I can see your sweet face and dance with you on them golden streets!"

Lion Country

I was just finishing the pile of paperwork on Friday afternoon when the phone rang. It was Dr. Snider. "How would you like to spend the winter in Palm Beach, Florida?"

"I'm sure the weather would be an improvement over the floods and tornadoes of eastern Kentucky last year!" I answered. "What are you thinking? Does that mean we can leave Alabama tomorrow?"

"Well, not quite, but how about two weeks?" Dr. Snider answered. "We are getting ready to open a new account at a 350-bed hospital in the Palm Beach area of Florida, and we would like for you to be our interim director."

"Tell me a little about it."

Dr. Snider continued. "There are five therapists and three aides and a secretary. The hospital is firing the director. He hasn't been able to keep up with current issues. They would like to be more progressive. This is all classified information, though. This is our largest account yet. We're depending on you to make it a real money-maker." Such was the spiel I was given as I was directed to the Gold Coast of Florida. "It should be a great place to park the fifth wheel. When can you let us know?"

"Hard to take, Dr. Snider. Hard to take!" I answered. "Better give me at least three seconds to say yes. Better give me three days to drive down, though. This forty feet of fifth wheel is much easier to live in than to tow!"

By Tuesday morning, Gracie Allen and I were preparing to leave for Florida. I was excited! I put the kitty litter box in the bathtub and took down the chandelier. I emptied the black water holding tank and filled the fresh-water tank. I checked the tires. All was well. I stuffed pillows in the cupboards to keep things from being broken and cranked down the roof vents. I rolled up the green-grass carpet and put the pots of red geraniums inside on the kitchen floor. Then I folded the steps and locked the door.

I opened the mouth on the heavy metal hitch in the bed of the truck and backed the truck under the overhang of the fifth wheel. This was the part I always worried about. What if I didn't aim right and had to try over and over again to get the ball into the socket? What if I didn't secure the hitch properly, and the fifth wheel became detached while we were moving down some turnpike somewhere? Never mind the what-ifs. I let the weight down onto the truck bed and held my breath. Snap! It sounded like the safety hitch had been engaged. I flipped the heavy bar and plugged the end of the big electrical hook-up into the reciprocal in the truck bed, then plugged the breakaway switch from the truck into the socket on the rig. I raised the electric jacks to let the entire weight of the hitch onto the truck. The springs on the one-ton pick-up began to flatten. One ton on the hitch and one ton on each wheel. That's a total of ten thousand pounds. The whole thing, including the truck, weighed 15,000 pounds. With that much weight in tow, you hope you don't have to stop quickly. I started the engine and put the truck into the "granny" gear. I liked this truck with its bass voice. The rig began to move, and we were on our way again.

> *The idea of being in a warm spot for the winter was incentive enough, but to have the added bonus of being where the nearest McDonald's is only five blocks instead of sixty miles would be big city stuff!*

The idea of being in a warm spot for the winter was incentive enough, but to have the added bonus of being where the nearest McDonald's is only five blocks instead of sixty miles would be big city stuff! Gracie and I rolled cheerfully down Interstate 65 toward Birmingham.

Gracie Allen and I found a campground about forty-five minutes west of Lake Worth. It was the only campground I saw in my campground guide, so I took it. It was a lovely new campground on the flat sandy soil of Florida. The trees had been planted only last year, so weren't tall enough for shade. But just now, I was a sun worshiper! The bathhouses were spacious, and smelled of bleach. I looked in the corners for signs of those huge Florida water bugs. None! The problem was that the showers were metered, and you had to keep depositing quarters to continue with the shower!

"Well, what brings you here, Elizabeth?" a male voice called from the office as I stepped from the truck.

I looked toward the direction of the voice. There was a tall, gangly man of about thirty-five, his brown hair pulled back in a ponytail. His blue jeans were a snug fit, and his biceps bulged beneath his T-shirt.

"Jim!" I exclaimed. "The last time I saw you was at a campground in Corbin, Kentucky. What are you doing here?"

"Jean and I are the managers of this campground now," he answered. "We had enough of the cold weather. We've been here since it opened. We like it here. Tell me about yourself."

"The company sent me here for the winter this year. I'll be the director at JFK Hospital in Lake Worth. How much of a drive is it going to be every day?" I asked.

"Well, with the traffic the time of day you'll be driving on the two-lane road from here to Palm Beach, and with all the stoplights and all, it will take you about forty-five minutes. You had a really long commute in Kentucky, too, didn't you? They do have a campground closer to the hospital, but this one is much nicer," he said with a smile and a twinkle in his brown eyes. "You might check it out, though."

I smiled and filled out the paperwork for the campground. The warm air felt good. It was September, and the air would be getting nippy at home in Maine. Kids were splashing and jumping into the water over at the swimming pool. Wow! A pool. Some gray-haired ladies with Kelly green hats sat at the white metal tables sipping iced tea. They seemed content to stay under the shade of big red and white umbrellas. I wondered if I would have any time to use the pool. *Well, I at least have today,* I thought to myself.

Gracie Allen and I opened all the windows on our big rig and spread out the plastic green-grass mat for the yard. Maybe we could even get some more flower pots and put out the awning and hang pink fuchsia and petunias from it.

I unhitched the truck and hung the chandelier. I unpillowed the cupboards and screwed in the hose. It only took about a half-hour to make things appear normal again. I could clean the whole fifth wheel and even wash and wax the kitchen in two hours. There was time to swim while the sun was still hot.

I donned my black bathing suit and grabbed my white towel and goggles, and was off to the pool. "Too bad you can't swim, Gracie," I called as I closed the door behind me.

The water was a pleasant lukewarm. *Much warmer, and it would be too warm for exercise,* I thought.

I pushed off from the edge and did a breaststroke to the other end of the pool. I had to dodge a little girl in a red bathing suit, but really, the pool wasn't too crowded now. The water felt good on my back, and I moved easily. Stroke, breath, kick, stroke, breath, kick, I moved effortlessly.

I wonder if I'll have time to do this every day? I thought to myself as I glided through the water. *I wonder how the therapists will take this new company? I wonder how things are at home?* Well, there were plenty of unknowns, but this moment was sheer joy!

After about forty-five minutes, I climbed out and dried off. *I wonder if the other campground has a pool as nice as this one,* I thought. *Forty-five minutes each way will take an hour and a half of my day times five days a week equals seven and a half hours of travel time. That's almost an entire workday. I could be using that time for something else, like swimming.*

Gracie was ready for her Meow Mix by the time I got back to the fifth wheel. I fixed a fat tomato sandwich and sat outside at the picnic table under the awning. How lucky I felt to be here for the winter. The breeze was gentle as the campers started campfires. Now and then, there was the squeal of a child. The puffy Florida clouds turned gold, then pink, then purple as night settled down over the campground. The lights came on in the other recreational vehicles, and I went inside to prepare for the night.

The sky was just beginning to show signs of dawn when I awoke the next morning. There was a loud roar, followed by another, and another. I wondered where I was. As consciousness dawned, I remembered.

"OK, Elizabeth," I said to myself. "You are in southern Florida on an assignment here at one of the largest hospitals in the area. Today is Sunday, September 29. Now, are you oriented?"

Again I heard the roar. "We should be able to go back to sleep, Gracie Allen," I said sleepily, as Gracie tiptoed under the covers and nestled under my armpit. "You don't need breakfast yet, do you?" But Gracie seemed a little agitated.

The roar didn't seem to be bothering any of the other campers. It was still only early dawn. "Come on, Gracie," I said, "Let's take another catnap before sunrise."

We woke with the sunshine streaming in on the kitchen table with the roar a thing of the past.

On my way to the bathhouse, I asked a fellow camper if he had heard a roaring noise this morning. "Oh, yes," he said. "You'll hear that every morning about daybreak. This is 'Lion Country Safari' campground, you know! Those were the lions. They feed them about dawn, and they roar over their food like a cat purrs, meows, and rubs against your leg. You ought to tour their setup sometime. You stay in your car with the windows rolled up and drive through. They have monkeys, elephants, giraffes, and hippos, and they all look at you as if you were some kind of specimen as you drive through their property."

After I ate a leisurely breakfast and pressed my uniform for the coming day, I drove over to the Lion Country setup. The twenty dollars for a carload seemed expensive, especially when I had only one person in the car, but I thought I should take advantage of everything I could!

The fifteen-foot-high gate opened, and I drove into the lions' den. A safari armored car was parked by the gate to discourage any escapees. I drove slowly along the curving two-lane blacktop to a row of trees. There, in the shade about thirty feet away, rested three lionesses and a couple of half-grown cubs. The male rested his shaggy head on the ground with his eyes half-open. I wished for someone to play with. It's not as much fun to see a pride of lions only thirty feet away and not have a soul to squeal and point and smile with. Flies buzzed around the nearby carcass. It was beyond recognition but looked like it could have been a cow. I wondered where they would get enough to feed all these hungry mouths. Then I remembered the twenty dollars I had left at the front office and ceased to worry about the price of the lion feed.

Another armored car with two attendants clad in khaki pants and shirts was parked about twenty feet from the lion pride. I stopped my truck to watch. The big boy lifted his head and stood. His tail switched. Immediately, the men in the armored car moved toward the shaggy lion. He glanced, annoyed, at the armored car, and moved back to his pride. The attendants motioned me to move on. I wondered if that big, shaggy lion would think to hop up into the back of my pickup truck and smash my windshield.

The lions had their own roaming range with the fifteen-foot chain-link fence around it. It seemed large enough, probably about forty acres, but I wondered if they ever had a lion climb the fence and visit the campground.

I drove out another guarded fifteen-foot gate and on into what looked like about 100 acres of rangeland. There were zebra and wildebeests and antelope ranging over the area along with monkeys and a hippopotamus and a family of elephants. This type of a zoo wasn't too bad. The animals seemed happy and content. The people were the ones in the cages. I stopped to watch the elephants squirting water on themselves. I've always been especially fond of elephants. It seems that trunk can do almost anything. I supposed they could go on a rampage, but at this moment, they seemed so benign.

Next, I came to the giraffe family. I wondered what it would be like to try to ride one of them. I thought of Jack and his easy canter. If I could just climb up onto this giraffe's back, I could hold around his neck to keep from sliding down his steep back, and we would canter away.

My daydreaming stopped. This tall, graceful animal was looking at me. What big brown eyes he had and what long eyelashes. He blinked and moved to another pile of hay.

At last, I drove through the last gate and back into the real world again. The gate closed behind me. I felt as though I was leaving friends. Maybe I could come back sometime with a significant other and laugh and squeal and play. But life must move on.

I strolled throughout the amusement park at the entrance to the lions' den. There were the usual crowds of people eating cotton candy and hot dogs. There were tourist traps where people could buy souvenirs and T-shirts. I bought a little packet of grain to feed the peacocks. I've always enjoyed the brightly-colored plumage of the handsome males. One of the big guys spread his fan with iridescent blue and green and black for me to see. Well, maybe it was for the lady peacock nearby, I don't know.

The pathway led over a little bridge with goldfishes in it. You could buy little packets of fish food for twenty-five cents, but I resisted. To me a fish never seems to have much personality. I followed the crowd to a small clearing among the trees where a riding elephant stood with his trainer. They told me it was an Indian elephant. It looked like any other elephant to me. It had the ropy tail and the little finger on the end of his trunk that he uses to pick up peanuts. His skin was rough and wrinkled, but I noticed it had a little hair on it.

I reached out my hand to pet this magnificent prehistoric mammal. "Oh, don't do that," the trainer said. "They can't feel you petting them, anyway. They have such a tough hide.

I didn't answer, but I bought my ticket and stood in line for a ride. I thought to myself, *If Dixi could feel a fly on her flank, it seems to me that an elephant should be able to do the same.* I looked at that little "finger" on the end of his trunk again. How fascinating. It was able to move almost as well as mine. I climbed into the big basket that was used for a saddle. Three other people climbed in with me and seated themselves on the red Indian cushions placed there for our comfort. The basket swayed from side to side as the elephant walked slowly around the clearing. I felt sorry for the beast. I wondered if it had a family back in India. I wondered if he missed them. I could understand how it feels to miss the people you love. I wondered how Tina and LeRoy were doing. I wondered if Tim was still missing Marbie. *How lonely it can be in a crowd,* I thought.

I reached over and patted the elephant's shoulder again as I dismounted. His big brown eye looked into mine. Did I really detect a look of appreciation and affection in that soft eye?

The walkway led through some jungle plants to another clearing where there were some kiddy rides. There were little cars that went round and round in a circle, and there were little boats you could rent that bumped one another. I wasn't even tempted. Not tempted at least until I spied the merry-go-round. A merry-go-round has always been a favorite of mine. The organ grinder carousel music reminds me of my childhood when my cousin and I would be allowed to go to the circus with my uncle.

The colorful wooden horses went round and round and up and down in time with the music. I had to do it, I just had to for old times' sake. I bought a ticket and climbed up on the child-size black horse with the red trim. Mothers and fathers escorted their children to the horse of their choice, and the music started. Maybe I shouldn't have done it. Maybe I should have just gone on back to the campground for another swim. But I did it. I found out that it's not the music or the rhythm of the horses or the memories, but it's who you are with. I had no one. There was not a soul to play with. Maybe someday I would have children of my own and even grandchildren. I could pick them up and put them on top of the merry-go-round horses and laugh and squeal with them. But not now. I felt lonely inside.

Lion Country Safari was an experience, but soon we found a campground only blocks from the big hospital. A big city campground was noisy, and it seems it never got dark. How would one look at the stars in a place like this? The only attraction was the proximity to the hospital. The sirens whined all night on their way to the emergency room. The campers were crammed into as small a space as possible. There were other "lifers" there, too. There were construction workers contracting local jobs. There were retired people with bumper stickers that read, "Retired, no phone, no home, no money." There were migrant farmworkers that worked in the farmland west of Palm Beach, and there were Gypsies. Real Gypsies! They read palms and made huge fancy puffy fake flowers out of bright colored feathers and sold them at flea markets, and to me!

"Well," I said to Gracie, "I guess we're Gypsies, too. I never thought I'd grow up to be a migrant worker. At least we have a home. I guess we're really lucky, even if home will never be the same, at least we have a community we belong to! Do you think we should think about going home someday, Gracie Allen?"

"Neow?" she asked excitedly.

"No, not yet. This assignment may be really great. Who could beat winter in Florida!" Gracie Allen looked a bit wistful as I spoke of home. She could hunt for mice in the hayloft, watch birds from the kitchen window, and dig holes under the forsythia bush. I noticed she had almost doubled in bulk since the day she first stepped into the trailer. She didn't ever ask to go out of the fifth wheel, but when I spoke of home, she looked wistful.

The Catch

There was a catch to all this build-up about this wonderfully exciting Rehabilitation Department! The political situation was volatile! The rehab team didn't find out about the transfer to Dr. Snider's company until Monday morning when they came to work! I was to be the new acting director!

When I arrived on Monday morning, the old director was gone, and I, as the representative of the new company, was their boss. Dr. Snider was there to introduce the new acting director and present the therapists with contracts to continue serving under their new leadership, but the natives were livid!

"They didn't even tell us he was leaving!" glared the dark-haired young male therapist. "Why didn't they just tell us! Wait till I see the administration!"

I looked around the group. There was a slight, young Filipina therapist. She made no eye contact. There was a tall, attractive, blond therapist who had been out of school only one year. She seemed to be the leader of the group and looked daggers through me with her hard blue eyes. There was a pleasant-looking Filipino male therapist who made no comment. There was a motherly-looking therapist who would probably have a good bedside manner, but at the moment, looked to be in a state of shock. Would these people decide to sign the contract with the new company? Where else would these people find jobs in the area if they decided not to join? And where would we find therapists if they decided not to! I waited.

I noticed them standing in little knots now and again throughout the day as I tried to find my way around this strange new hospital. They became quiet and gave side glances at me as I passed.

I introduced myself to the director of nurses and the chief financial officer. Dr. Snider proudly introduced me to the administrator. "This is Elizabeth Boyd, Mr. Haught. She has been with our company for a year as our lead therapist. She has some background in the type of new philosophy you are purporting for your hospital now."

Mr. Haught extended his hand. His palm was damp. His eyes darted about the room. "Pleased to meet you," he said. "We need to talk sometime. I'll have my secretary give you a call to set up an appointment."

I excused myself and allowed him time to talk to Dr. Snider alone.

The next morning, Dr. Snider called the therapists together to receive their signed contracts. On cue they all ripped the contracts and walked off the job.

I was left alone! Not only was I in a strange city and a strange hospital, but I was the only one to treat the entire caseload that six therapists had been treating in a 350-bed hospital! I geared to work twenty-four hours around the clock!

It was then that I learned an "Elizabethan truism." Not every problem is mine. Life is for living. I've always been a "type-A" personality. My middle name is Immediate. I've always thought that if I worked long enough and hard enough and fast enough and efficient enough, that I could do whatever I set my mind to. But now I hit the wall. There was definitely a problem, but the problem was not mine. This was a problem for the administration of the hospital! Even if I worked twenty-four hours around the clock seven days a week, there would still be patients untreated. I vowed that from now on, I would set reasonable goals and even take time to smell the roses.

The south Florida sunshine was warm. *How far am I from the beach,* I wondered? I took my tomato sandwich and drove east over Interstate Highway 95. At the top of the bridge, I could see the turquoise waters of the south Florida coast. I found a parking spot at the edge of the beach and took off my shoes. The sand felt warm to my bare feet, and the breeze flitted my hair. I took a deep breath. Moments like these put life back into perspective.

There were a couple of young, suntanned men trying to fly a yellow and red two-fisted kite. The snowbirds from Brooklyn, New York, were wading with bare white legs in the shallow water. Four Pelicans flew south just skimming the water.

The Lonely Judge

I broke for supper about 6:00 p.m. and went to the hospital cafeteria. "Another hospital cafeteria," I said to myself. "You've seen one, you've seen them all!"

I filled my plate with the usual green, leafy vegetables. They were fresh and well prepared, but I hardly noticed. I was too preoccupied to notice my food. I was too preoccupied to notice anything.

Then, there he was in front of me, holding his dinner tray and looking at my name tag. "Elizabeth Boyd?" he read out loud. "My name's Tom. Come sit with me, or we'll both be alone."

I was in no mood to entertain a man. My mind was on the impossible situation at the hospital. How could I possibly treat all those patients!

"This cafeteria is the best-kept secret in all of Palm Beach!" Tom began.

"It is?" I asked, looking at my pile of greens. "Do you eat here often?"

"Yes, I work in town and live alone. At least the food is healthy.

"Oh? You live alone? Do you have any pets?" I asked, really wanting to tell him about Gracie Allen.

"Pets? Interesting you asked. I have a parrot that I've had since my wife left me some ten years ago. Her name is Pickle. I felt so sorry for her, being there alone all day that I decided to get her a friend. I bought a myna bird named Charlie. They both talk. I thought they could talk to each other all day while I'm at work. But they don't! They wait till I get home, then both want to talk to me!"

> *The next morning, Dr. Snider called the therapists together to receive their signed contracts. On cue they all ripped the contracts and walked off the job*

We laughed together.

Just then I heard my name being called over the PA system.

"Elizabeth Boyd, Elizabeth Boyd, please dial the operator for a long-distance call."

I couldn't believe my ears! It was the renters at the farm. "It's all over now, but I thought you should know as soon as possible. We just had a chimney fire in the Franklin stove in the kitchen! I don't know how badly the place is damaged yet.

"We called LeRoy and Tina as soon as we saw the shower of sparks covering the roof. He was up the hill in a flash and took the garden hose. You wouldn't think he could move that fast at his age, but he almost flew up that ladder. The Harpswell volunteer fire department was here about the time LeRoy got to the roof with the garden hose. They smothered the fire in the Franklin, then checked the attic to see if any sparks had escaped into all that old stuff stored up there. Then they raced down to the cellar. They opened a hole in the chimney from down there, and put something in there to retard fire. I guess that's the last we'll be using the Franklin."

I was numb. I walked back to the table and buried my face in my hands.

"What happened!" Tom exclaimed. "Did your house burn down or something!"

"Exactly!" I moaned. "They didn't even know the damage yet. What's more, I live in the state of Maine and can't even go home!"

"What are you doing here?" he asked. "This is a long way from Maine!"

Tom was sympathetic as he listened to my story. As he pushed back his chair, he put his business card in my hand. "Call me if you ever need anything."

"Thomas E. Smith, Circuit Court Judge, Palm Beach, Florida" A couple of weeks later, I pulled his business card out of my purse. "Tom," I began when he picked up the phone, "This is Elizabeth, that physical therapist you met in JFK cafeteria a couple of weeks ago. I'm having problems with the truck. A little light comes on that says 'check engine.' Where would I go to have this looked after?"

"How 'bout if I meet you tonight after work at the hospital cafeteria. I've got a good mechanic I use for my own cars. He has his shop over on Military Trail. I'll see that he does you right. You can follow me out, and then I'll give you a ride back."

That evening, we left the truck and headed back to the campground. "How would you like to stop by my house and meet Pickle and Charlie?" he asked.

"Do you think they'd talk to me?" I smiled.

The guards at the gate lifted the barrier and waved as Tom drove into the restricted housing development.

I wonder why anyone would want to live here, I thought. *I like my friends to be able to come see me anytime without having to pass a guardhouse. What would they say if they saw Sally taking rhubarb from my garden to make me a pie?*

Tom spoke. "I like living in a secured area. In a job like mine, I get threats on my life now and again. You never know if some kook may make good on his threat!"

He pulled into his drive and flipped the garage door opener. *More protection,* I thought.

Before Tom had a chance to put his key in the lock of the back door, I heard a woman talking inside. "Hello! Hello! Come in, come in!" the woman's voice called.

"Who's in there, Tom?" I asked. Surely with all the security, he wouldn't find a woman in his house calling, "Hello! Hello!"

Tom laughed, and his steel-blue eyes twinkled. "That's Pickle. Wait till you hear Charlie."

About that time a man's voice called, "Hello, Charlie! Hello, Charlie." It was my turn to laugh. "Is he talking to himself?" As Tom opened the door, a white ball of fur came flying into his arms. "This is Tuffy," Tom said, handing me the little white dog. He was more interested in licking Tom's chin than in having anything to do with me.

Tom flipped on the kitchen light. There on the white tile countertop was a graceful tabby tomcat. He stretched his back, yawned, and jumped to the floor with a thud. "This is Boomer," Tom introduced me. "Come, Boomer." Boomer was more interested in his cat dish than being introduced to strangers, so padded to the refrigerator and waited.

"You can take a look through the house if you want to while I feed these animals," Tom offered.

"Sure," I said. "I always like an open house tour."

I walked into the living room and groped for the light. I thought I saw a large, tawny animal with his back to me looking at the front door. My heart skipped a beat. What was it? It looked like one of those tigers I had seen at the Lion Country Safari. Surely, Tom wouldn't have a tiger chained up in his living room! After all my travels across the country, in a little pink hat, driving a forty-foot fifth wheel, why should I be terrified of a tiger in Tom's living room? I took my life in my hands and snapped on the light. Sure enough! It was a life-size stuffed tiger sitting on its haunches looking at the front door. I got it. If a burglar tried to break into the house, the first thing he would see would be the tawny tiger. This guy must really be spooked out!

After a couple of TV programs, Tom took me the mile and a half back to the campground. "Could I take you to get the truck tomorrow night after work? Maybe we could go out for dinner afterward."

"I definitely need transportation, and I'd love to keep you company for dinner. You probably need to know I'm a vegetarian, though," I said as he walked with me to the door.

"A vegetarian!" Tom sounded shocked. It was as if he were observing a specimen of some strange creature. "What will I feed you?" he said seriously. "What will I feed you?"

I laughed, "Oh, Tom, you don't need to worry about what to feed me! Just consider me an easy keeper. You can eat whatever you want, and I can always get a whole plateful of side orders. Almost everyone has a baked potato! Stop your worrying! The reason I go out to eat is for the company!"

"We'll go for Italian food," he said with a smile. "You can eat spaghetti, can't you!"

I laughed and waved as he pulled away.

Gracie Allen was there to meet me when I opened the door. She sniffed me all over as I opened her Meow Mix. "Interesting evening, Gracie," I said. "I think we have a new friend."

Making Good Old Times to Remember

He called in early February. "Can we meet for dinner tonight at the hospital cafeteria? You wouldn't believe everything that's happened!"

"Sure. We need to catch up. See you then," I answered.

"Could we get together this Sunday?" Tom asked. "How would you like to go out to Lion Country Safari and see the animals? I know you love animals."

"Really, Tom!" I answered excitedly. "I'd love to. I did it before all by myself, but there was nobody to squeal and laugh and play with. When shall we go?"

"I'll pick you up around eleven a.m. after my golf game."

"I used to live out this way in Loxahatchee," Tom commented as we drove west on the two-lane highway toward the sugar cane farms.

"Tell me about it," I said, sitting sideways in the seat.

"We had five acres and two show horses."

"Show horses?" I asked. "What kind?"

"We used to show Tennessee Walking horses. You know that picture in the hallway at my house? That's me on my sorrel gelding, Midnight Man," he answered.

"You're kidding!" I exclaimed. "Jack and Dixi were Walkers, too. Ever think of getting a horse again?"

"No. I don't miss all the work, especially if you show them. You have to give them a bath and beauty treatment the night before, then hope they don't roll in something during the night. Then you have to bring them home and put everything away. You have to get hay and grain all the time. You have to be sure they always have water. It's a lot of work."

In about forty-five minutes, we drove up to the guardhouse by the big chain-link fence to buy a ticket.

"I don't do this very often," he said, "it's too expensive."

"That's OK," I answered, "I'll pay my own way. This is really a fun thing to do. You like animals, too!"

"Oh, ugh, that's OK, I didn't mean it was too expensive to take you!" He sounded a little embarrassed.

"Oh, Tom, could we do the amusement park first? I want to play on the merry-go-round!" I bounced on the seat of the car like a little girl.

"The merry-go-round!" he exclaimed. "You want to play on the merry-go-round!"

"Try me," I answered. "Come on, you gotta play sometimes!"

He grinned like a little boy. "I haven't been on one of them in a long time!"

As we stood in line with the mothers and fathers and little kids, Tom chuckled. "What if somebody sees me doing this?"

> *"Oh, Tom, could we do the amusement park first? I want to play on the merry-go-round!" I bounced on the seat of the car like a little girl*

"Put a bag over your head if it bothers you, Tommy," I answered with a giggle. "They'll just laugh at you and wish they could do it, too."

We climbed up side by side onto the child-sized circus horses. Tom's was black with a gold saddle and bridle: mine, a brown and white spotted pony with bright blue trimmings. The organ grinder music box started, and the horses rose and fell to the rhythm. Tom glanced at me with a big grin. "I can't believe we're doing this!" he chuckled as he gave me a sideways glance.

"Are we making good old times to remember, or what!" I laughed.

The music stopped, and the merry-go-round horses came to a whoa. I didn't really want the moment to end. But I didn't dare ask for another round!

The afternoon went too quickly. We made our way through the lion's den and the elephant jungle. We watched the gazelles grazing and the hippopotamus bathing in the mud. Then it was time for him to take me back to the fifth wheel.

I had to admit to Gracie Allen that night that I saw a part of Tom that day that had probably been buried for a good while. It was hard to picture that grinning little boy on the black and gold carousel horse, sitting as the black-robed, silver-haired judge on the bench in the courthouse.

A Real Money-Maker

The situation at work deteriorated. Only top priority patients got attention. One evening, Dr. Snider took me to the restaurant at "The Breakers," overlooking Palm Beach. We ordered an appetizer of stuffed mushrooms and began to talk shop.

"Is there anything we can do, Elizabeth, to be sure you are happy here? We are happy with your work and would like you to stay on as the permanent director. I think we can make it a real money-maker. There are lots of rich people in the area. We need to get all the treatment units possible out of each visit. With your expertise, you may be able to get some of these well-heeled individuals to donate to the physical therapy department."

Money-maker, I thought. *That's the name of his game. I feel like throwing up! I want out of this company!*

"What about the replacements you promised," I asked, "for the therapists who walked off the job? There were five of them plus a director. We now have only myself and two other physical therapists. It seems that we may be sacrificing quality care on the altar of saving the salaries of three therapists."

"Oh, uh," he stammered, reaching for the fresh whole-wheat rolls. "We are looking for some."

"Let's see what you can come up with," I continued.

The evening wore on. What do you talk about when you go out to an elite restaurant for the evening with a man you don't respect? *Money-maker*, I thought to myself, *Money-maker!*

I stopped by the grocery store to pick up Meow Mix for Gracie Allen and some tomatoes and mayonnaise for me. From Hazard, Kentucky, to Palm Beach, Florida, was almost culture shock. The stores seemed to be littered with lonely, little old men and women with Kelly green Bermuda shorts and white sun visors, pushing grocery carts here and there about the store. The skin on the face was brown and weather-beaten. Some wore a tight-lipped perpetual smile put there by some plastic surgeon. Their legs were flabby, and their gait unsteady. What struck me most was the vacant, woebegone look on the face. Had these people no one to love them? I thought of my church family back home that comforted me when my dad died, and little Tim who brought the grocery store pink and blue and white daisies when Marbie died. I thought of the night I called Tina at 2:30 a.m. to get a ride to the emergency room for treatment of a kidney stone. And I thought of Ruth standing on her wisteria-covered porch waving as I pulled out of the driveway. "Remember, we love you, Liz!"

That evening as I drove back to the noisy, crowded campground, I thought of the peaceful farmhouse on the coast of Maine. I wondered if "the frost was comin' out o' the ground" yet. March was always my least favorite month—mud season. As the days grow longer and the sun moves northward, snow begins to melt and forms little streams. Green moss appears as if by magic, and even before the snow has melted, the "May flowers" appear. In Harpswell nobody calls them Trailing Arbutus. They are just "May flowers." Their small, white blossoms nestle under the tough green leaves all winter. When spring comes, they are the first to bloom. I thought again of the light fragrance of these delicate petals. It seemed a sweet alternative to the bright lights and golf courses of Palm Beach. I thought of my quiet woods and the walk along the trail to the rocky coast. "Gracie," I said as she crunched her Meow Mix. "We've done what we can here. We'll give them two weeks. It's spring, and we'll pull this fifth wheel back to the farm. These are not the kind of people we want to work with. Yes, we can go home again!"

"Neow?" Gracie Allen asked in her sweetest kitty voice.

"Not yet," I answered, "but we'll start looking for a new way to earn money to buy your Meow Mix and my tomato sandwiches."

The bright yellow flowers were out on the Jacaranda trees when Gracie and I hitched the fifth wheel to the truck. We stuffed pillows in the cupboards to keep things from rattling around. We took down the swinging lamp over the kitchen table, and we emptied the holding tanks. We could go home to the lilac-laden breezes and the chipmunks in the woods. We could walk to the shore and watch the tide rise and the tide fall. We could sit at the kitchen table with our old friends and recount the stories of what was. The parting words of my neighbor as she waved from her porch rang in my ears. "Remember, we love you, Liz! "

"We Believe in You, 'Lizabeth!"

It was March, and there would still be snow in Maine. I decided to swing by Uncle Felix's. I needed the stability of family right now. Uncle Felix has always been more than a father to me. As we were walking back from the barn together after feeding the horses, I told him about Tom. Uncle Felix just put his arm around my shoulder and said in his midwestern farmer's way. "Your aunt and I believe in you, 'Lizabeth. I'm sure you'll do the right thing."

I felt tears spring into my eyes. It was comforting to know that he really did believe in me.

5. Almost Home

Spring Beauties

I needed to give my full-time attention to finding a job. There were no jobs in my hometown. No problem, there were plenty of ads in the Physical Therapy Bulletin. I could find a job for myself in Maine, surely.

With the Physical Therapy Bulletin full of want ads for physical therapists, and the telephone at my side, I started job hunting. I placed the phone on the mahogany coffee table and stretched out on the gray-green antique couch. I loved this couch. I wondered just how many geese had to bare their downy chests to supply all those soft pillows. I looked around the room at the antique dusty-rose overstuffed chair in the corner. It was such a massive chair. I guess they didn't have recliners in those days. Long, long ago, they must have put a footstool in front. It wasn't particularly comfortable. I prefer goose down. The seven vertical rolls in the back of the chair were stretched tightly over horsehair stuffing. Men seemed to migrate to this chair. I think it was the massiveness.

The house had been remodeled. A sand-colored wall-to-wall rug covered the "punkin' pine" boards of the floor, and a couple of oriental rugs with a sandy background rested on the wall to wall carpet. I wondered what stories these elderly pieces of furniture could tell. They came with the house, so I didn't know the stories.

There was a windowless "borning room" in the center of the house that was just large enough for a cot and washstand. It was absorbed into the living room with the remodeling, but I sometimes wondered about the women who had given birth there. Did any of them die? What happened to their babies? New England is cluttered with small ancient graveyards with mossy tombstones that might read, "Rebecca Bibber. Born March 2, 1734. Died March 4, 1734."

I looked out the big front window at the horse pasture. I remembered how Dixi and Jack used to stand looking over the split-rail fence and into the living room, and nicker at me come feeding time. I smiled at the memory. With time comes healing. We remember the good times.

For a few moments, I reveled in the comfort of being home, then picked up the phone. I began my spiel. "I noticed your advertisement in the Physical Therapy Bulletin for a staff physical therapist. May I speak to the person in charge of hiring for this position?"

It was usually the secretary that would answer the phone. "I'm sorry, that person is away from his desk. May I have him call you back?"

If the director did call me back, it was usually, "We're looking for someone as soon as possible. It's a great department, and it's a friendly community with a twelve-grade school. We pay to have your household goods moved. How soon can you come?"

When I answered, "I am a traveling therapist, and I'm available for temporary relief while you are attempting to locate a permanent hire." They would answer, "Oh, no, we don't really want a temporary person. We're looking for someone who will relocate here permanently and fit into the community."

The healthcare community wasn't used to having mobile therapists who were free to travel about on a locum tenen basis. A few had heard of traveling nurses. I still held licenses to practice in fifteen states, however. This increased my chances of being able to fill a temporary vacancy immediately.

It was good to be home again. Part of me wished that there was a local job. The phone began ringing off the hook, but it wasn't hospitals calling for a therapist. It was the neighbors wanting a report on the travels. "Can you come for suppah?" Sally asked. "Tide's in down here, and I'm fixin' chowdah."

Of course I would come! I needed to catch up on the news as well as fill my stomach with New England boiled dinners and chowder.

Later in the week, I sat with LeRoy, Tina, and Katie around the hard, wooden table and felt the comfort of the wood range in the corner of the kitchen.

"Tim is married now, you know, and has a little boy. Looks just like Tim did at that age, except he's blond. Tim is such a good father."

"They've got a new preacher at church. He's from away. Don't think he'll last long. Nice young fellow, though."

"They cut down those big pines at Bowdoin College and made a parking lot, of all things. Nobody could stop 'um. Money talks, you know."

"Buster's retired now, from LL Bean. He's only thirty-nine, but they gave a one-time retirement option for people who had been there twenty years. He took it. He's bought a house and is moving north to Greenville. Got a good deal on a house and some property on Moosehead Lake. The house is all furnished and everything."

With all the gossip and the chowder under my belt, it began to feel like home again. I went to the local supermarket to lay in a few supplies. There were actually people in the grocery store that I knew!

"You're home!" Margaret called from the other side of the bananas.

"You're home!" Rosie called as she lifted her head from sorting over the store-bought Florida oranges.

Suddenly, there were two thin arms thrown around my waist. It was little Katie. How she had grown.

I walked down Maine Street and looked in the familiar shop windows. This was home. I knew where to get the car fixed, I knew where to get the dry cleaning done. I knew who to go to if I got sick. Yes, and I remembered Ruth's parting words as I drove out of the driveway. "Remember, we love you, Liz!"

It was early April now, and the sun streamed into my bedroom window at about 5:00 a.m. I blinked in the sunshine as I opened my eyes and looked around my bedroom. I didn't have to ask myself this time if I were in Kentucky or Palm Springs. I knew. I pulled the white bedspread up over the pillows and straightened the white alpaca throw rugs. I liked the contrast of the white fur rugs on the dark red carpet of my bedroom. I hadn't thought I'd like it when my friend suggested I use dark red wallpaper, too. "… and bright white cotton curtains," she said. "You'll like it. It will be very stunning."

It was stunning, all right. I liked it.

I put on my red jacket and show boots and started on my morning walk to the shore. It seemed like a page from the past. It was still mud season, and the "frost was comin' out o' the ground." In spots the mud was over the toe of my boot. I checked the striped maple and the fiddlehead fern. It would be too early for lady slippers. Gracie followed, glad to be home where the field mice were plentiful, and she could lie in the sunshine on the green steps of the front porch or take her walk with me through the woods. I guess she still thought she was my loyal dog.

I blinked in the sunshine as I opened my eyes and looked around my bedroom. I didn't have to ask myself this time if I were in Kentucky or Palm Springs. I knew

The woods smelled of black warming earth and leaf mulch. I sniffed again. Yes, it was the pungent odor where a red fox had crossed the trail. I checked the dogtooth violets again. Their faces were bright in the sunshine.

I walked on down the trail to the spot near the water where the spring beauties bloom in the spring. I needed them. I wanted the assurance that although the snow may cover the sod, spring will come again. Spring beauties always give me assurance that although hope may fade, that, come spring, the world will come alive again. The spring beauties will bloom again like they do every spring. I touched their pinkish-white petals and picked one for the little vase on the kitchen counter as I had every year. Gracie rubbed my leg. I looked. Eider ducks paddled in the cove and talked to each other with sweet cooing sounds as they had done every spring since time began. It wouldn't be long until the brown mothers would have a line of fuzzy brown and yellow little ones.

No Way Out

Shortly, an assignment opened in Millinocket, Maine. Only a five-hour drive seemed so close to my home after being 1,500 miles away! I was excited! No more rush hour traffic jams, no more flat Florida landscapes. This hospital was located at the edge of the wilderness. Mount Katahdin peered into the picture window of the hospital lobby, and the locals all had stories to tell of moose and white water rafting on the Allagash River. They told stories of hiking the rugged "Knife Edge" along the trail to the peak of Mt. Katahdin, where the Appalachian Trail begins. I was almost home again.

I stopped at the local Timberline Cafe on my way into town. I had found that lunch at the local restaurant was a good way to get the flavor of the community.

The people were tough loggers who had been working in the woods since youth. The Timberline Cafe served the best pumpkin pie with real whipped cream!

"So, you're going to be working up at the hospital?" The waitress asked. "They just built up there on the hill about five years ago. It's a really nice hospital. My sister's little girl has cerebral palsy. The therapist up there, Susan Lifer, is a specialist. They say she's the best there is between here and Canada."

Mt. Katahdin, Maine

I thought to myself, *And just what is there between here and Canada? It looks like all the land is timberland that belongs to the paper companies! There's nothing but the Dead River and the Allagash as far as I can tell! But never mind, I'm almost home. Well, I will be on weekends, at least.*

"Could I have a piece of that pumpkin pie for dessert?" I asked as I watched a logger finishing off his last mouthful. "Do you make that here?"

"Oh, yes, she gets up early and makes the pies first. We have apple pie, too," the waitress offered.

I pulled my rig into the campground. It was really too early for campgrounds to be open in northern Maine. The buds were swelling on the horse chestnut trees, and they had just finished "sugaring out" the maples. The "frost was still comin' out o' the ground" up here, and the mud squashed up around my feet. One must put up with a few inconveniences to have the location one wants ... and the pie!

It was a beautiful site for a campground. "The ice was out," as they say when it has melted off the lake. The water was clear and sparkled in the sunshine. Ancient pine and spruce trees were here and there throughout the campground. *What a peaceful spot,* I thought, *to spend the summer. And I'm the only camper here so far. I think I'll enjoy the peace of no neighbors for a while after the noisy campground in Palm Beach.*

The owner of the campground helped me back my rig through the mud and into the campsite and unhitch, and then took me inside to fill out the paperwork and pay the price. He didn't look me in the eye. I felt uneasy. He led me into another room in back of the office. The smell was of wood smoke. The windows were closed, and I noticed there were no handles on the inside of the doors! Before I had time to think it through, I shot past the man and out the front door. I was into my truck and back at the hospital before I stopped!

With my heart still pounding, I burst into the administrator's office. "I'm scared! Do you know anything about the man that owns Evergreen Campground? He just took me into a room that didn't have any door handles! He looked like he had something on his mind other than filling out papers for the campground!" I paused for breath.

"Oh, no," Mr. Lively cautioned. "I'm glad you got out of there! Last summer, an older woman was taking a shower in the bathhouse. She didn't think much about the open rafters overhead. Lots of campgrounds have open areas above the shower. But after she was in there all soaped up, she happened to look up, and there was Butch on the rafters directly above her, looking down at her taking a shower! She grabbed her towel and ran back to her husband, screaming. They pressed charges, but all they could do was give him a fine for a "peeping Tom."

"I know I don't want to ever see that man again!" I said, still pale. "But, my rig is over there."

"I'll send a man with you to pull your rig out of there right now!" the administrator said. "You can park here in the hospital parking lot until you can find something else. I'm glad you played your hunch and acted immediately!"

It took us only three minutes to back under the rig and hitch up.

"What's the matter?" asked the campground owner as he came around the corner.

By then, we were pulling out of the campground. I didn't answer.

Mount Katahdin

The Millinocket Hospital was friendly and well-equipped. The locals wanted to hear stories of my travels, and I wanted to hear stories of Baxter State Park and Mt. Katahdin.

My patient, Mr. Murry, was in excruciating pain. The cancer had gone to his bone, and he knew, and I knew that there was nothing more that could be done.

"I had this man back in the hills of Kentucky that really got a lot of good from the TENS unit." I told him the story of Bill and the gunshot wound to the femoral nerve.

"Well, it can't hurt anything," he said as he turned his face toward me. "Let's give it a try."

I wired him to the little gadget and started it working while we visited. He seemed so young to be dying of cancer. His light brown hair was thin from the radiation treatments.

"What do you do for fun when you are able to be up and about?" I asked.

"For fun?" he asked. "My work has been my fun all my life. I'm in charge of Baxter State Park and Mt. Katahdin. I can remember it before Governor Baxter set it aside. He made it into a wilderness park, you know."

"Where do you hurt right now, Mr. Murry?" I asked.

"You can wear it constantly if you need to," I said. "It will sometimes last for several hours, though, after you take it off. Let's leave it on for a while and see what happens.

"Did you say you have lots of slides of the park? Do you think your wife could get things set up, and you could give us a slide show some evening? I don't have much to do in the evenings. I'm staying in my fifth wheel during the week and driving home to Harpswell on weekends."

"Well, if this thing keeps working, maybe I could even go home. You could come over, and I could have things set up to show you," he answered, much encouraged.

"Yes, tonight's the night. The wife will be here to help," he said.

"Let's see your Baxter State Park pictures, Mr. Murrry," I suggested.

His wife set up the show of Mr. Murry's pictures of a lifetime. There were pictures of moose at sunrise. There were pictures of lady slippers in the spring. There were scenes of brilliant leaves in autumn. There were chipmunks nibbling acorns. I sat entranced. Each picture had meaning to Mr. Murry. He was there again as he showed the view from the top of the mountain. The hazy blue hills stretched on and on to the horizon. It was as if he were reliving each moment, then putting it to sleep until that morning when everything will be fresh and new and beautiful in the hereafter.

The wife finished the last carousel and turned on the light. Mr. Murry was asleep and resting comfortably. We left the room.

That night, Mr. Murry slipped into a coma and never awoke.

Alone Beside the New York Throughway

As the leaves turned red and gold and covered the ground instead of trees, the regular therapist was due to return to work at the Millinocket PT department. I was glad she had time to bond with her new baby all summer, but I was ready for another location. I thought again of the seashells and salt waters of Florida, and maybe even Tom.

Poor Gracie had no choice. "Here we go again, Gracie," I said.

"Neow?" she asked respectfully.

"Yes, Gracie."

It was on the New York Throughway, east of the Tappan Zee Bridge, on Friday afternoon when I heard it. The loud bang came from a major blowout on the traffic side of the fifth wheel. I pulled off the road and onto the shoulder. I adjusted my little pink straw hat and stepped out to look things over. The blowout was on the tire directly under the refrigerator and the washer/dryer combination. This was the heaviest part of the fifth wheel. I wondered what had caused it? I usually went the speed limit. Never over sixty-three mph. I wondered if this was a bad batch of tires. I always took a walk around the rig whenever I stopped because I saw the professional truckers doing it. They always beat the tires with a club and checked the hitch. They jiggled the electrical cord and tightened any tie-downs. Three times I had found bulges on the tires. There had always been a place to get the tire repaired close by, so this was the first, and I hoped, the only blowout of my entire journey. The shoulder was steep and rendered the fifth wheel too low to the pavement to get a jack under. Even if I had been able to get the jack under, I don't know how I planned to get the tire off!

The eighteen-wheelers roared past, buffeting my rig. The four-wheelers looked the other way. I got on the CB radio and began to try to make contact with someone who might help. I could hear the truckers talking among themselves about the predicament they could see I was in.

"Where's her Buffalo?" one crusty trucker crackled into the CB.

"She got an escort? Check that pink hat!" said another.

"Ten-four!" laughed his partner, but no one stopped.

I asked myself again, "What's a nice girl like you doing in a place like this?"

The sun began to sink low behind the trees, and the cars began to turn on headlights. The New York Throughway would be a poor place to spend the night at best, but the thoughts of being alone with a flat tire frightened me big time. My father had a stockpile of stories about little ladies, with or without pink hats, who were stranded along superhighways. Sometimes people stop, but not to help. Sometimes it's people with ill intent!

I thought of home and the smell of fresh, warm strawberry-rhubarb pie the neighbor left steaming on my kitchen table. I thought of the safe place where you can take a walk alone by moonlight through the quiet woods to the rocky shore. I thought again of my neighbor, Ruth, waving from the wisteria-covered porch. "Remember, we love you, Liz!" Loneliness and fear began to creep in around the edges of my heart. Why wouldn't anyone pick up on my SOS?

Then a huge mobile-home-hauling tractor pulled up behind me and sheltered me a little from the traffic. Although there was no mobile home in tow at the time, the tractor gave ample protection. The driver, a tall, lean man with dark hair, jumped from the cab and began to assess the situation.

> *"What's a nice girl like you doing in a place like this?"*

"Got any spare boards?" he asked.

"I got the pressure-treated four by fours I usually block the wheels with when I park. They are beveled on one end. Is that what you're thinking?"

"Just what we need," he answered. "I'll make a little ramp with a couple of those, and we'll be all set."

"Now get in and pull forward slowly," he instructed. "With those extra inches, we should be able to get your hydraulic jack under the frame."

"You'll never make it!" some cranky truck driver bellowed over the CB.

"Yeah, better just take her to a motel and call the wrecker," another one crackled.

"Too steep. You'll turn the whole thing over if you jack it up any more." another said.

Where were all these know-it-all men when I needed them? I thought.

The tire changed, the tall truck driver stood up. "You don't have a spare tire now, and you shouldn't travel without one. Follow me up the road. I'll show you where to get off at the truck stop that has your size tires.

"Thanks! I mean really!" I breathed a sigh. "What's your CB handle?"

He paused and looked me in the eye before he answered. "Spirit," was all he said and drove away.

6. Florida Again

Walter and the Dance Band

I dawned my pink straw hat and sped cheerily down Interstate 81 south, planning to stop in Abington, Virginia, for the night. The late afternoon sun shone into the front window of the truck, and the air was warm and comfortable. I rolled down the truck window and began to sing:

> I love to go a-wandering,
> Along a mountain track,
> And as I go, I love to sing,
> My knapsack on my back.

I glanced in the side mirror. *Nice-looking car following me in the hammer lane. Looks like an antique of some kind.* I thought. I watched as it began to pull past. It was a restored model of one of those old cushy Chevrolets. I always thought those exaggerated fins looked funny, but right now, it looked quite sporty. The convertible top was down, and it was really rolling. The blur of white metal with red seat covers sped past me. I laughed to myself. It was full of college-aged young men out for the ride of their life in the autumn air. Suddenly their brake lights came on, and the car slowed to fifty-five mph until it was abreast of my cab. I looked down and smiled and waved. The fellow in the passenger seat held up a little black box and snapped a quick picture. Then with a wave of their arms, they sped on down the road.

Two days later, I pulled into Alligator Mobile Home and RV Park in Punta Gorda, Florida. I remembered Lion Country Safari and the roar of the lions early in the morning. I hoped I didn't wake up in the morning with alligators snapping under my window. I liked the campground immediately. I pulled in and parked in front of the clubhouse. The manager was gracious and filled me in on the rules and activities. "And since this is a retirement community and we want to keep it as quiet as possible, we only allow patrons fifty and older."

"I guess that counts me out," I said, looking out the window at a couple of hoary heads peddling past on oversized tricycles. "I have a ways to go before I reach fifty, and I'm not in any hurry!"

"Do you think you could make an exception?" I asked, standing in front of him in my pink straw hat and ruffled white blouse. "You see, I'm a single lady starting work at Medical Center Hospital as a traveling physical therapist tomorrow. I really need the security of your nice facility here."

"I think we can do that," he smiled. "You are a professional person. I'm sure the club would welcome you. You can take a drive around the park and pick out your site. It's still early in the season, and all the snowbirds haven't arrived yet. You may find this side of Florida a little more laid back. Most of the clients that come to the west coast of Florida are from the Midwest and the South. Lots of them come year after year."

I pulled into a corner lot near the back of the campground and spread out my little grass-green mat and pulled down my blue and white striped awning. The Florida sand seemed even whiter here on the west coast. The grass was well-kept, and a few long-needle pines grew here and there on the campground. I noticed that there was a section where there were mobile homes with neat little flower gardens. There were bright red impatiens and Dusty Miller with florescent blue lobelia growing in the flower boxes. Some mobile homes even had hand-carved wooden signs that gave the name of the owner.

Punta Gorda was just off the Tamiami Trail going from Tampa to Miami. It was out of the mainstream tourist traps and traffic jams. The facility was also ideal. My assignment was in the outpatient department. This department was operated in conjunction with an outpatient wellness program. Sliding glass doors opened onto a neat patio with a little birdbath in the center. Adjacent to the clinic was the gym with rowing machines and stationary bicycles and exercise weights of all sizes and shapes. I was ecstatic. I remembered the cramped quarters under the eaves at the Mattie Williams Hospital in Virginia. What they could do with all their patients if they had a setup like this. And to top it all, there was a spacious indoor therapeutic pool. I stuck my finger in the water. *Ah, about eighty-eight degrees!* I thought. I think most of my patients will be needing pool therapy.

The week went quickly. "How far is it over to Palm Beach, Judy?" I asked my assistant.

"You don't want to drive all the way over there on a weekend!" she exclaimed. "It takes hours! And besides, it's crowded, and most of the people are from New York City!"

I laughed. "How true! What's there around here to do?"

"Have you checked out Sanibel Island? It's the seashell capital of the gulf. The surf is blue, the sand is warm, and the people are friendly. You can walk along the beach for hours and find all kinds of shells," Judy answered.

Judy was right. I took along my tomato sandwich and a plastic bag for shells. But mostly, it felt good to squiggle my cold white toes into the warm white sand and let the sea breeze blow my hair.

I picked up four white flower planters from Walmart on Sunday morning and stopped at one of the ubiquitous plant nurseries along the road. There were dwarf lemon and orange trees. There were red and yellow and pink hibiscus, the kind Hawaiian hula dancers wear in their hair. There were orchids and gardenias. Wow! I felt like a kid in a candy store with a pocket full of change.

The fragrant gardenia was an absolute. Surely, there would be a place for it at home in the farmhouse. But for now, it could stay outside all winter. I settled for some bright red impatiens. I found myself even looking forward to the winter in this balmy weather.

Midafternoon, there seemed to be some noise coming from the clubhouse. I put down my garden tools and walked in that direction past the neat flower boxes of the other seasonal residents and past the swimming pool where little old people with Kelly green shorts sat under the shade of the green and white umbrellas.

I stepped into the back of the recreation hall. It was cool, but not cold. An older couple gave me the nod, and I slipped in beside them. I looked around. There were about sixty people sitting toward the back of the room on wooden benches and metal folding chairs. In the center of the cement floor, a group of older ladies with little white polo shirts and Kelly green Bermuda shorts was line-dancing to the tune of "Golden Slippers."

On the low wooden platform in the front of the room, about fifteen of the old folks had gathered with their musical instruments. There were fiddles, banjos, a bass, and a washtub! There was a gentleman with bib overalls sitting over at one side playing an amplified harmonica. I looked more closely. His harmonica was supported by a little stand. He had no arms.

Then, "Walter! We want Walter!" called a group of folks with a Tennessee accent.

"Yes! We want Walter!" echoed the rest of the group.

I watched. Walter stood unsteadily and shuffled to the front. People shouted again. "Go, Walter! Give us the Tennessee Waltz. Both hands were shaking as he reached for his electric guitar. His head shook, and he looked so unsteady on his feet, I thought of offering some physical therapy.

The rest of the band joined in as Walter's faltering baritone voice began: "I was waltzing with my darling to the Tennessee Waltz ..."

The folks from Tennessee found partners and danced to the rhythm. Others joined them.

"My friend stole my sweetheart from me," Walter crooned. His voice was strong now. The folks still sitting in their seats were humming along.

"The night they were playing the beautiful Tennessee Waltz."

It was beautiful. If they would treat old tottery Walter with such respect and love, maybe I could even join them with my French horn! I never had really enjoyed playing by notes, anyway! At least I could take the off-beat. Um-pa, Um-pa, Um-pa pa.

My eyes were moist. These people were professional campers. They had no real roots. Most of them had retired and sold their homes. They were footloose and free. Florida in the winter, and Montana in the summer. They would take in a few campgrounds in between. Some of them wouldn't live to go home again. Some had no friends or family who really wanted them. Nobody really cared. We cared for each other. We shared stories and babysat the neighbor's cat. But we were each alone, really. When we parted, we knew we'd never see each other again.

In the center of the cement floor, a group of older ladies with little white polo shirts and Kelly green Bermuda shorts was line-dancing to the tune of "Golden Slippers."

This Land Belongs to You and Me

My daily routine included a quiet walk along a sandy little road that made its way through the palmetto palms and the pastureland in back of the campground. No, it didn't lead to the rocky coast of Maine, but I learned to appreciate its own unique charm. At least it was a safe spot to be alone and do some thinking as well as get exercise in the fresh air. I got someone at the clubhouse on Sunday afternoon to teach me a polka step and found the sandy trail a handy place to practice. Of course, one has to have music if they are going to dance. So I sang as I skipped down the sandy lane.

> This land is your land, this land is my land
> From California to the New York island

From the redwood forest to the gulf stream waters
This land was made for you and me.

Yes, there was something about this traveling thing that gave me a bond with my country. I am a part of the whole. I thought of the black earth of Minnesota and the men in the blue denim overalls, and the Spanish moss and little Lucy in Alabama. I thought of the whippoorwills and mountain laurel in the hollers of Kentucky and Dreama and Lofton. I thought of Tom and the bright lights of Palm Beach. I remembered the desert sunsets from my youth in the Southwest and the smell of sagebrush. I thought of the pristine lakes on the Olympic peninsula. *Yes,* I thought to myself, *This land belongs to you and me!*

But I wondered, "If I didn't have my Old New England Farmhouse on the rocky coast of Maine, and if I had no Tina, LeRoy, Tim, Ruth, Sally, Charlotte, George, and Eugene to come home to, would not my travels throughout my country be meaningless? Yes, my home was on the rocky coast of Maine, but there was a completeness about belonging to the whole United States of America.

I thought of the days on the farm before Jack and Dixi died. I remembered when I moved to Maine after college. The old farmhouse needed lots of remodeling. "After I get the place fixed up, we'll have a party!" I said to myself. But as the days and weeks went by, I realized that if I waited until the house was perfect before inviting people to enjoy it with me, there would never be a time!

So I invited the other single people from the church to come over on Saturday night for a "Hootenanny." "Bring an instrument if you have one, if not, just come and sing, or be an audience!"

Nobody seemed to mind if the wallpaper was coming off the wall, or the doors hung funny. We were all together.

As time moved on, some of the charter members of the hootenanny gang fell in love. Some got married and had children! Some can no longer sit cross-legged on the floor. But it matters not. We still all get together on a cold Saturday night in January with the north wind howling around the corner of the old house. The house smells of popcorn and hot apple cider with cinnamon in it. Cy plays the spoons and sings the "Wabash Cannon Ball." Alice plays "Glow Worm" on the big grand piano. Charlotte sings "Enjoy Yourself" and strums her guitar. George does "Go Tell Aunt Rhody" on his bass harmonica.

We've compiled the words to lots of the old songs we learned from our fathers and grandfathers into a little hootenanny songbook. I had to smile. A couple of years ago, we talked about revising the old hootenanny book but got quite a squawk from the kids. "No!" Eugene insisted. "These songs are our heritage. You can't take that away. Where would we find all these old songs if you revise the hootenanny book!"

"Right, Eugene," Beth confirmed. "When your mom dies, I want to inherit the books. This is our legacy."

COMING HOME

Diesel Fumes, Again

As the little pink spring wildflowers began to bloom in the backyards and along the white, sandy lane that made its way through the palmetto palms and the cow pastures, the campground began to change. The snowbirds, who had been camping in Florida for the winter, began to roll up the awnings. The little grass-green carpets that made up their front yards disappeared, and they began to head north. The Sunday afternoon hootenannies dwindled. Soon it would be just me and my French horn at the clubhouse on Sunday afternoon! Walter and his electric guitar, the old man with no arms and his harmonica, the big guy with his washtub would be heading north.

As the snowbirds left, the patients in the outpatient clinic dwindled. It was time to make my way back to the faded green feather couch and the telephone.

I rolled up my own awning and little grass-green carpet and set out for Maine again. Gracie Allen and I headed north on Interstate 75 then east to Interstate 95 bound for home.

It was 11:00 p.m. when I pulled into a crowded truck stop just south of Washington, DC. Diesel tractor-trailer rigs lined up side by side in the parking area. I pulled in between a Peterbilt tractor hauling steel and a UPS truck. Bright lights blazed overhead. The smell of diesel filled the air. These eighteen-wheelers never shut off their engines. I wondered if I could sneak back to the fifth wheel and lock myself safely inside before some lonely trucker noticed that I was traveling without an escort. I don't know why I thought they didn't already know that little bit of information. They had been whizzing past me in the hammer lane going downhill all day and slowing down to a crawl on the uphill. The bump, bump, bump of the road made me feel jiggly when I stood up. Why hadn't I planned better and found a nice campground? This was no place to spend the night. I was glad I didn't do this for a living. Well, maybe I actually did!

I waited until everyone was out of sight, then scooted quickly into the fifth wheel. In the semi-dark, I filled Gracie's dish with Meow Mix and climbed the three steps into the overhead. I felt exhausted. So what if there were exhaust fumes and grinding gears and bright lights. I could just sleep in my clothes until I awoke, then get in and start driving again. Maybe I could get through DC before the commuter traffic in the morning. I fell asleep even before Gracie finished her meal.

About 3:00 a.m. I heard the UPS truck pull out. *He must know something I don't,* I thought to myself. *I better start rolling, too.*

The landscape was hidden in the darkness, but I followed the trucks back on to I-95 north. No four-wheelers out this time of morning. I followed the herd of truckers north.

I wonder where we'll go next, I thought. *I still have fifteen state physical therapy licenses. I'd really rather spend the summer in Maine, but I don't know about jobs.*

I thought of the time I spent here when I first got out of college. I remembered the good times on the Appalachian Trail. I remembered my first Christmas away from home. Benita owned Dixi's mother and used to invite me to ride with her around Conn Dam. Come Christmas, her family invited me to spend the day and to have Christmas dinner with them. It would have been pretty lonely without them.

I remembered Carol and the times we spent together, playing the organ and the French horn together, or hiking the Appalachian Trail. I remembered her illness and God's comforting presence. *I'm glad He came into my life,* I thought as I sped northward on I-95.

Gradually, a plan began to form in my mind. Perhaps I would be able to offer placement to other therapists and have my headquarters at home. That word "home" sounds really good after four years on the road.

I wondered aloud, "How many therapists would I need working with me to be able to make what I'm making now?"

"It's doable!" I said, "I'll do it!"

I sat on the big soft couch in the living room, staring out at the empty horse pasture. The leaves were turning green. It was my favorite time of year.

"How did a nice girl like me go about founding a corporation," I asked myself. "Well, when you find out that you didn't grow up to be a housewife," you gotta do what you gotta do."

In front of me was a blank white sheet of paper. Beside me lay the Bible open to my most recent motto: "Wars are won by skillful strategy. For want of skillful strategy, an army is lost."

The goal, objectives, and strategy began to take shape. The action and tasks followed.

TRAVELING MEDICAL PROFESSIONALS, INC., must be an ethical PT/OT temporary placement company providing high-quality services. But it must also have that added "compassion factor." We must treat both facility [patients] and professional as we would want to be treated if we were in their position.

Founding a corporation seemed such a stupendous task! But I remembered once long ago when I was complaining to a friend about the years it would take to complete my education. "Never mind," he said. "You'll be alive all that time!"

And so it was now. The goal of establishing a company seemed distant, but the thought that life is a journey, not a destination, was comforting.

View from Stone Mountain

Stone Mountain

At home I had time to visit with old friends and walk to the shore again. I breathed the fresh Maine air and the scent of lilacs that grew beside the old farmhouse.

But they needed me in Atlanta, Georgia. Diesel fumes again, but the campground near the hospital was clean and friendly. Maybe I could do Stone Mountain this Sunday.

The crowd was gathering at the foot of Stone Mountain as the sun set in the west. I watched as the smooth granite surface turned gold then pink in the setting sun. I needed to be here. The crowd around me didn't know I was a little girl again, playing with my cousin in the cool streamlets that trickled down the rock in the springtime long ago. They weren't living again the peaceful moments in the Sabbath evening sunset with my uncle and aunt there alone on Stone Mountain. The crowd would see only what is now. The little girl making circles with the florescent snake was making her own memories, but she didn't know.

From my perch on one lone boulder, I watched the crowd spreading blankets and munching popcorn and swilling soda pop.

The music started, and the laser searchlights played to its rhythm upon stone faces on the now-dark surface of the mountain. I watched the children scampering about, then returning to the arms of their parents like lambs to their mothers. I felt lonely. There were no little children scampering back to my open arms and climbing up on my lap. There was no cousin to squeal and point and dance to the music. I sat silent and alone. Families passed on either side as if I were only a part of the lone granite boulder. I stood and turned to leave while the lights still played upon the mountain.

I tried to make eye contact with a plump gray-haired woman in a navy blue T-shirt. Her balding husband walked a few steps behind, his eyes wandering to the figures of the scantily clad group of teenaged girls walking beside him. "Come on," she called. "Quit gawking! We'll never get there!" Her face was hard, and although her cold, gray eyes looked at my face, she didn't see me. I was alone.

I made my way back to the fifth wheel. Gracie Allen was there to meet me and rubbed and purred against my leg. "It's OK, Gracie," I said, taking her in my arms. "We'll go home someday where the people smile when we walk down Maine Street, and the babies gurgle and grin from their carts at the grocery store."

"Neow?" she asked for the hundredth time.

"No, Gracie Allen, not now, but someday. Someday really soon!"

7. "Remember, We Love You, Liz"

I knew in my heart that home would never be the same because a different person was coming home. My hometown, though still the same, had gone on without me. Some of the patriarchs had been laid to rest. I would be a stranger to some of the youngsters. Yes, I would be welcomed home. "Remember, we love you, Liz!" was still ringing in my ears, but I wasn't the same Liz who had left.

Sabbath came, and I sat alone in church in my usual church pew. I looked around. I loved these people. They were there for me when my mother died, when my father died, when the animals died.

I'd been there for them, too, when Cliff and Vi's son was hit by a car as he got off the school bus. When Ruth's husband was killed by a drunk driver, I was there. When Susie was nine months pregnant, and her husband ran away, I was there. When Johnny had to go to jail, I was there.

Yes, I had changed, but it was alright. I loved these people! I was bringing home to them a depth in my heart that neither they nor I had known in me before. My love for them was stronger, deeper, more tender, and more open. I could nurture their children and support their aged. I could laugh and sing and dance with them ... or cry.

But from the broken pieces of my life, I learn to love more gently, to risk rejection and failure, to be less judging, to carry on with courage. I learn to live.

... And Then Are Gone Beyond Our Reach...

Today as I stand on the rocky coast of Maine and hear the seagulls and smell the salt water, I wonder. I wonder whatever happened to Lofton, to Mommie Lone, and Tom. How thankful I am that there is a hereafter. There is a land where we will never part again. The earth will be new and fresh. All the gentle, the loving, and the pure will be there. And Jesus Himself will be there, and God will wipe away all tears from our eyes.

Yes, just what is a "Nice Girl Like You Doing in a Place Like This!" Again, it was circumstances that limited the options. Gracie and l just needed to reconnect with our home on the rocky coast of Maine. But at age fifty, the openings for an experienced physical therapist are scant to non-existent. The population of Maine at that time was only one million! Jobs? Gracie would need her Meow Mix! So how does a fifty-year-old woman who has never attended Harvard Business school start a traveling medical professional company? Eventually "you gotta just do it!" So when the client in California didn't pay his bill, it was time to pray a lot and catch a flight.

What's a Nice Girl Like You Doing in a Place Like This?

"You leave my office now!" he shouted. "I didn't ask you here!" He got up from his leather swivel chair and stomped, fuming to the other side of his walnut desk, and towered above my chair, his dark eyes glowered. A heavy gold chain was about his neck, and gold rings with precious stones were on his fingers. "Get out!" he shouted again.

My palms were sweating, and my mouth was dry. "What's a nice girl like me doing in a place like this?" I said for the hundredth time.

It was just this morning, during my quiet time with God, that He took me to the story of Abigail. You can read the story in Second Samuel. She was married to a mean-spirited, rich man. Yes, even abusive. But she was a meek, quiet, and capable woman. When she heard that David and his 300 men were coming to wipe out every man in her husband's household, she went to work immediately. First, she packed enough food on her donkeys to give all 300 men some raisins and figs to raise the blood sugar level and put them in a better mood. Then, when she saw David, she got off her donkey and humbled herself. She told David that surely, he wouldn't want to do something that would damage his good name. David calmed down and enjoyed the attention. A month later, when Abigail was widowed, David took her to be his wife.

But now, here I was in the plush office of one of the Fortune 500 companies. The wood paneling in Steve's office was dark walnut. The green wall-to-wall rug was soft and squished when I walked on it. There was an Oriental rug in front of the desk. In every way it was a man's cave. There were no windows, only a huge picture of a golf course in Hawaii. There was a huge bookcase. Here I was, a single woman in this man's cave, attempting to collect the money they were refusing to pay. Was there was a chance they would even try physical force!

I leaned back in my chair and began to pray. I thought of Abigail and began to relax. "Father, this is beyond me. I don't know how to handle this! Amen!"

"Get out!" Steve shouted again.

Suddenly Steve's attitude changed, and he walked back to his chair. His dark eyes softened, and his tantrum subsided. I listened. He opened his top desk drawer and took out his checkbook. "I don't know why I'm doing this," Steve said with a little smile playing around the corners of his lips. "A few minutes ago, I was getting ready to throw you out of my office!" He handed me a check, and as I left his office, something said, "Send him a book about Jesus." I did.

I met with Steve three more times, and each time I took him another book about God.

The last time I saw him, he took my hand and said, "I'm a committed Christian now too, you know!"

Birth of a Traveling Physical Therapy Company

It was not as if I just woke up one morning and said, "This is the first day of the rest of your life, Elizabeth! You are going to be president of your own multi-million dollar company! Now, get out of bed, and get going!" No, God usually has to back me into the horse trailer. I've had to do that a few times when there just wasn't any other way to get my horse to load. God knows I'm terrified of the unknown. I want to have all the plans for my life given to me all at once. Then maybe I could think up a few shortcuts!

It was in West Palm Beach, Florida. While I was staying at the Safari Campground next to the Lion Country Safari Animal Park. Each morning, I would wake up to the roar of the lions waiting for breakfast.

Sunday morning, the sun was streaming in the east window of the RV. Yes, just what was a nice girl like me doing in a place like this! I was sent here as a traveling therapist by a company who provided temporary physical therapy coverage. I was here to clear the swamp, but I was up to my neck in alligators! The company I worked for had this new contract with a huge acute care hospital in West Palm Beach, Florida. I was to be their new chief physical therapist and director of rehabilitation. Great! The company had not told the Indians they would be getting a new chief. The administration had not advised them of the "Take-over." The professional staff loved their present supervisor, and were livid when he was dismissed! The take-over company just assumed that all the present staff would be staying, and rehabilitation services would rise to a new level, as would the revenue.

Surprise! When the president of the take-over company presented the contracts to the therapists, they simply ripped up the contracts and walked out the door!

Now, as the only therapist in this huge facility, I needed to get busy and treat patients! *All of them,* I thought! As I ran madly from one floor to another, bounding up the stairs two at a time and rushing through patient care, I began to realize that if I worked 24/7 as a solo therapist, I would never be able to finish the patient load that had been put on my plate. This was an administrative problem, not mine! I stopped, caught my breath, and proceeded to triage the patients.

So, as the sun shone through the east window of my little camper home that Sunday morning, I began to make plans for the first day of the rest of my life.

"Well," I said to myself, "I've been on the road for four years as a traveling physical therapist. I have licenses to practice physical therapy in fifteen states across the nation. I have my own one ton Ford pick-up truck, and a forty-foot fifth wheel travel trailer complete with washer and dryer. I even had a sweet little gray and buff kitty. But it is most terrifying to jump ship with no safety net. I have always worked for someone else. An employer has always traded me security for services. Now here I am, planning to be my own boss! "When you're your own boss, you have to do what the boss says!"

Gradually, a plan began to form in my mind. Perhaps I would be able to offer placement to other therapists and have my headquarters at home. That word "home" sounded really good after four years on the road traveling from one health care facility to another, one state to another, and one campground to another.

And so began the first day of the rest of my life as a solo therapist without a safety net!

Nuts and Bolts

After serving in this traveling health care industry for four years, I had some knowledge of the nuts and bolts of how to operate a traveling physical therapy company. There was a weekly magazine called the PT Bulletin which contained a few articles about treating patients but was supported by page after page of want ads for physical therapists. The timing was right. I would test the market by selling my own services.

I wondered aloud, "How many therapists would I need working with me to be able to make what I'm making now?" It appeared that twelve therapists out on the road should bring in what I was currently making plus expenses.

"That's doable!" I said, "I'll do it!"

Then came words of reality from my own brother, who already owned his own business. *"When you're your own boss, you have to do what the boss says!"* It worked! I was my own boss!

> *"When you're your own boss, you have to do what the boss says!"*

There are lots of hidden costs and surprises in owning and operating your own business. But I didn't know all that yet. Had it not been that God was watching over this "nice girl in a place like this," I would have gone underwater and stayed there! God knew I couldn't swim! There were mentors with encouragement and words of wisdom that God had stationed along the way. There were books about owning and operating a business that God had scattered in all the airport book stores. There was even a very valuable syllabus put out by *Entrepreneur* magazine that proved to be most valuable.

But for now, I chained myself to the telephone and began telemarketing my own services to the facilities in the *PT Bulletin*. At least I was home. The big Old New England Farmhouse with the attached barn opened its arms wide and welcomed me. Memories were tucked into every corner of the old farm. It was here that I came immediately after graduating from physical therapy school. The old place rang with laughter on Saturday nights when friends would come over and sit on the floor and sing all the old songs together. Together, we ate popcorn and fruit salad. Together, we dreamed the long, long dreams of youth. Friends were married, babies were born, and the old place just absorbed more laughter.

But now, after four years on the road as a traveling therapist, I was the one who had changed. An intensity took possession of me. I used every waking moment to focus on getting this new business up and flying! Starting a new business is something like flying a kite. You run and run, you tighten and loosen the string, you change direction with the wind, then a puff of wind takes your kite, and it's off the ground! Had it not been for my commitment to keep God's Seventh-day Sabbath sacred, I would never have taken a break. I began to resent the time people took from my daily schedule. I felt presumed upon when Charlotte called on Sunday with, "Can I bring the kids out this afternoon?"

"I have only a couple hours, Char, and I have no horses for them to play with, but maybe we could walk to the water and see if it's calm enough to skim those flat rocks they always like to throw."

I hung up the phone. "Why," I said aloud, "did I say yes? That just means that they wanted a big chunk of the time I had set aside to work on the business plan for the bank, or figure taxes, or to make calls to therapists. The nuts and bolts of the company still have to be done!" But I couldn't say "No" to old friends. I really did want them to take a walk through the woods to the shore to let the wind blow through their hair and listen to the seagulls cry and smell the sea.

I didn't realize it at the time, but now I can see all the distractions! They are called people! Everyone wants a part of me. Each wants a bigger part than the other, and I would like to have given more of myself than I was able. It would have been more than a full-time job just to nurture all the people who thought they were number one! I'm not sure I have learned how to balance the demands of friends and family yet! But I find that the older I am, the more friends and family I have lost. Death takes its toll. Old friends become more and more precious.

The Business Plan

I sat on the antique feather couch in the living room of the Old New England Farmhouse, staring out at the empty horse pasture and reading a book about how to put together a business plan. How will a "nice girl like me" go about founding a corporation." My brother, who already owned his own company, gave me his words of wisdom again. "WHEN YOU'RE YOUR OWN BOSS, YOU HAVE TO DO WHAT THE BOSS SAYS!"

Interlude. Life must have interludes. There must be moments of awareness to put things in perspective. Interludes actually freshen the body, the spirits, and the mind.

The ice was bending the birch trees, but the sun had come out, and the world seemed to sparkle. I was immersed in business projects as usual, when my neighbor, Sally, called. "Liz, the ice is just perfect for sledding on Will Proctor's hill."

"I can't do that, Sally. I'm trying to get this business going. I'm in the middle of it!"

"Liz," she insisted quietly. "I've got two sleds. I'll meet you at the top of the hill."

No excuses. Sally, bundled in her blue snowmobile suit and me in my red, pushed off and went whizzing down the hill toward the frozen bay. Sally's big black lab sat on the sled between her legs, and the golden retriever ran along beside me on my sled laughing and poking fun!

Sally looked over at me and grinned as we whizzed down the hill, scarves flying. "Liz!" she laughed, "We're fifty years old!"

And so we were. Living didn't stop just because I was immersed in my all-absorbing project! I still needed to make "good old times to remember" with old friends. The boss told me so! I remembered once long ago when I was complaining to a friend about the years it would take to complete my education. "Never mind," he said, "You'll be alive all that time!" And so we were.

Old Friends

It was May when Tom, my lawyer friend, called from Palm Beach, Florida. He was being "sworn in" by the Wisconsin state board. He'd always wanted to be sworn in by his home state.

I stopped on the way back from business in California to spend an afternoon with him and see him achieve a dream. The apple trees were in bloom, and the grass was fresh green in the yard around the Capitol in Madison. It was a happy time. But Tom was married to Ginger, now. I couldn't let myself think about loving Tom. He was another woman's husband. But I did love Tom. Not as a lover, but as a friend and mentor. It was refreshing to enjoy this beautiful day of spring with him.

Was "letting go" what the experiences of the last fifteen years were all about? The little girl in me wants to be close to people. Maybe even to lean a little.

An old roommate from college days always seemed to be one that I could lean on. We talked, but our paths had taken different directions, and she couldn't understand the pressures of owning and operating a nationwide traveling therapist company. Her life was quiet and settled. Maybe there was something to be said for that. I walked away.

One of my mentors once said to me, "Never let anyone make your decisions for you. It's your company. You can delegate authority but never responsibility."

Skillful Strategy

In front of me was a blank sheet of white paper. Beside me lay the Bible open to my most recent motto: "Wars are won by skillful strategy. For want of skillful strategy, an army is lost. "Victory is the fruit of long planning" (Prov. 11:14. NEB).

The goal, objectives, and strategy began to take shape. The action and tasks followed. It was my major professor, Ingrid, who always insisted that any of our papers began with "aims and objectives."

Traveling Medical Professionals, Inc. must be an ethical, for-profit PT/OT temporary placement company providing high quality services. But it must also have that added dimension of the "compassion factor." We must treat both facility and professional as we would want to be treated if we were in their position.

Founding a corporation seemed such a stupendous task! And so it was. The goal of establishing a company seemed distant, but the thought that one of my mentors had left with me long ago was encouraging. "You'll be alive all that time."

Picking a Partner

My friend, Diane, had just quit her job as an OB nurse at the hospital near her home in California. Diane was bright, and her experience in the health care industry would be beneficial. She was a very people-oriented person. She genuinely cared about people. I knew we worked well together. We had been doing life together since college.

I really felt I needed some help with this venture. There would be lots of phone calling, and I needs someone who would come through well on the phone. But she and her husband and three children lived in California!

I called. "Di, what would you think about the possibility of working with me on this traveling therapy project? I've told you about it before. Could you and Doug come out, and we can talk?"

"Really, Lizzy! Really? Let me talk it over with Doug!"

Diane and her husband, Doug, came to the Old New England Farmhouse for a visit. Di and I were hyper. We invited a houseful of friends over to sing and play instruments with us. Doug can play anything on the piano and also the guitar, and Diane knows all the words.

The next day, Diane and I sat on the soft antique feather couch and looked out through the greenhouse into the empty horse pasture. The blank page began to turn into a real business plan like the one in the book about starting your own business. When we felt as though we had the basic details hammered out, Diane and Doug went home. The next working visit would be mine.

Boning up on Management Skills

There was a bright star in the eastern sky as I pulled out of the driveway heading for the airport. And as the plane climbed to our cruising altitude of 37,000 feet on the way to California again, I watched the world below me. It was waking up. Newspaper trucks tossed out bundles. Delivery trucks backed up to loading docks. There was a middle-aged woman bundled in a gray overcoat and a worn red hat waiting on the comer for the bus. Must be a waitress. She'd go get the coffee started and unlock the door for the salesmen and laborers that would stop in before work.

At 37,000 feet I pulled out my book on time management and began to read. "Wow! Let's get organized," I said to myself. Everything was focused on getting TMP off the ground. Like the airliner carrying me to meet with Diane again, the bulk of the journey's fuel was required to get this thing off and up! I felt exhausted.

There was time at 37,000 feet to think. It's too bad I had to wait for a trip across country to do focused thinking. But I was thankful for it. Sometimes at 37,000 feet, there was even time for "the poetry of living!"

Advertising

The Physical Therapy Bulletin, the primary source of advertising for therapists, was full of want ads for physical therapists. There were full-page color ads from huge hospitals all over America. There were only two ads for traveling physical therapists. One was from a company in Boston that did traveling nurses, and PT was more of a sideline. The other was for the company I had been connected with before starting

TMP. They had a large ad with a picture of a woman's hand placing "people" on a chessboard. The caption read, **"We know the right move for you!"**

Diane was looking at the Bulletin with me. "Look at this ad, Di!" I blurted out. "No self-respecting physical therapist wants somebody planning their moves on a chessboard! The traveling therapists want to manage their own future!"

"What do you think of this?" I grabbed a pencil and scrawled, **"Pull your own strings! Call Traveling Medical Professionals, Inc. at 1-800-64-travl."**

It worked. Diane and I were in the hot tub in her back yard in California, working on the business plans and waiting for the phone to ring. Suddenly it rang! We both jumped, startled, and looked at each other. Diane answered in her most professional voice. "Traveling Medical Professionals. This is Diane."

Who would have known that we were working in the hot tub! Diane's spiel sounded believable! We signed on our first physical therapist, and we were able to place her in Hawaii! We were psyched!

Suddenly, we were catapulted into the real business world! Now we had one a real employee! I felt like a first-time mom with her new baby! All the books and all the experience was helpful, but when the baby wakes crying in the night, you walk the floor and pray.

Diane worked in setting the foundation for Traveling Medical Professionals, Inc. for two-and-a-half years. Her feeling heart endeared her to the therapists and contributed immensely to the "compassion factor" that was the distinguishing factor of the fledgling traveling therapy company. Only God could have seen us through! I discovered that I am a type A person and sometimes harsh. Without her compassion factor and forgiving spirit, there would have been more than one train wreck!

Moments of Sanity in the Insane Rat Race

It was always good to be home after sleeping in a strange bed night after night for ten nights. Oh, I enjoyed the moments of awareness I snatched while on the road, but there was always the comfort and security of tradition. In the autumn I came home and was comforted and revived by a raw November day. I put on the LL Bean water-repellant outdoor wear and stepped into the barn. Someday, there would be the stomp of horses' hooves again, the happy yip of a dog. There would be the smell of hay and molasses feed and apples.

The remaining leaves were swirling from the trees and piling up in big colorful heaps. I stood in the midst of November and watched the colored leaves swirl about me. I lifted my face to the driving rain and felt it spatter on my cheeks. I listened to the streamlets laughing and gurgling over the rocks and into the bay. There was the smell of autumn in the air—wet earth, leaves, and apples. God has always sandwiched beautiful moments among the hectic pace of living life. He still does that. I wonder if I took more time in His presence if there would be more beautiful moments when I would be aware of the beauty, peace, and contentment He wants to give me.

> *There was the smell of autumn in the air—wet earth, leaves, and apples. God has always sandwiched beautiful moments among the hectic pace of living life*

In the years of owning and operating the Traveling Medical Professionals, Inc. business, there were deliberate moments to keep the sanity and the peace. I live about a five-minute walk from the shore of Casco Bay on the Maine coast. There is a trail through the woods to the shore. The delights change with the seasons, but there is always something to draw the soul heavenward.

Come summer, when the lilac-laden breeze wafts through the open window, and the clean white curtains tickle the red-checked tablecloth, and the kitchen smells of fresh-baked bread and fresh-waxed floor, I smile. The neighbor kids drop in for a tea party with "Mrs. Jokoski," and I say to myself, "Maybe I did grow up to be a housewife."

Sometimes It's OK to Cry

My sister's little girl, who calls me "grandma," had her thirteenth birthday. Why is it that little girls age thirteen like a slumber party with friends? We baked a cake, walked to the shore, played dress-up, and told stories. Some of them were sad. Her mom and dad had split up, and her new father wasn't married to her mother. Life happens. And there's not a whole lot one can do about it … except maybe just love them!

But I didn't have time to do a lot of loving. There were the long calls to the western office for encouragement and direction, and calls to therapists and facilities. Just how important is loving a thirteen-year-old!

I walked to the bay and stood on the shore in the dense early morning fog. I could hear the waterfall plunging into the ocean at high tide. Fog wraps you in a cloak. It's safe and peaceful. And nobody can see you if you cry.

The Boss Says There's Not Enough Money for Payroll

There's more to payroll than meets the eye! You have payroll taxes to pay each pay period, and worker's comp insurance, and a few other little details. Cash was in short supply, as it usually is when a company is in a growth phase. I found myself walking the floor and wringing my hands and wondering what to do. There was no money in the bank to pay the payroll taxes, and they were due that very day! What was I going to do? But God was not walking the floor wringing His hands, neither was He waking up at all hours of the night in the grip of fear, wondering what He was going to do about my situation. This was His business, and over and over again, He provided an "out" just when I was ready to panic. I think He delighted in showing Himself strong, as is mentioned in 2 Chronicles 16:9. "For the eyes of the Lord run to and fro throughout the whole earth, to show Himself strong" (NKJV).

Just before the banks closed that afternoon, the mail came with all but three dollars of what was needed for the payroll taxes! For the rest of the day I walked the floor, but this time I was singing,

> Lord, what can I impart
> When all is Thine before?
> Thy love demands a thankful heart;
> The gift, alas, how poor!

Interludes

Through the intensity of living life as a female executive, there were interludes of time to become aware of the moment. There were times to become aware of life. Nature hadn't changed; only the seasons, like my life, had changed. The peepers came in the springtime, then Mayflowers. In the early springtime, the pussy willows still graced the woods along the trail to the shore. The robin's lilting melody gladdened my heart. In the summertime the lightning bugs and the sweet scent of new-mown hay gave me peace after a day of intensity. The whirl of the red and gold of autumn leaves made my feet dance and seemed to give energy and cheerfulness. The first snowfall gave a peaceful wrap-up to another year.

I stood alone in the middle of life. I was not in love or beholden to anyone. I was a part of the whole. I sensed the part my own sometimes-hectic life played in the grand symphony of living, and I stood aware of the moment and my own significance in God's overall plan. Like the flowers in the springtime and the sweet scent of hay in summer, and bright leaves in autumn and the silence of the snowfall, I felt a part of life.

The Banker

There was daily pressure to get on with the to-do list. There was no way I would be able to "bootstrap" a traveling therapist registry! I learned that bootstrapping is the term used for people who choose not to borrow money, but to grow as the money comes in. Fine, the therapist had to be paid. But the facility could not be billed until after the services were performed! There would obviously be a gap between the time the therapist had to be paid, and when the money would come in from the facility!

So, a nice girl in a place like this begins to take the humble, new business plan to the banks. Bankers never want to loan money to people who are in need of money. It's much easier to get a loan when you don't need one!

In the days when we were starting TMP, the idea of a nationwide therapist registry was something new. Bankers don't like to loan money to people who are risking a new industry! There was the ecstasy of getting an appointment with a bank, and the agony of the shaking head and the closing door.

But, at last, a bright young lady banker seemed to catch the idea. Somehow, she was able to coach me into a more corporate business plan. "Sit right here in this little cell where people come to paw through their safe deposit boxes. I'll come check with you between clients and make a really professional business plan. This idea is workable."

She took it to her boss and was able to convince him that this was doable! The funding was small, but so were our numbers. In a few months, we had four therapists actually earning money! We thought it would be only a matter of months before we would have fifty working. Diane and I were ecstatic!

Interlude

I have this hurry sickness. You know how it is. When you are in school, there's always somebody hounding you about a deadline. Then you get out, and there's always a boss hounding you about a deadline. Then you get to be your own boss, and you really get hounded by the boss. It's like my brother says, "When you're your own boss, you've got to do what the boss says!"

Sometimes, the boss will let me steal some time, though. One of the early contracts led me to Daytona Beach, Florida. I got a motel on the beach the night before visiting the facility. Just before sunrise the beach was empty except for the low-flying pelicans and some sandpipers. The foam lapped along the sand as I walked, and the waves washed in, and the waves washed out. What a peaceful, calm moment. The sky began to turn pink, and I thought of my mother, who used to play on this beach. Her honeymoon with my father was here at this beach. It was her favorite place of all. I had almost forgotten. How blessed I was to be alive and able to walk along this same beach! As I stopped to watch a sandpiper bobbing up and down (doing push-ups) at the edge of the water, I noticed the foam was a delicate pink. The sand was pink! I looked up, and the sky was pink with gold and green! I savored the moment.

But there are promises to keep. I really should be in a hurry! Or should I? The song, "We Have This Moment, Today" put things in perspective.

Chained to the Desk

The peonies and iris and poppies were blooming when I finished my trip to check out the facility in Lincoln, Maine. But there was no time to play in the flowers. Things at TMP needed a mighty push. It seemed that nothing got done while I was away on a business trip. So I chained myself to my desk and pushed on. I listened to one of these motivational tapes. It was full of pearls of wisdom. I had to swallow hard, though, when it said, "Don't let your batteries get too low. They're harder to recharge when they get too low!" Some days I felt that the batteries might get too low. But the goal seemed worth it. Someday, it would be worth it all. I could just relax and hug my "grandchildren" and visit with my friends, and play the French horn.

I looked at the calendar. It was twenty years ago that I first set foot in Maine. I needed time to ponder and evaluate. Oh, I would get around to it someday, "The apple tree, the singing, and the gold!"

Office on the Move

In late February "the ice went out." The open saltwater is so beautiful after being frozen over all winter. The eider ducks start making love almost immediately!

When the ducks start making love, a woman needs to play house. This time my assistant, Karon, and I decided it was time to move the office from the mudroom downstairs to its own space in the upstairs of the Old New England Farmhouse. The mudroom in an Old New England farmhouse is the room that is first entered when coming into the house from the barn. You see, these 200-year-old New England farmhouses are connected to the barn! The mudroom collects snow boots and snowmobile suits. It contains the cat box. It's a good place for the washer and dryer. And, of course, it makes a good place for a start-up business and a telephone.

We were no longer a start-up now. We appropriated the master bedroom upstairs. The fifteen-by-twenty-four-foot area seemed expansive! We put a flat wooden door across two file cabinets and made a handsome desk. Karon teased me when I wanted to put a little handmade cloth drape across the front as a privacy panel and storage cabinets. "Oh, how cute," she teased, "I see you made this yourself!"

That was enough, we picked out an inexpensive, but business-like storage cabinet!

Friends When in Need

The cash flow problem was ever-present. As more people began to work, the problem escalated! There were all those mouths to feed, and there was lag time before the facilities could be billed. John offered $20,000 for three months. Jackie plunked down her retirement of another $20,000, and Ingrid offered a loan of $12,000. Our life-long neighbors, LeRoy and Tina, gave us a long-term loan of $5,000. It's comforting to know there are friends who believe in you and are willing to put their money where their mouth is.

The smell of hay and the stomp of feet and the crunch of grain were relaxing to me. There's some thing about a horse that won't let you really keep your hurry sickness

Interlude

Charlotte and I met at Linda-Lee's barn to work on breaking Linda-Lee's big black filly. The smell of hay and the stomp of feet and the crunch of grain were relaxing to me. There's some thing about a horse that won't let you really keep your hurry sickness. They just look at you and say, "What seems to be your problem? I only chew one speed!"

The day was over, and the sun was setting red behind the Old New England Farmhouse. I walked out into the cool evening and looked around the farm. There was the empty pasture with a web of fresh green grass—empty. There was the clean box stall with fresh sawdust—empty! And in my heart, there was a lonely spot for what used to be. I went inside and picked up a horse magazine. My eyes grew moist with tears. What was then could never be again, but maybe someday there would be the stomp of horse hoofs in my own barn again, and the smell of hay again. And maybe even a foal to frisk at his mother's side in the sunset.

But for now, I needed to work on the Therapist Handbook. How could I expect clients to know what was going on if we didn't have anything in writing? Where would one start? How do you create something out of nothing? Well, you don't do it by standing in the yard at sunset, dreaming of days gone by! You pull out the blank piece of paper and fill it up. Even loose ideas are better than no ideas. You've got to start somewhere! The good news was that there were some paydays now that we didn't have to access the line of credit!

Worry Is Blind

The ever-present cash crunch continued. One morning, I woke with the sunshine streaming in my bedroom window. I lay there for a few moments, reviewing the last few weeks. Suddenly, I realized that the Lord had made arrangements to have two therapists prepaid by the facility! Wow! Without my even asking them, a company in Florida offered to prepay! The second one just paid a finder's fee and kept the therapist. I wondered why I should ever worry about cash flow again!

When the Boss Says, "Do the Right Thing"

A call came from a small facility in Podunk, Nowhere. Yes, we would help. But it was hard work and time-consuming to try to fill our obligation in such an out-of-the-way place! Karon, now one of the recruiters, complained. She threw up her hands and wanted to just quit and walk away and leave Podunk with no one to treat patients.

I went to the Lord alone. He reminded me of the text in Psalm 15:4: "Blessed is the person that swears to his own hurt and changes not" (Author's paraphrase). That verse took on new meaning. The reason for having a Christian-based traveling professional company was to make God look good. Often, I told the office staff, "If it's the right thing to do, do it. You'll know what the right thing is."

Now it was my turn. I had to do the right thing. It was costly. We lost money on filling the position, but we kept a promise.

The Company Vs. Friend

In quiet moments when I assess my values, I put old friends and family high on the list. What happened? Beth and Betty were here for five days, and I felt pushed to get on with TMP stuff! I wondered if I were seeing a change in priorities. Well, so if I was. I still had to get therapists on the road! Will TMP cry at my funeral? Not at all. Only friends and relatives cry at a funeral. Better keep my friends. When TMP is a thing of the past, they will be the only ones that care. How blessed I am to have people who love me and care when I hurt.

Integrity

Early one morning, when leaves were on the trees again, the phone rang. It was Mr. Jones.

"I'm sorry," he apologized, "but something has come up, and I won't be able to serve at that facility in Florida. I know I had promised to start on Monday morning, but I just won't be able to."

I started to sweat. My heart went lub … How could I tell the little hospital in Melbourne that their patients wouldn't get treated on Monday? This was Friday!

God and I had quite a bit to talk about on the way to the shore. There was nothing I could do!

I made some calls to people already licensed in Florida, but, of course, there was no one who could start on Monday morning. How I dreaded making the fateful call!

Early afternoon, I knew I must tell them. But before I had a chance to pick up the phone, it rang.

"I hated to make this call," the lady said. "I know you have a therapist all lined up and ready to serve our facility here in Florida on Monday, but we won't be needing him. One of our previous therapists called and wants the job starting Monday."

I could have hugged her. Or maybe it was God I should have hugged! I walked along the trail through the woods to the shore. The white-throated sparrow has such a silver-throated song on an evening in June. The little lapping of the water on the rocks at the shore sang its own song. I sang, too.

In life we don't remember days; we remember moments. One needs to collect beautiful moments. They are needed in a crisis.

Pay Yourself What the Boss Says

I'm not always sure where God gets His money. But I know where it appeared on November 18. The bank sent me a statement of an old checking account that had been closed for some time. To my surprise, the statement indicated that there was $2,000 in it! I quizzed the bank, and they insisted that I did, indeed, have $2,000 in that account! Needless to say, I closed the account again and supplemented the payroll! I don't quiz God. He can take care of His little company any way He chooses.

It was hard to feel justified in paying myself a salary when there was a loan at the bank. Everything went back into the company. But, at last, there was a day when my advisory board told me to start taking a regular salary. I had tax advice and financial advice from the Ernst & Young company in Portland, Maine. One day, after going over the financials for the tax returns, one of the advisors looked at me and said, "Elizabeth, you are no longer a 'small company.' You are a multimillion-dollar company." The possibility of being a multimillion-dollar company hadn't occurred to me. I just drove myself and everyone else day after day and prayed a lot. The bottom line showed a profit, yes, I could take a salary! After not having a real paycheck for a few years, my eyes began to glow green! What does a nice girl like me do in a place like this when her Father gives her an allowance? What does the boss say? Well, you already know. A nice little girl goes shopping. Nice girl goes shopping for shoes, of course! Heels! Very high heels!

Interlude

One day when the lilacs were blooming, Charlotte and I went to Eliot, Maine, to check out a horse. She was a big, black Walking Horse mare. She looked sad. She was kind of old and had been to lots of homes. She didn't have a very good running walk. She seemed gentle enough, though, and she looked at us right! I brought her home.

She was quiet to work around. I kind of liked the old girl. They called her Lady. All I needed was to have a horse again, and to ride through the woods again, and smell the hay again, and just stand in the stall sometimes and feel the hurry sickness drain from me. And, well, there would be the added benefit of having an excuse to get exercise.

New Foal

Lady dropped her foal while I was gone. I guess I didn't need a colt, but it was a distraction from the intensity of TMP. And it gave me more exercise, too. He was a cute little sorrel fellow and full of spunk. What a joy. But the time crunch kept me from really giving him the attention he needed. They say if there's something you don't have time for, it's probably the thing that most needs your attention. We found a good home for the stud colt and felt happy to let someone else break him.

But looking out on the pasture and seeing Lady stand sad and silent, did pluck at our heartstrings. That morning, Karon brought her four-year-old son, Garrett, into the office for a few hours. In our prayer time, Garrett prayed, "And dear Jesus, please help Lady not to be lonesome."

Not long after that prayer, one of my friends told me of someone who wanted to find a good home for her black Walking Horse mare. She looked quite like Lady, and when we checked the papers, we discovered that Lady was actually her mother! When we put the two horses in the pasture to see how they would get along, the old mare squealed and actually jumped up and down in one place!

I guess part of me wanted to have things like they used to be. I wanted a garden, too, and time to really clean house, and entertain, and maybe even sing a little! I forgot, "You can never go home again."

Instead of living in the past, though, I was forced into the present. That was then; this is now. There was TMP as top priority. Maybe someday I'd be able to do all those things that give life meaning.

Child Magnet

The farm is a child magnet. Summer evening is a time to lay aside the intensity of getting a business up and running and to bring in the horses for the kids of the neighborhood. They bring apples and carrots, and, of course, want to brush their satin coats. The horses thrive on attention. I must admit, though, that when there were placements to be made between a facility and a professional, I felt an intense urgency to get the work done instead of playing with God's little ones in the cool of a summer evening. My human resources client at the big hospital in Palm Springs, California, put it this way, "When you've got a contract pending, don't go to lunch!"

Old Friends

Keeping in touch with old friends "from away" was important to me during this time of intensity. If, while on the road solidifying clients and encouraging therapists, I was near enough for a chat or a lunch or a hug, I took advantage of it. In fact, it pays to find clients near points of interest and near old friends. Therapists like to go to Colorado in ski season and Florida in winter. They like the great Northwest and the Olympic Peninsula. And, of course, we made every effort to place them in New England in summer.

Mentors

Tiny, baby maple leaves have always been an important happening in my life. They are so delicate and so perfect. They grow up and get old by late autumn. They have warts and snags and discoloration. But in the spring, they are so fresh and new and perfect. And when they turn their brilliant colors and float to earth in the fall, they leave a promise. A promise of spring again.

McCann called one day, during my lunch break. McCann was a quiet, self-assured, Southern country gentleman. He was the oldest of seven children. When McCann was a child, the father had a drinking problem and was not supporting the family. At age eleven McCann started work. He rode his bicycle down the Virginia mountain every day to work on cars. He pushed it back up the mountainside after a hard day as a mechanic. Soon, he bought his own tools and began to repair and to sell cars on his own. His business grew. He was able to hire his brothers and sisters.

His first marriage broke up, leaving him with two wonderful, hard-working sons. His second marriage broke up, leaving him almost bankrupt. (His wife was the business manager.)

"Oh, no!" I sympathized. "What did you do?"

"There was nothing to do, but to start all over again."

He purchased real estate and traded wisely. When I met him, he owned not only the Ford and Mercedes dealership, a Lear jet, and private pilot, but most of the small Virginia town!

I needed a mentor. I told him my fears. "What if I lose my shirt! Or worse, my home!"

"Don't worry, 'Lizbeth,'" he said in his Southern drawl. "I won't let you starve!"

I was ashamed of my lack of faith. If this man could give me this kind of encouragement, surely my heavenly Father had plans for peace and not of evil.

McCann was a good mentor. His words were not just for this little start-up company. They were words I would remember throughout life. "Don't let anybody else make your decisions for you. It's your responsibility and your company."

> *I was ashamed of my lack of faith. If this man could give me this kind of encouragement, surely my heavenly Father had plans for peace and not of evil*

On the board of directors was a wise, unassuming gentleman who had been the administrator at the hospital where I worked when I first came to Maine. One of the pearls of wisdom he left with me was the fact that one should "never take responsibility without authority." Think about that one. I could have saved much worry had I learned that earlier.

Another mentor and board member was Ingrid, who had been my major professor in college. She also owned and operated a traveling nurse registry in Chicago. "Well, Lizzy," she said, "you won't make a lot of money doing this, but you'll learn a lot."

Cousin Gwen gave me her father's quote of a lifetime! Simply, "Don't let anybody else drive your car."

I wish I had learned that sooner, too. Seemed I was always feeling under pressure. Looking at it from this angle, I wonder whose fault that was! Must have been letting someone else drive my car! Or were they? Could it be that I am my own worst enemy! I can blame it on other people and on circumstances, but the buck stops with me. It's my own hard-driving will that puts me under pressure. My body was expected to toe the line and keep up with a will that was both stubborn and unreasonable. My body made complaints, but I just told it to shut up and keep breathing! I'm having to do quite a bit of apologizing to my body for being such a ruthless tyrant! Yes, don't let anybody else drive your car. Even your own stubborn will!

Especially for Presidents

I was attending a few days of networking and seminars, "Especially for Presidents," when I learned another truism. I was complaining to one of the other presidents about a situation that needed a firm hand back at the office. Our mothers didn't teach us to play the game this way. Nice girls sometimes need the guys to teach us things our mother never taught us! So when I told this president about my situation, he just looked me in the eye and said, "It's your company." I got the point.

In the *Entrepreneur* magazine, I saw an ad for the "Inc. Conference" just for entrepreneurs. I went. Entrepreneurs are a unique group. I was aghast when, during the first seminar lecture, I saw men get up, grab the attaché case, and hurriedly leave the room. At first, I thought they must have a very important appointment or need to go to the men's room, but lo, when I got up during the break, I saw where people were going! They were in any one of the other break-out sessions. No self-respecting entrepreneur will waste time sitting in a meeting just to be polite! No way! Time is too precious. If what you are getting is nothing you need, don't stay just to be respectful! You just get up and go to the next room, where there's another meeting that is more what you need. Hey! This is business. If you don't take care of "Number One," nobody else will!

Growing Broke

Over and over again, I watched God have just enough money in the mailbox to cover our needs. If left to myself, I would have let the company grow too fast. They say that too much money is worse than too little. You see, a company that is growing too fast can "grow broke!" God would always bring the money in just in time, but never give me opportunity to say to myself, "Soul, thou hast many barns full of dough. Take your ease now!"

I didn't know there was such a thing as "growing broke." But God did. He carried His "nice girl," controlled the finances, and sometimes even played horse with her!

Lessons About Life

The Lord also took advantage of the situations that come about through running a business to teach me some things about myself. Some of those lessons I'm still learning, and fitting the pieces of the Traveling Medical Professionals, Inc. puzzle into what is today. Some of the lessons I would have been better off to have learned then instead of now! If you don't catch on the first time, God will bring you over the ground again until you learn it and learn it well.

One of these lessons is about my own personality type. I tend to be a hard-driving intense boss when I'm my own boss. My mind is a hard-driving, intense boss over my own body, too.

My first lesson in trying to drive my body with the intensity the mind demanded was long before TMP. It was the summer between my junior and senior year in college that the first shoe fell.

I was taking a full load of summer school plus working the 11–7 shift as a nurse's aide at the local hospital. Sleep was something I hadn't calculated into my schedule. I was of the impression that sleep is something that just happens, and the body would just need to adjust and deal with it, like it or not!

Yes, sleep just happens. It happened in class as I was attempting to stay with the program and take notes. When I woke up and looked at the paper, it was obvious that my hard-driving mind had commanded my right hand to keep moving and my eyes to stay open, but my brain had disengaged. The squiggles on the notepaper were totally unintelligible! I'm thankful my mind didn't make this major plea for mercy as I was driving to work at 11:00 p.m.!

With a slave driver of a mind to boss my protoplasm, I realize I haven't always been temperate. They say my middle name is "Miss Immediate!" Sometimes, I've made my poor little body cry! When the Lord brought this character flaw to my attention, I made a deal with God to help me change. It's called "a God thing." I promised my body that by God's help, I would give it the things it needed to do its job. But during the TMP years,

I hadn't thoroughly learned that hard lesson yet. My body was exhausted most of the time. The 25 percent of my time away from the office and in the air was usually jumping time zones!

Do What the Boss Says

The time flew by, and the stresses of operating a viable business continued. When you're the boss, you've got to do what the boss says! I had to roll a few heads. I had to collect hard receivables. I had to make hard decisions about the directions the company needed to move. I lost some life-long friends in the process.

Stress

Sometimes, the stress gets to a person. As I lay awake at night thinking about the traveling company, I could hear my heart beating. Lub-dub, lub-

Whoops! There was a lub without a dub, then a long pause! When one lies awake at night thinking, it's scary enough! There are bills to meet, advertising to think up, brochures to print, contracts to put together, equipment to purchase, policy and procedure book to put together. You'd think that would be enough to think about without hearing your heart stop beating! But sure enough, there it went again! Lub-dub, lub-dub, lub!

The doctor checked it out. Yes, there was a heart murmur. Lots of people have those.

Yes, I thought, *But they are not me! Minor surgery is what happens to someone else. Major surgery is what happens to me!* Maybe it was no wonder that my energy level was low.

There was some medication. That helped. But still, I wondered when it went lub-dub, lub-dub, lub ... Would it start again?

Interlude

A journey through the woods to the shore in the spring is like a class reunion. I wonder every spring will the Spring Beauties make it through the winter? There's a promise in their delicate petals. Once, when I was shriveled and aching over rejection from the man I hoped to marry, the Spring Beauties had to remind me that there will be spring again, and life and beauty—and love!

It was early spring.

On the south side of Maine National Bank, the crocuses were up. New life! People were beginning to get out of their shells and nod and speak to each other. The frozen patch of ice where the kids had been skating all winter had melted and was showing a web of green. Were the birds singing a different song now? I took a quick walk through the woods to the shore. Streamlets pure from the winter snow tinkled over the rocks and down the side of the hill into the bay. The eider ducks were wooing their mates. Such a beautiful spring day. Maybe I could steal some time to get out in the sunshine.

Back at the house, I slipped on my bathing suit and sat in a sheltered, sunny spot on the south side of the house and watched the snow melt and read *Entrepreneurs Manual*. Maybe someday, I could just sit in the sun and watch the snow melt without feeling pushed to read for profit instead of pleasure. I wondered, "Whatever came of that little girl who wanted to be a housewife when she grew up? What's a nice girl like me doing in a place like this!" But when you're your own boss, you've got to do what the boss says.

Personnel

A very obvious thing I learned was the fact that if you've hired someone for a task, and then you have to hire someone to make sure they've done the job right, it just may be that you don't need the original person you hired. A case in point was the accounting department. The lady we hired to send out the invoices and pay our bills was leisurely about doing both! Sometimes, one day's loss of time in getting the invoices out can be very costly. The money won't be in the mailbox in time to pay the employees if you don't even let the facility know what they owe! So, what's God to do to cover for someone who hasn't done what He asked them to do!

Learn to fire people. I smile now at the thought of one of the ladies who worked as support in the office. She was enjoying her job, we all loved her, but she was not getting the work done! The day after she was terminated, a lovely bouquet of flowers arrived at the office! A nice note read, "In all the times I've been fired, I have never left with such hope and dignity as I felt yesterday." I smile now, knowing I wasn't the first one who had to fire her!

But I should have known that! The best way to keep competent people is to hire competent people!

Sabbath Rest

Sometimes there were peaceful moments of Sabbath rest. I would curl up on the puffy bed with a book and my kitty, Gracie Allen, who had been my traveling companion in the days before TMP. Gracie and I had shared the forty-foot fifth wheel RV as we did the "Safari Survival Stories." We shared our lot together, traveling from campground to campground and health facility to health facility as an itinerate physical therapist. Now,

Gracie could curl up on the big antique feather couch or go out and catch mice in the big old New England barn that was connected to the big Old New England farmhouse.

Sometimes there were breaks in the clouds when I could evaluate the business and my own life and plan a strategy. Sometimes, yes, sometimes I almost figured out what a nice girl like me was doing in a place like this!

> *Just knowing there is one Being in the whole universe who totally understands you is freeing and life-giving*

Once, in my deep sleep, I dreamed of closeness to people again. There was time for music and dancing and popcorn and apple cider. Alice and Dick were there, and George and Mary. It wasn't the music, although at the time I thought it was pretty good, you know, sitting on the floor strumming and singing Mockingbird Hill. No, it wasn't the music, it was the closeness to people again. I enjoyed the dream. Maybe someday there would be time and energy to play again. Maybe.

When the "buck stops" with you, there's not really any person you can turn to that fully understands except your heavenly Father. He not only understands, but He can also do something. Just knowing there is one Being in the whole universe who totally understands you is freeing and life-giving. "My God will supply all your need." He supplies not only the temporal needs, but also the emotional needs.

The She-Bear

Another firing incident could have turned into physical harm. She was a young girl just out of high school. This was her first job in an office. Her only previous employment was diving for sea urchins off the coast of Maine with her father.

The day came when we were able to "free up her future." She was angry and tearful, OK, understandably. I wasn't prepared, however, for the stormy, noisy entrance of her mother an hour later! When the mother came screaming up the steps, everyone else in the office went into hiding—you know, under the desks, behind doors, in the bathrooms! I stood alone and unarmed against a raging she-bear, (fortunately, also unarmed!), who would have torn me limb from limb if she had possessed the proper tools! I felt as if I were in the presence of one possessed of demons. After what seemed like forever, she retraced her steps and retreated from the property. I didn't have to say a word. Fact is, I probably couldn't have had

I wanted to! As she screeched out of the parking area, the pale faces of the support staff began to appear from hiding. Sometimes, we are more aware than others of the protection of our guardian angels.

Neighbors

I woke one night with a severe pain in my back. I started vomiting! Called the neighbor, Tina. As soon as she heard my voice, she said, "I'll be right there, Liz!" She jumped into her LL Bean jeans, and before I could put on my coat, she was there. Not only did she take me into the hospital, but stayed with me until the doctor had my kidney stone under control! It's moments like that that bond a person with the neighbors. There are a strength and solidity with the neighbors on my road in Harpswell. I'm more than lucky; I'm blessed!

Fear

Yes, there were moments when fear would grip me. "What's the worst thing that could happen?" I wondered. "Well, I could lose my shirt and have to start all over again like McCann and carve out a new company with my bare hands. But if TMP fails, I will no longer be fifty! There may not be physical strength or mental courage to do it all over! I'd better enjoy the journey!"

One of the fears of a traveling professional is that something incapacitating will happen while they are alone and far away. This fear is grounded! Nancy injured her back while in Tucson. Alone and far away, she called the home office. One of our local physical therapists based in Tucson took compassion on her and walked her through the experience, but meanwhile, the facility needed coverage to cover the traveler! What were we to do? There was always such a lag time between the need and getting the therapist licensed, having the therapist give notice to the present employer, and getting tickets in the hands of the therapist.

But God had someone licensed, ready to go, and willing to cover! Nancy was cared for, and the facility was able to keep its obligation to the patients. There was just no way all this would have worked out without direct intervention from the Lord. My faith is always strengthened when God opens the Red Sea! Then, just like God's people in the past, I panic when the next crisis comes along. I forget how God is looking for ways to show Himself strong.

Play Sometimes

I released myself to spend money and play dress-up. In the "Burn Out" book, it says that you burn out when you are putting more energy into a project than you are getting out of it. If you are putting more into it than the reward you are deriving, you will burn out! Life must have balance.

There was nothing but navy blue corporate uniforms hanging in the closet. While in Tucson, I stopped in at my favorite boutique and bought a whirly, swirly square-dance dress! Now, it's been years since I did any square-dancing, and even then, it was just in P. E. class in the fourth grade! The new dress was dark blue with big pink and red flowers and lots of ribbon and ruffles! Did I wear it? Well, some, but the most fun was when my class of little girls from church came to play house. They would try on all the dress-up clothes in the closet. And how they loved the swirly, happy dress from Tucson!

Stay Focused

The rain was coming down in torrents and making little soldiers in the puddles. I stepped into the bookstore and rustled through the magazines. There was *Entrepreneur*, but I already had that. I wished I had time for reading *Horse Illustrated* and *Writer's Digest*. But I needed something to help me grow TMP. Ah, ha! *Growing Your Business* looked helpful. Maybe someday I could read those other interesting magazines. There would be life beyond TMP, wouldn't there? But for now, I needed to stay focused.

Interlude

Winter has a different kind of beauty. The sunset on this shortest day of the year was clear and cold, and just the sliver of the silver moon hung as if suspended in the tall pine trees on the other side of the pasture. I stood in the middle of the front yard and looked at my home. How cozy and warm it looked as I gazed in through the picture window. The cuckoo clock ticked away on the wall, and the Franklin stove sent a puff of smoke into the cold December air. There was a lining of frost on the window, and I was glad there was a warm kitchen to go to. Maybe there would be the smell of hot potato soup with onion! But no, if there was any hot potato soup, I was the one to make it. I was alone.

Nice Girl in a Place Like This!

Over and over I kept saying to myself, "What's a nice girl like me doing in a place like this!" I was sure that well-deserved rest would come as soon as I brought on another office worker, or when we placed the next therapist, maybe then I could rest. I was exhausted but didn't know how to jump from a runaway horse without causing permanent damage. Only way to manage in a situation like this was to lean forward and go with the dead run. I couldn't see the crisis looming in the traveling physical therapy industry. And besides, I was actually enjoying the ride! The ride reminded me of the days on the farm in Missouri when I would undo my long copper braids and let my hair flow with the horse's copper mane as we would gallop bareback at top speed down the east road.

But the bridge was washing away, and I didn't know. Would I be able to ride it through with the exhaustion at my elbow?

Know the State of Your Flocks

The quote of the day was from Proverbs 27:23–27. "Be diligent to know the state of your flocks, and look well to your herds: for riches are not forever; does a crown endure to all generations? When the hay is gone, the tender grass shows itself, the herbs of the mountains are gathered in. The lambs will be for your clothing and the goats will furnish you the price of a field. And there will be goat's milk enough for your food, for the food of your household, and for the maintenance of your maids" (AMPC). I detected a note of hope and a promise that God would see me through.

The Dream

Seems that all my life I've been afraid of water. I would dream of huge tsunami waves almost ready to engulf me. I would wake just before the tsunami hit and lie there in bed, shivering and frightened. Then, one night in my dream, the wave overtook me. I was in a ship on the ocean when the wave towered

First, she discovered a gas leak in the heater, and then a door with only one flimsy lock on it! And there were cockroaches in the bathroom who scurried away when you turned on the light!

above the ship and came crashing down on our helpless ship. It swallowed the ship and all its occupants and sucked them to a watery grave in the gray Atlantic. Just before I was overcome by a breath of water, my Guide was by my side and calmly asked if I would like for Him to hold my nose so that I wouldn't be overcome by water before getting to the surface.

Now, there's only one thing more frightening than being overcome by a tsunami, and that is someone holding my nose. But when my Guide asked permission to hold my nose, I nodded and slumped, unconscious into His arms. The next thing I knew, we were both above water.

From that time forward, I no longer had the dream until here in the middle of the chaos of handling Traveling Medical Professionals, Inc. One night, I dreamed I was in a huge, powerful ocean liner, moving through the waters toward the destination. The seas were like the mighty waves we encountered on our way to Japan when I was a child. At that time, they told us the waves were –fifty to sixty feet high! Yes, these waves were about to engulf the ship, but this time, the ship plowed through each one, and without even a shudder of the propeller rising above the waterline, our ship seemed to just slice each wave and move on.

The dream wasn't the same as all the previous dreams. There was no longer any terror. Could it be that all God wanted was for me to let Him "hold my nose?"

The Health Care Professionals

Cockroaches and no phone. My phone rang at 10:00 p.m. It was the mother of one of our prize therapists. I have great respect for parents who can bring up a child to be such an outstanding adult. Nancy was serving at a new facility in Blythe, California. Blythe is on the Arizona-California border about halfway between Los Angeles and Grand Canyon. Her first day on the job, the administrator took her into the desert to teach her how to shoot a gun. "You'll need to carry a gun. Everyone else does!"

That in itself would be enough to strike terror to the heart of a well-bred young lady from Boston. Then she went to her motel room. First, she discovered a gas leak in the heater, and then a door with only one flimsy lock on it! And there were cockroaches in the bathroom who scurried away when you turned on the light! The hospital was responsible for the housing and was trying to save money. Besides all that, there was no phone in the room!

Having been a "nice girl in a place like that" before, I could understand the situation without much explanation. During my assignment as a traveling therapist in Hazard, Kentucky, the girls who worked with me took me aside the first day, and yes, they told me, "You better carry a gun. Everyone else does. We all carry one either in the glove compartment or in our purse. And don't stop if you're being followed. You'll know when you are being followed. Don't take the same route home every night."

It didn't take any time for me to get back to Nancy, telling her to get the best motel she could find, complete with pool and hot tub. She was not to stay in that situation another minute. Her traveling company would pick up the tab! The next day, I called upon my aunt, who lived about eighty miles west of Blythe and asked her to drive over and approve Nancy's accommodations.

Nancy finished her assignment, but from then on, we made sure the facilities knew we needed safe, clean accommodations with secure locks and a phone! You gotta do what the boss says.

Will There Be Any Friends at the End?

The pressures of the office were constant, like a correspondence course in ancient civilization. If there's even a spare moment, it seems you should get a little more done on the correspondence course.

No matter how much time I spent on Traveling Medical Professionals, Inc., there was always an endless supply of "woulda, coulda, shoulda." It was something like that job in West Palm Beach where all of the therapists ripped up their contracts and walked out the door, leaving me with the entire load of patients to treat in the 350-bed facility! At that time, I realized that this was an administrative problem, not mine. But now I am the administrative decision-maker! It's all my problem. I'm where the buck stops! They say one should never take responsibility without authority. One could delegate the authority, but it was still the hospital administrations' responsibility! Now it was mine.

Interlude

At home I opened the office window. Spring was in the air. A robin chirped, then warbled! The peepers in the pond chimed in. The crocuses and daffodils lined the fence. There was that which called me into the out of doors—to life, to living, to poetry, and love. "So, what's a nice girl like me doing in a place like this?" When you're your own boss, you've got to do what the boss says. All the problems and projects would be there when I returned—so what!

The sunshine was warm on my face, and I no longer had to wear my snow boots. My feet wanted to skip; my heart wanted to laugh! The chickadees whistled their "Hi, Sweetie" to me, or was it to his mate! Was the water ever this blue, the seagulls so white, the air so pure? Why does a "nice girl like me" chain herself to a maga-mahogany desk! And so I played. I tickled the Spring Beauties, stooped to breathe the fragrance of the mayflowers and earth. I petted the moss and looked for fiddleheads, even when I knew they weren't ready yet. Pussy willows? Yes! There were pussy willows!

Back at the office, I fielded a call from our therapists, Jean and Katie. Should they testify in court about a suspected child abuse case? There would always be problems, but they would be interspersed by moments of awareness.

"Get Him out of Here"

Our therapist, Red, had only been in Millinocket, Maine, a few hours when he called. "I don't like it here. This place is a pigsty and a dump! I only came because you came to visit me and twisted my arm." He hung up.

The hospital called. "Get this guy out of here! He's using some unorthodox methods of treating patients, and he came in with a chip on his shoulder. He says his apartment is a pigsty and a dump! He is aggravating the patients and the employees, and we want him out of here!"

What was I to do? It was two days before Christmas. I had no replacement for him. And he was foreign!

There were not many alternatives. But, "when you are your own boss, you gotta do what the boss says."

So, to Millinocket, I went. Sometimes a nice girl like me had to do hard things. I found myself detaching and doing what had to be done. But really, I just wanted to bake cookies and hold the children on my lap and tell them stories.

I bought Red a return ticket to Gary, Indiana, and hand-delivered it to Millinocket. Red showed me his methods of treatment. As a therapist myself, there was no way I would want him to treat one of MY patients! I gave Red his dismissal and left.

Six weeks later, there was a letter in our mail from a lawyer in Indiana. He wanted blood. I had fired a perfectly capable therapist, and that, the day before Christmas!

When Red left Maine, we found a lovely foreign-trained female therapist from Africa. She stayed for almost a year and loved the area and the people. How thankful I was for Nava. But sometimes, "you gotta do what you gotta do." To fight in court would have pulled us off-center at a crucial time. We settled out of court.

Interlude

It was a couple of days after Christmas, and the dirt road to the shore was frozen solid with ice. The bay was frozen solid down to four feet. The best thing I could think of to keep myself from freezing solid was to stay indoors near the fireplace. But no, I decided to take a walk to the shore. I bundled up in almost everything I owned, including a face mask, and started down the snowy road to the shore. When it's below zero, the snow has a special crunch to it. I knew it was well below. All the rhododendron leaves were curled as tight as possible, and the pine twigs snapped in the cold.

At the shore I found the bay frozen over. Because of the tide, it freezes in chunks. Between the four-foot-deep chunks, depending upon the tide, one could see cold, green ice water. The hike was worth the effort. God has precious gifts when we come into His presence. He is a lover of the beautiful. As I turned from sea level to trudge back up the hill through the snow to the warm fireplace, I looked at the snow-covered path at my feet. The sun, though lacking in strength for warmth, was strewing diamonds at my feet! Tiny diamonds of red, orange, yellow, green, and blue surrounded me! They seemed to dance at my feet, and then, through my frozen tears, they surrounded me like a rainbow! I know God smiled. He did that just to play with me! He does that, sometimes, you know.

I remembered, too, that He loves rainbows! There is a rainbow surrounding His throne. It's also His promise of His watch care and His promise that He sat enthroned above the deluge, and He still sits enthroned. Nothing is out of His control.

L.A. Combat Zone

On a clear day, right out of the blue, in the middle of our usual routine of an office busy with therapy placement, payroll, and filing, the phone rang. It was Belinda, one of our prized therapists serving at the huge, gray LA County Hospital, looming above the surrounding landscape in the middle of Los Angeles. This area of LA is where the gangs rule. You could call it a combat zone. The first words out of her mouth were, "I just thought you'd like to know we are all safe."

Now, what does that do to the heart of the nice girl trying to place prized therapists in safe facilities throughout the nation? Mine skipped a beat. "What's up?" I managed.

Her voice was still shaking. "This guy came into the ER this morning, brandishing his pistol and looking for drugs and for doctors. Then he started shooting. Before anyone could stop him, he had killed three doctors!"

"No, Belinda!" I said, aghast. "You must have been terrified!"

"I'm still shaking," Belinda said. "They herded as many people as possible into the hospital cafeteria and bolted the door! That was the emergency plan!"

"What do you think, Belinda. Do you want to come home!"

"Oh, no," she said, "I'll be all right, but it really shook me up, I've got to admit! I called as soon as I could get a line out because I was sure you would see it on TV and be worried."

We were glad the bad news came with the good news!

Something Special

It was a relief to walk to the shore in the early morning. Lobster boats were chugging, and the lobster men were pulling traps. It was peaceful at the shore. I always like to absorb the peace before a grueling day.

This particular morning was even more special. As I turned to leave, I stopped. There on the edge of the clearing, not twenty feet away, was a doe. She gave a short bleat, quite like a sheep. Out of the woods bounded a little spotted fawn! He trotted quickly to his mother, dropped to his knees, and began to nurse vigorously! I couldn't believe my eyes!

Compassion

Then there was Annette. She was licensed and ready to go in both California and in Hawaii. She was eager. Her references checked out great. I was on the phone with all the health care facilities where we had previously served and all the possibilities in the National Hospital Phone Book. I checked all the ads in the PT Bulletin. There was nothing! Just nothing! It's hard to let a good therapist go with another company just because you don't have a facility in your stableful of possibilities. But it seemed there was no choice.

Later that day, Annette called. "I hate to do this," she apologized, "but my boyfriend and I just patched things up, and I need to stay home in Kansas City." She was apologetic, but as far as I was concerned, she wasn't apologetic enough! I have to admit I was so thankful there wasn't a facility all pre-paid on this one!

I was to learn later that relationship problems with a significant other would account for the high percent of therapists who thought they wanted to travel.

Greater Compassion

Another crisis. The therapist, Susan, we sent to Iowa for three months, wanted to leave and go home. We were still obligated to the facility. What would be the ethical, compassionate decision here?

"Oh," sobbed Susan. "Oh, I just don't know what to do! I'm all alone here." she sobbed again.

"Dear, dear Susan," Karon tried to comfort, not knowing just why all the tears.

"Oh!" she sobbed again.

"Tell me, Susan, what happened."

"Oh, I can't. I just can't!"

"You can't what, Susan. Did someone hurt you?"

"Well, not exactly. Well, I've just got to go home!" she sobbed again. "You see, the pregnancy test came back positive, and now he wants nothing to do with me!"

"Do what you have to do, Susan," Karon said, trying to stay calm. Susan absolutely had to leave. We listened to her as she sobbed out her story. The facility absolutely had to have a therapist. Then we listened as they sobbed out their story!

Sometimes there are no options. Not everything turns out like you hope it will. Someday we'll understand, but at the moment, we supported Susan in her decision.

Promises to Keep

Then, there was the issue of trying to fill an obligation in Modesto, California. It was another one of those times when the promised therapists called the day before she was due to start at the facility and said she had changed her mind. What were we to do? We were praying, walking the floor, and wringing our hands again when God really came through.

We called one of our former therapists who lived in the Modesto area. "Any way you can give us a week to pull things together at the hospital, Kelly," I asked, hardly daring to hope.

"Well, our patient count is down right now, so I could probably ask for a few days off and help you out," she said.

"Believe me, Kelly, you are a real God-send! I owe you big time!"

When will I ever learn? I could have just done the praying without the hand wringing and the floor walking! It would have been OK just to leave things in God's hands and listen to His directions. Yes, He pulled it off again, and we were able to have a fine therapist ready to treat patients on Monday morning!

Shoot Out

The headlines of the newspaper were about the shoot-out in Las Cruces, New Mexico. Apparently, there was a drug deal going on in the bowling alley near the hospital in this border town. Things went wrong! Two people were shot dead!

Ordinarily, this would only have raised one eyebrow, but not when one of my prized therapists was serving there! All the what-if's come to mind. Just what if Sharon had been at the bowling alley! What if she had been the line of fire! What if she had been held hostage! If these kinds of people were having a shoot-out in the bowling alley, was the rest of the town safe?

> *When will I ever learn? I could have just done the praying without the hand wringing and the floor walking!*

I called Sharon early the next morning. "Are you all right, Sharon? We saw the headlines, and the first thing we thought of was you! Is it a pretty rough town?"

"Well," she answered, "It is a border town, and there are drug deals on a regular basis, but really I like it here. I just don't go to places like the bowling alley!"

Again, there was no way I could control every situation. I could not be everywhere at once and foresee every emergency and make preparation for it. But God can! And He did! Our therapists were safe!

Earthquake in San Francisco

I hung up the phone and turned to Karon. "Guess what now! That hospital in San Francisco that was so desperate for coverage found a permanent placement, and they don't need Dana after all!"

"Oh, no!" Karon sighed. "What about Dana? He wanted so badly to serve in San Francisco!"

"Well, I've got to tell him, I know, but first, let's see what else is available," I said, picking up the list of openings.

"Looks like there's one in Fairfield. Let's give them a call."

They were delighted, but I did detect disappointment in Dana's voice when I had to tell him he wouldn't be serving in San Francisco, that jewel by the sea. He would have to travel about eighty miles to enjoy the city on weekends.

We were, of course, aggravated by the fact that the facility backed out at the last minute. Yes, we were aggravated and put the facility on our blacklist. But our aggravation turned into relief when, about a week later, the earthquake hit! Entire sections of the freeway were demolished, and people were trapped for days in the rubble. The death toll was high. San Francisco was cut off for a while from the rest of the world! It was months before the commuting system was restored to any semblance of normal! Our therapist would have been in grave danger, and perhaps lost life or limb! There is no way we could have prepared for this emergency. It was a God thing!

Pile-up on I-95

I was just completing a visit to encourage facilities and therapists in Palm Beach, Florida, and to collect receivables. God took care of the details of my own life and comfort. He woke me at 4:00 a.m. and impressed me to check out of the motel and get to the airport immediately. I had been encouraging therapists and solidifying contracts and visiting with Tom for several days. I was to leave late that morning and was prepared to be on the road to the airport about 8:00 a.m. I was sleeping soundly in the motel room when suddenly, I was wide awake and knew I needed to be on my way to the airport quickly. I turned in the rental car and had time for a leisurely breakfast while watching the world wake up. I was in plenty of time for the flight.

I would never have known why God was so insistent that I get to the airport quickly had not Tom called that night. "Are you all right?" he asked.

I detected something in his voice. "You seem quite concerned, Tom," I said. "I woke up early and went on to the airport. Had time for a leisurely breakfast before boarding. Why do you ask?"

"I'm glad to hear your voice! They had a major pile-up on I-95 this morning about the time you would have been going to the airport! Of course, I was concerned! The interstate was tied up for hours. Hospital emergency rooms were full, and several people died in the collisions. What would have happened to the nice girl like you in a place like that?"

"Oh, Tom! Only God knows! I can only imagine!"

You gotta listen! You gotta get up and out of bed and be on the way to the airport instead of hitting the snooze button. Do what the boss says!

But back home the happy moment came when my neighbor, Sally, showed up on my front doorstep with a little baby duck in her pocket. Made us smile. Life goes on.

Personal Impact

Now and again, God would give us a glimpse of the impact we had on someone's life. When Heidi stopped traveling, we got some feedback to encourage us through the tough times. Karon opened the letter and read it to me.

"Listen to this, 'through working with TMP, my faith has been strengthened. By my association with you, I feel like a stronger person.'"

I looked at Karon. Her face was rather red, and I detected a tear in her blue eyes as she put the letter back in the envelope and handed it to me.

"It is encouraging words like that, Karon, that kept a nice girl like me staying in a place like this. Sometimes, I think I see how He is using us! I like it!"

Success

On a cool evening in late May, with the peepers peeping and the scent of lilacs in the air, I was in my office with the windows wide open and my eyes on the financials. It finally hit me. We were not really that far behind! Applications were coming in from the therapists. Health care facilities were calling for help. The team was pulling together. We were going to make it! I knelt by my chair. "God, you have been so good to Your little girl and Your growing company! How can I ever thank You for the way You have carried us!"

"The Apple Tree, the Singing, and the Gold"

There were days when the poet and the artist in the nice girl would cry for attention. More often than not, I would tell them to be quiet; we had things to do and places to go. Someday, we would be free to play and laugh and dance! Someday!

There were sometimes stolen moments, sweet, stolen moments to ride Lady along the trail to the shore and watch the tide rise and watch the tide fall.

May came with all the friendly flowers. I petted each one and breathed in the smell of spring and saltwater. I thought of all the days as a traveling therapist when I longed for moments like these. Now the moments were at my fingertips. What happened? Why did I feel like I had to steal these moments for the "Apple Tree, the Singing, and the Gold?"

Presidential Perks—Hawaii

One perk of the job as president of a nationwide traveling therapy company, is, of course, travel! Duh! You place your therapists in places you want to visit. There's even a travel allowance! But it comes out of your own pocket! Well, we call it pre-tax dollars. But they are still dollars off the bottom line!

Never in my life would I have thought of Hawaii as a place to visit. But guess what! Some of my therapists thought it would be really exotic to do an assignment there! And sure enough, hospitals sometimes get short-handed, even in the island paradise! So what could I do but laugh and go!

I took advantage of the chance for a tax-deductible trip to the garden island. Kathy was serving on the island of Kauai. I knew she shared my love of horses. "Elizabeth, any chance you would go with me for a breakfast ride on the beach Sunday? You aren't going to go right back to the mainland, are you?"

"Wow! Kathy, how did you arrange that? You know me! I'd love it!"

"Oh," she said, "I've got connections. There's a stable not far from the beach, and they let me ride if I help them muck out stalls."

It was all I could do to keep from clapping my hands and jumping up and down. "Oh, we absolutely have to do this. What time?"

I'll pick you up at 7:45 Sunday morning." Kathy looked almost as excited as I was!

It was an unforgettable day. The sun was warm, and a gentle breeze tickled my hair. The group rode along a quiet dirt road beside the sugar cane, and then through the jungle to the shore. The sunshine sparkled on the sea, and the waves lapped the sand. There on the beach, the breakfast crew had spread a fine meal of fresh papaya, mangos, fresh sweet breads, and juice. I kept saying to myself, "I can't believe I'm doing this! What's a nice girl like me doing in a place like this?"

The time went by too fast, but the memory is there of the smell of sugar cane, the sound of the sea, the feel of the sunshine on my face, and an agreeable horse under me as we rode through the sugar cane to the stable.

And the facility even paid their bill!

Collections—New Bedford

I packed the camper and headed south to New Bedford, Massachusetts.

When I climbed the steps into the facility, I wondered how they could keep their accreditation. I was very disappointed that I had put a therapist in a facility like this!

"May I speak with Mr. Jones?" I asked the receptionist. I had no idea whether or not they would even speak to me. Every time I tried to contact them by phone, I would be told the administrator was in a meeting, or away from his desk, or with a client.

Mr. Jones was a thirtyish gentleman with blond hair and a worried look on his clean-shaven face. I presented the statement and told him I needed to take a check home with me. Mr. Jones assured me that we would be receiving payment. Unfortunately, there was no money in the bank to pay vendors at this time.

> *"Fine," I said. "I brought my camper and am prepared to stay until I can take the check with me"*

"Fine," I said. "I brought my camper and am prepared to stay until I can take the check with me."

That plan is dangerous, but this time I had a pile of administrative tasks that needed attention, so the plan worked.

His secretary ordered me out of the building, but there was a convenient parking lot just outside the president's window and adjacent to his parking space (and in the shade). Three days later, my office notified me that I could pick up the check at the switchboard.

A Loner

Back home again I stole some time on Friday to play house. As the sun set in the west behind the bright red maple trees, the house smelled of kitchen floor wax, spray starch, and fresh bread. I set the table with the red-checked table cloth and lit the red candle. Gracie Allen curled up and purred in the big recliner in the corner of my country kitchen. But I was alone.

The lady on Olivera Street who analyzed handwriting said, "You have made yourself a loner." Maybe I had. I have learned to enjoy my own company. But that doesn't mean it's not lonely when on a Friday night, you light the big red candle and set the table for one and cry.

"Next week," I promised myself, "I'll invite some of the other people who are sitting alone at their tables on a Friday night!"

But the pressure of TMP prevented my thinking about it until Friday afternoon, and by then, I was so exhausted that all I wanted to do was crash! "What was a nice girl like me doing in a place like this!" I said to the little gray and buff kitty curled up in the soft chair beside the table.

"Do you want to go to bed, Gracie Allen?"

"Neow?" Gracie asked in her sweetest voice.

"Yes, Gracie, now," I said and scooped her up and carried her to the bedroom. There's something about the purring of a kitty that makes one fall asleep and maybe even dream sweet dreams.

Taos

New Mexico presented a different problem. Taos was a prime location for travelers, and it was orthopedic outpatient, the love of most young male therapists. A solid Christian gentleman named Brett was licensed and wanted to serve.

It was only his second year out of PT school, but no sooner had he arrived than the owner left on an extended vacation. She was a wiry little lady on the verge of burn-out and "had to get away."

The payments lagged. Brett was in charge of paying bills while the owner was away.

I called. "Elizabeth," he said, "she just doesn't have the money in the bank! I think we can work out a plan, though," he continued. "I think I can make a success out of this, and I can stay here with her and get her on her feet. She's back now, and we are having Bible studies every night. She knows she needs the Lord."

I wrote her a letter, stating that I could understand how one could get in a situation like this, and we would be willing to work with her. I also reminded her that there is a God up there who is in control of everything and wants only to see us with Him in the hereafter.

A week later, I received the following letter along with a check for the $14,000:

"I have never been so happy to write a check before! I mean, I cringe every time I write a check at Smith's food store for even $2.53! And this one is big! I want to thank you for all of your prayers and the effort and understanding from you for us out here. At a time when people I loved and cared about and trusted in deserted me, betrayed me, and let me down, God gave me people who didn't even know me to help me. Hey, I get it now—you're really guardian angels! Thank you so much for helping me and caring and for going so far out of your way businesswise. I've never seen a contract with encouragement and blessings written into it. But you know, maybe the business world would be better if all contracts were that way.

"But you have really changed my life—you have helped to introduce me to God and having God in my life, and I can even feel Him in my heart and golly, He feels good there. All through each day now, I can feel and see God's working and doing, and I'm in awe! I'm learning, and I'll get there, but what an excellent adventure. And to think, He's been there all along, and I was the one who didn't have a clue. I only hope to be able to help other lost people out there like you helped me!"

"Karon," I said, showing her the letter, "Look at this! Sometimes I know why God is letting us have this business! He has to tell 'um!"

Almond Blossoms

Palm Springs

They don't all turn out that way. It was a small business owner in California. I had not really consulted the Lord about either getting the account or about the collection.

After the therapist left, and I stopped in to pick up the funds, he said simply, "I'm not going to pay you. So sue me."

I checked into legal services, but decided it would be counterproductive and pull the president off-center to attempt a lawsuit over the $5,000, to say nothing of the court costs! I walked away. But I can't say I walked away cheerfully!

Springtime Interlude

While in California, I took a rental car and drove to check on other facilities and therapists in the Sacramento area. The hills were green with fresh grass, and there were soft, white fragrant almond blossoms in the almond grove. I took a side road off the freeway and parked on a farmer's dirt lane. I slipped off my shoes and let my bare feet feel the healing cool of the fresh green grass. The sun was warm on my shoulders, and the earth felt comforting to my soul. The bees were humming over the almond blossoms, and so was I. If one waits to be happy until some major elation comes, one could wait a long, long time. I'll take the short exuberance of the moments. Yes, exuberance mixes well with the more somber colors of life. Shouldn't I have just stayed another day? Could I have missed it? Now, twenty years later, I wonder. I thought I would miss a chunk of change if I extended and played in the green, green grass and the almond trees another day. But really, it seems to be these small breaths of reality in the rush and pressure of the present that give energy.

In the reading and studying of books, we sometimes forget the book of nature. It's OK to study this ever-changing book. The lessons are new with every breath and every shift of the eye and every step along the path through the woods to the shore.

Back at the Old New England Farmhouse, I am constantly amazed at the beauty of the changing seasons, the changing tides, and the changing clouds. Yet, God has put an unchanging stability and security in each.

Beauty is necessary for my health. I'm glad God put me in this little corner of the earth with all the changing beauty and the beauty of the neighbors and friends.

Marina Del Rey

The reception area was dim and empty except for a fat man sitting at the receptionist computer. On previous visits this area had been a hubbub. I wondered at this.

The man at the computer seemed a bit embarrassed. "May I help you?" he asked. "I'm not really supposed to be here," he said. "My name is Eric Abraham, and I'm chairman of the board."

I told him my errand. "I've come to pick up a check."

"Oh, won't you come in?" he said as he ushered me into the board room. "Would you have some coffee, tea, or water?"

We talked about his company, his plans, and his problems. "Eric," I said, "I want you to know that I'm praying for your company."

"You're praying for my company!" he asked, surprised. "Yes," I said, "we would like to see a mutual success."

He handed me the check, and as he ushered me to the door, he said. "Keep praying for my company!"

Out West

This one was the most fun of all. There was a facility out West that not only refused to pay, but the receptionist refused to let me connect to the decision-maker by phone! I had to do something. Just because I was back East and they were out West, did not give them license not to pay their bill.

It was summertime, and I happened to have a white cotton pantsuit with me. I bought a large bouquet of gaily-colored balloons and entered the office door. The ladies at the front desk squealed and clapped their hands when I entered. Little did they know I had come to collect a bill!

> *The ladies at the front desk squealed and clapped their hands when I entered. Little did they know I had come to collect a bill!*

"For me!" cried a cute little brunette.

"A singing telegram!" squealed the girl at the computer.

I didn't answer their questions. "I need to speak with Mrs. Schemelflenige." I smiled. "Are you Mrs. Schemelflenige?"

Their faces fell. One of them went into the back office and called for Mrs. Schemelflenige.

They were still wondering what was going to happen when Mrs. Schemelflenige appeared from the back office.

I was wondering, too! Now, what was I going to do? I had come with the invoices that were lagging.

There was nothing more I could do but sing! So to the tune of Happy Birthday, I sang!

"It's our money we want, It's our money we want, …"

They paid!

Back Home

The cool morning air hit my face as I stepped out the back door and into the shed. The big black mare nickered. There was the smell of hay and horse. Lady munched her grain as I brushed her and put on the saddle. How blessed I was. Friday morning, and a horse to ride, and strength to do it, and the crisis over. Whew!

Travel Expense Account

The travel involved in owning and operating a nationwide traveling therapist registry is highly romanticized. I was eating my scant vegetarian rations at 37,000 feet when my seatmate asked what kind of work I was in. She was a sweet young thing, probably a sophomore in high school.

"I'm in the traveling therapy business," I told her. "We have therapists across the nation that are filling in for relief staff. Right now, I'm on my way to visit one of them."

"Oh," said the sweet young thing, "that must be really exciting. You must even have an expense account!"

I blinked. "Yes," I said. Then thought to myself, *Yes, I can have all the money I want in my expense account. But the money will ultimately come out of my own pocket!*

Christmas on Lake Champlain

It was a week before Christmas, and it seemed the only way to renew Nava's visa was to go directly to immigration in St. Albans, Vermont, and make a personal visit to the decision-maker. I hopped a small plane out of Portland and headed for Burlington and picked up a rental car.

It worked. I got the visa problem straightened out and had a few hours to enjoy the college town of Burlington on the eastern bank of Lake Champlain. I drove down the steep hill past the college to the town. The sharp, icy wind was blowing off the frozen lake. The town fathers had blocked off one of the cobblestone streets for pedestrians-only traffic. Vendors with portable carts displaying mittens and earmuffs and bright woolen winter scarves parked in the middle of the cobblestone promenade. Vendors selling trinkets and toys were blowing on their fingers or holding a hot cup of coffee and turning their backs to the wind. Sleighbells tinkled, and Salvation Army pots sizzled. My breath turned to ice and fell plunk to the ground as I walked. The mood was festive. Shoppers were carrying gaily wrapped parcels and humming with the Christmas music that was playing from the speakers on the corner. Salvation Army bells jingled, and children bundled in snowsuits trotted beside their mothers. I liked it. I could forget for a moment the visa, the licenses, those needing jobs, those looking for service, and office politics and just enjoy the poetry of living.

I could see through the frost-covered windows of the corner restaurant and drug store. It looked like the place where the townspeople hang out. I stepped inside. It smelled of hot coffee and freshly baked blueberry muffins. I sat in the ladder-backed chair at the tiny table in the corner and watched the people. They all seemed to know each other. I was the only one who sat alone.

"The blueberry muffins just came out of the oven," the waitress said with a winning smile. "How 'bout some coffee to go with it?"

I smiled. "Blueberry muffins fresh out of the oven! Just what I wanted! Make that a glass of orange juice to go with it. Have you worked here long?"

"I'm a junior at the college and need to work. School is so expensive now."

"What's your major?" I asked.

"I'm taking physical therapy. When I finish, I would like to travel for a year or so to get more experience and see what's out there before I decide where to take a job."

I gave her my card and told her to give us a call when she was ready.

Looking out through the frosted window of the restaurant, I could see an old man with a white beard and white hair with collar turned up and head down, going nowhere. I wondered where he would spend the night. He didn't come inside, although he glanced through the frosty window at the warm, friendly people chatting with each other. I wondered, would he be warm tonight? Had he collected enough returnable bottles to buy some warm soup? Or would it be whiskey so he could fall asleep and forget that it was almost Christmas, and people were supposed to be joyful? Would there be hot food on the table? Would there be warm, loving arms to hug and hold? Would there be grandchildren to bounce on his knees? I'll never know.

I flew home on the small plane and thought how lucky I was to have only the set of problems of Traveling Medical Professionals, Inc., instead of those of the old man tramping the snowy cobblestone street on the eastern bank of Lake Champlain just before Christmas.

Thunder Clouds

It was the time of year when the kids go back to school. When the "summer people" go home, and the flow of life in coastal Maine begins to be normal again. There are no black flies and no mosquitoes, the days are cooling off a bit, and the sky is a bright blue.

I began to feel angry. Angry about what? I'm not sure. It's just that nobody moved fast enough, nobody was efficient enough, and there was always a cash crunch. I would wake in the morning again to the lub-dub, lub-dub, lub …

But I loved my job. It was exciting, exhilarating! And there was an "expense account." There was something to look forward to, there were things to learn, and there was the hope of someday, well, maybe, even being a housewife and having time to play "Mrs. Jokoski." Maybe I could hold children on my lap and tell stories.

I was crushed when I returned from a business trip to find that my team no longer wanted prayer at the morning meeting! Didn't they know that it was God and only God who had made it possible to have an honest traveling therapy company that afforded them a job! But I couldn't fire people for not wishing to pray together. I got a first-hand view of how the enemy used a perfectly good law to protect religious liberty to cause anarchy in a small company whose foundation was based on our trust in Divine Power.

No Pot of Gold

I reviewed the last few years. TMP was taking all my time and energy and money! I wondered what might be in that pot at the end of the rainbow. Was life really a journey, not a destination?

When I started TMP, there were only two other traveling PT companies. The one I worked for that turned out to be crooked, another one out of Boston that placed mostly nurses, and then TMP. But as the need for traveling therapists increased, so did the number of traveling therapy companies.

Foreign-trained therapists were brought in by the airplane-load. In fact, one of my competitors called one day. "Elizabeth, I have a whole planeload of foreign-trained therapists coming, but I don't have enough jobs for them. Can you use some?"

"Sorry, Allen. We're all set!" I answered. "Are there more jobs than therapists now?"

"Well, it sure seems to be that way right now. Hope this trend doesn't continue." I detected a note of concern in his voice.

Schools of physical therapy mushroomed at universities all over the country. I was at an alumni banquet at my alma mater, Loma Linda University, when the head of a new school of physical therapy asked about the market. "Sue, what I'm seeing at this point is a shift in the market. There are more therapists than jobs!"

She blinked. Then turned pale! Could it really be that by the time she graduated her first students, there would be no jobs? Managed care hadn't been turned loose yet, and it was a heyday for the industry. Within a matter of a couple of years, the thirty-five traveling physical therapy companies advertising with full-page color advertisements in the *Physical Therapy Bulletin* was down to twenty, and then ten. As I watched, week by week, the advertisements dwindled.

It was summertime, and we had lots of therapists wanting to go out West. Seattle was a prime location. I identified some clients that should be needing therapists and made a trip to the Seattle area. You know that song about "The Sky's the Bluest Blue, in Seattle?" Well, it really is! The weather was just perfect. Diamonds were sparkling on Puget Sound, and sailboats with brightly-colored spinnakers were sailing across the water.

I went to make a call on one of our facilities.

"Nope. Don't need any therapists now."

At the next facility, my contact person met me with, "All set, Liz. Thanks anyway."

The next facility told me, "We've got therapists knocking at our door."

It was Friday afternoon, and I didn't fly out of Seattle till Sunday, so I took the ferry across Puget Sound to the Olympic Peninsula for the weekend. I found lodging at an inn on Lake Crescent and got a cabin right down at the water's edge. It was beautiful—the snowcapped mountains towering above the lake and all. I slipped into my bathing suit and waded into the icy cold water. Swimming gives a person time to think.

> *Everything will NOT turn out exactly as you plan, but all things WILL work together to glorify our God*

Nine therapists who want to come to Seattle within the next month. All our facilities say therapists are knocking on their door for a job. Hmmm! Something's happening. I used to have nine facilities knocking on my door for therapists, but now I have nine therapists. Something has changed. My ear to the ground detected a rumble! There is a shift in the market. The words in Proverbs came to my mind with startling freshness. "Riches are not forever." The hay was gone. There would need to be a new crop! I closed the company.

Few of the other companies advertising in the *Physical Therapy Bulletin* with big full-page color ads are still in the business. In fact, there isn't even a *PT Bulletin* to advertise in anymore, it's all online.

We made a cash profit that year in spite of the outlay of cash for the office amenities. It was a hard year. But when a "nice girl" is the boss, she has to do what the boss says. Some of these things involved in owning and operating a traveling physical therapy company are hard things.

When I returned from the Seattle trip, I pulled the group together in the office and told them the situation. They should start looking at other options. I contacted the therapists that were on the road and told them to duck for cover. "When you're your own boss, you better do what the boss says!"

Today is the first day of the rest of my life. God has been so good to me. In Hebrews 13:5, He said, "I will not in any way fail you nor give you up nor leave you without support. I will not, I will not, I will not in any degree leave you helpless nor forsake you nor let you down nor relax My hold on you! Assuredly not!" (AMPC).

Everything will NOT turn out exactly as you plan, but all things WILL work together to glorify our God. When I turn around and look at what He has done, I KNOW He can be trusted!

All I can say is, "God! You have been so good to me! You carried your 'nice girl in a place like this!' You always will!"

Life moved on predictably again at the Old New England Farmhouse. Gracie Allen had plenty of Meow Mix and always left some for her mice. There were friends around the red-checked tablecloth again, but now it was the grandchildren of the aging Hootenanny gang. There were walks to the shore where the Eider ducks mate in the springtime. Ruth's little grandson, Tim, would always show up at the Old New England Farmhouse to help with emergencies and bring his own son to play with the black and tan puppy with the white trim.

But it is hard for a traveling physical therapist to keep from wondering how things are doing in the rest of the great United States because that's all her home. It's the heart that insists on a road trip with the puppy.

Journey of the Heart

This Is How It Happened

Here I am, lying at her feet, a dog. I'm only a dog. I do this every day, every moment she's not on her feet doing some kind of people thing. I know I'm her dog. I know I belong.

It hasn't always been this way. I was just a gangly teenage pup. I was nobody's dog. My owner had dropped dead of a heart attack when my brothers and I were only six weeks old. We all went to live on a crowded ranch with a bunch of other dogs and some horses. Life was easy; all I had to do was to eat and sleep. But sometimes, I would dream. I would dream of belonging to someone. I wanted someone to call my own. I wondered what it would be like to have my very own rug in a warm spot beside someone who loved me. But then, I would wake up with all the puppies yelping, horses stomping and snorting, and people giving orders. A wave of loneliness would sweep over me, and I would lie with my head on my paws, waiting, watching, longing.

One by one, my brothers would leave the kennel. Sometimes, it was with little boys in baggy pants or sometimes little girls with rosy cheeks talking baby talk to them. I wished someone would talk to me like that. All anybody ever said to me was, "Kennel, big puppy, kennel." I would obediently go back into the cage, and they would shut the door. Nobody came to get me. Then I would dream again about romping through the woods, chasing chipmunks and squirrels. Maybe there would be a horse to follow. Maybe I could splash in the lake in the summertime and make the children laugh and play. Again, it would be only a dream, and I would wake, longing for a nameless being to call my own.

Then one day, when I was almost a year old, I saw her. I was out and about the stable sniffing and minding my own business. She was looking at the roly-poly baby puppies and letting them pull on the legs of her blue jeans. I wondered, could this be the one my mother told me about? Could she be the one I could trust with veto power over all my decisions for the rest of my life? Could she teach me tricks and scratch me behind the ears and love me in the ways that people love dogs? I wondered; I watched. I watched the way she handled the baby puppies with gentle hands and voice. At last, I made the decision to take a chance. What did I have to lose? From across the arena, I ran toward her at top speed. I wanted to throw my arms around her neck and ask if I could belong to her forever and for keeps.

Then it happened! To my shock, she met me with her knee doubled up and aimed at my solar plexus! It was too late! I was in midair. I yelped and fell to the ground. As soon as I could gather my wits, I ran back to the other side of the arena and lay in the dirt with my head on my paws and my eyes wide open, watching, waiting. What would happen next? Would she be like all the rest? Would I be rejected again, and have to go back into the kennel, only to dream of sleeping beside her bed. Would I wake and find myself all alone in the cold, lonely kennel? I watched. I waited.

Our eyes met. She smiled and called me to her side. This was the one my mother told me about, the one I could trust with veto power over all my decisions for the rest of my life.

"Come on," she said, "let's go home!"

Liz and Tip at Tidy Coon

"Journey of the Heart"

I'm not sure how long I had been there when I saw Lizbeth and our friend Linda-Lee packing the little A-liner camper. I wasn't sure what was going to happen, but they packed my dog food and water dish. It was when Lizbeth put my feather pillow on the floor beside her bed that I knew for sure we would be going together. I don't know how she would get along without me. I supervise the details of her life, like watching while she sleeps and takes a shower. That's my job. She tells me I am a Very Fine Dog, so I must really be a Very Fine Dog. She trusts me.

This must be a very important trip. I'm not sure where we are going, but I peeked at the paper she gave the folks at home. It had lots of names and phone numbers on it. She called me to her side and bent down and tried to explain things to me. "Tip," she said, "This will be a long, long trip. You see, I feel lonely. I love our home. I love to watch the tide rise and watch the tide fall. I love to watch the lilacs bloom in the springtime, and the leaves turn bright red and orange in the fall. I've lived here almost fifty years. I've worked here to make the Old New England Farmhouse into a place where people can come home and find love and joy and peace. They can sit around the red-checked tablecloth on a Friday evening and eat fresh homemade bread and hear the peepers in the springtime.

"But there was a life before I came here, Tip. My country is lonely for me. There are friends far away. I want to feel the heartbeat of my own, my native land again. I want to feel the heartbeat of a friend. I guess you could say this is the Journey of the Heart. I want to feel the heartbeat of America!

"Let's go!"

It was earlier than usual this morning when we took a walk to the shore. The ice is out down there now. We've been iced in all winter. It's good to see open water again. I wonder if it is warm enough to go swimming yet? I walked over to a tide pool and stuck my front paw in. No, not yet, I shook my foot, and we started back up the hill.

Mayflowers are blooming. Folks seem to get so excited about Mayflowers. I don't know why. Their gray-green leaves always look like some squirrel has been nibbling on them, but Lizbeth lifts the leaves, and there are tiny white or pink flowers. She bends down to smell. There's nothing there that appeals to a dog, so I just take a little walk into the woods and look for squirrels.

Lizbeth and I ran outside and stood in the front pasture and watched the geese flying over the Old New England Farmhouse day before yesterday. Their bellies look gold then pink in the setting sun. But now, she and I are the ones planning a trip south! I roll in the fresh new spring grass, trying to scratch my back. It always itches in the spring, and then my winter coat falls off.

I never ask where we are going or why. It is enough that we are together, but I heard her talking to somebody on the phone. She said that we are taking a Journey of the Heart. I think that means we may need some extra Kleenex.

As we drove down the lane toward Route 123, I saw Ruth standing on her porch in the sunshine waving to us. I saw her wipe her eye with her hand as she called after us, "Remember, we love you, Liz!"

Yes, there are people to come home to.

I was stretched out across the back seat as we drove. Lizbeth thought I was asleep, but I wasn't. I was just playing possum.

She began to talk. No, she wasn't trying to wake me; she was just talking to our country. "I watch your springtime come softly as we drive south out of New England. How beautiful you are, how soft your gentle countryside, how strong your mountains, how powerful your Maine.

"Your springtime comes so gently. You unsheathe the icy brook and let the tinkly music bounce happily over the rocks and on into the Casco Bay. I love the smell of springtime and life. There'll be lilacs laughing at the door come Memorial Day. And there'll be lady slippers and peonies and promises of more."

I dozed off again. This will be the Journey of the Heart. Our hearts will feast on beauty and love.

First Night

We were having trouble trying to find a place to stop that first night out. We thought we could make it to Ingrid's, but it was dark and stormy. The wind was terrifying. The rain was coming down in sheets. We were far from the Old New England Farmhouse, far from Ingrid's and far from any campground, but we were together! Lizbeth finally pulled into a service station. It was terribly late, but they said they would be open all night. The downpour let up just long enough to let us set up the camper. The salesman said it would only take thirty seconds. But they didn't figure on wind and rain. I don't think people should be trying to lift the lid on a tiny seven-by-seven tag-along A-liner in weather like this! The little thing shakes in the windstorm, and so do I.

Old Friends Are Gold

There's a song that says, "Make new friends but keep the old. One is silver and the other gold." Lizbeth was singing that as the truck hummed along the highway. We made it to Ingrid's. She, along with several others dear to our hearts, is turning ninety this year. It was with sadness, yet joy that we stopped to spend time. Their lives breathed a God-given fragrance from the collection of God-given experiences.

Each of these "golden" friends is unique to her because of the experiences they have shared together. I like Ingrid's little white poodle. She likes me, too. But I slept with Lizbeth in the little camper. I was on the rug beside the bed. We just pulled the camper into Ingrid's yard for the night.

Lizbeth always gets up and lets me do my chores first, and then she spends some time with God. I like it when she does that. Her God is my God and her people, my people. On our walk we could see row after row of blue mountains and a kind of haze as the sun came up. "See this, Tip?" she said. "I used to live here. It was beautiful, but I missed the sea and the seagulls and the smell of homemade bread on a Friday afternoon in the Old New England Farmhouse. Everywhere you go, you have to make new friends. I did that, Tip, but you see, it takes a long time to make an old friend. They are irreplaceable."

"Make new friends but keep the old. One is silver and the other gold"

Just then, I saw a squirrel! He was fat like he had been eating birdseed for a while. Everybody in the retirement community feeds birds—and squirrels! I figured I could catch him before he got to the tree! But he scrambled up on somebody's housetop. The house was near a dirt bank, so I took one flying leap and landed on the roof with him. Lizbeth called and called, but I knew she wouldn't be able to jump from the bank to the rooftop, so I ignored her until I made up my mind it was time to get back on track. So I went on down the road with Lizbeth, hoping to find another squirrel. If there's one, there will be two, just like the javelina (also known as collared peccary) we saw in the Arizona desert! Lizbeth stopped to let one cross the little two-lane road, and here came another one. Must have been his wife because trotting along behind was a baby javelina! Oh, how I wanted to round them up, to herd them, and show Lizbeth what I can do!

But, alas. Ingrid had a bird feeder, so I just bided my time, knowing the squirrel would be back.

The time with Ingrid made me happy. I heard them talking and sharing "good old times to remember." I could tell that these experiences have bonded their hearts together with ties that can never be broken. They relived the time Lizbeth and Mary sat together on the gymnasium floor with their coach, Ingrid. The spring sun was shining through the high windows and onto the gym floor, warming their souls as they opened their hearts and shared significant experiences of their young lives. Ingrid listened. Little did they know that when time had fled, they would still be sharing their lives, this time, on Ingrid's couch in her neat little apartment in the retirement community. We had a great view of the Blue Ridge Mountains of North Carolina right out Ingrid's big window.

The two of them review their sacred history and the way God has given them the gift of lifelong friendships and the abiding comfort of His own personal Presence. Tashi, Ingrid's little white poodle, and I stretched out there on the floor together. I knew "The Teach," and Lizbeth felt encouraged by each other's faith. There's a song they like to sing. It's about a "Pearly White City John saw coming down."

Lizbeth thanked Ingrid again and again for helping her through undergrad school and then giving her support when she started the traveling physical therapy business. They tell me that Ingrid was on Lizbeth's board of directors. You see, Ingrid too, had run a temporary health care service. "Well, Lizzy," Ingrid said. "You are in for a lot of hard work and stress. You don't really make much of a profit doing that either, but you'll learn a lot!"

Yep, Lizbeth was there for Ingrid through thick and thin, too. She told me about the time Ingrid was stranded in the Colorado Rockies because of a cardiac episode.

Lizbeth wanted to go to her and give her moral support. As she did her morning swim, she counted and thought, *Lap number ten, lap number eleven*. Her mind kept racing as she swam through the cool water doing routine laps.

Ingrid had just undergone emergency heart surgery while vacationing far up in the high country of Colorado. How would Lizbeth feel if she were all alone in a strange place and had to have emergency cardiac surgery!

Lap number twelve. She wanted to go. She didn't know what she thought she could do, but she wanted to go.

Lap number thirteen. Wasn't there a business trip she needed to make to Colorado Springs? Well, does that matter? Does one have to have the excuse of a business trip to support a hurting friend?

Lap number fourteen. Of course not! She must go!

The next day she walked through the door of Ingrid's hospital room. "Lizzy! You came!" Ingrid said as tears came to her eyes.

It was worth the trip! Did Lizbeth do anything? Well, no, not really. All she could do was, "just be there."

Today, here they are together in Ingrid's cozy little apartment, looking at the Blue Ridge Mountains and talking about old times. I stretch out with Tashi on the rug. Ingrid is a good cook! She made some chili beans, and I saw them put a scoop of cottage cheese on top of the bowl of chili beans. Then they laughed and talked about how they always did this on camping trips! Makes Tashi and me happy to hear them laugh.

Then it was time to go. I saw their tears fall on each other's shoulders as they gave each other a long hug. I knew we had touched the heartbeat of a friend.

"But Lizzy," Ingrid said, "it won't be long, and we'll all be together again. All of us, you and me and Tip and Tashi and Mary and Di …" Her voice drifted off. I knew they were thinking of heaven.

We drove on down the road, and I didn't ask any questions. But in my heart, I knew this would be the last time until then, until the Pearly White City. I wonder if there will be squirrels in that Pearly White City? Maybe they'll be tame, and we can all play together.

Sometimes Lizabeth sees something that reminds her of days gone by. I'm glad she brought me along to talk to. She told me about Mr. Lincoln there in Washington, DC.

"Again, it is nighttime, and I'm driving a bunch of college kids home from a field trip in Shenandoah Valley back to the college in Washington, DC. The streets of the nation's capital are almost deserted. I take a side street and make the circuit around the Lincoln Memorial. A light snow has begun to fall—big floppy flakes. The light shown on Mr. Lincoln sitting silently in his big stone chair at the top of the stairs between the tall stone columns. I stop the car. No one stirs. The kids are fast asleep. It's as if Mr. Lincoln looks down on the carful of youth and smiles. Maybe he belongs to the ages, but he belongs to us, Tip. He is a part of our home, our native land.

Yes, our country, our own, our native land. I love you.

Make New Friends but Keep the Old

The mountain laurel was blooming along the Blue Ridge Parkway, and we could see forever. We could feel the heartbeat of America as we drove south again.

The campground was spacious and friendly. There was warm Georgia sun on the meadow, and we breathed a sigh. We unloaded the camper and repacked so we could find things. I laughed to myself. All I needed was my dog dish and my feather pillow. The truck was full, but Lizbeth told me most of it was for the auction. Lizbeth's nephew was planning a big deal of an auction when these treasures from generations past would be passed on to the kids.

We didn't hurry on this Journey of the Heart. There was no deadline. We stopped at a nice lake and opened the lunch box. There was homemade whole-wheat bread Lizbeth made just before we left. She tossed me a slice, then proceeded to slather hers with mayo and put a huge slice of tomato on top. I lay in the shade of a crape myrtle tree and watched.

Lizbeth spread the blanket on the fresh green grass and took time to jot a few notes in her journal. Then she just talked to me. "Tip," she said, "I lived here as a child. My folks left me here while my Dad finished medical school in California. My mom worked in food service, so they'd have enough to live on. There was no choice. I was left with Mama Frankie and Granddaddy in the little cotton mill town here in south Georgia. I loved Granddaddy especially, Tip. When he would come home at night after a long day as a postal carrier, he would pick me up and rock me in the squeaky rocking chair on the front porch. I can still hear him singing as he rocked back and forth: 'In the sweet by and by, we shall meet on that beautiful shore'."

I crept close to the blanket there on the grass and licked her toes. I liked this Journey of the Heart. I, too, listened to the heartbeat of my country.

"Oh, Tip, I wish we could go to Savannah," Lizbeth was talking again. I think she saw the sign on the interstate that said something about, "Savannah, Next Right."

"Tip, you know me. In my heart I hug my country and say a prayer. I feel very tender toward my country. In my heart I walk down one of those suburban streets in Savannah, Georgia. I gaze at the splendor of color. In my memory the azaleas are in full bloom! What a joy to my sight after the stark white and spruce-green of New England. The contrast is dazzling! In my heart I touch the delicate petals and put my cheek close to the bright magenta flowers. There is a fragrance sometimes. Only sometimes! Each little flat home that I stroll past is surrounded by such exquisite beauty! There are mounds of azalea bushes higher than I can reach. Oh, Georgia, I cannot hold you close enough! I want to hug you to my heart, My Country, My Own, My Native Land!"

"Keep the Old ... One is Silver and the Other Gold"

By nightfall, we were in Florida. It was friendly and peaceful there under the table at ninety-year-old George's place. Lizbeth and George sat comfortably on the couch. Florida was warm, and the azaleas were actually blooming there. There was color everywhere.

George and Lizbeth have always shared music together. He has a magnificent bass harmonica, and they just sat there "breathing" together. Then, when they couldn't stand it anymore, they sang together in harmony!

I wish I could sing. I'm sure I could with the right training. Maybe I could sing tenor. George is the bass. The songs they used to sing were just as dear to their hearts as ever. They laughed, they sang, they prayed, and encouraged each other in the Lord. I know their hearts were full as they hugged warmly and affectionately, knowing this would probably be their last embrace on this earth. George is another one of those who turns ninety this year.

"Elizabeth," he said, his face showing deep emotion from his heart, "Jesus is coming soon, very soon! Oh, how I want us all to be together there! As you know, my wife, Ruth, passed away three years ago. I took care of her myself as long as I could." His sobs made his body shake as he talked about her. "I think of the youthful face I will see when we are all together again.

"We must be there, Elizabeth! And we'll see Jesus! I can imagine the look on His face when our eyes meet. He knows all about me and loves me anyway. I know that what I'm going through right now is part of the process of His creating His own character in me! When an old ninety-year-old man breaks a hip, people figure that's the end. But I know that my Redeemer lives and that He is able to keep what I have committed unto Him against that day!

"Elizabeth," George said, "my son and I have been thinking we would like to invite you to live down here when you sell your house. There's plenty of room, and if something should happen to me, my son says you could stay here as long as you want to."

I wondered what Lizbeth would say. Would we be moving to Florida!

"Dear, dear George. It touches my heart that you would make such a generous offer. I am moved almost to tears by your love and thoughtfulness! You are the only one who has seriously offered to give me a home, should I no longer be able to stay at the Old New England Farmhouse. I know that the timing would be off should I make a move now, but it gives me security to know that you would be to me as Boaz was to Ruth, and spread your wing of protection over me. You are very dear to my heart, George. Let's wait upon the Lord."

I wondered, but I couldn't ask. "What about me?" So I studied her face.

"Tip," she said, "It's not time to worry yet. You are my dog. Where I am, you will be!"

> *I wish I could sing. I'm sure I could with the right training. Maybe I could sing tenor*

When we drove away, Lizbeth and I had a peace and confidence that there will be a reunion in that land that knows no parting. I want to be there, too. I think God can work that out. George, Ruth, Jackie, Lizbeth, and I will be united again as a prayer "Platoon." I think of Hosea 2, "And she will sing there and respond as in the days of her youth …", as well as 1 Peter 5:7, "He cares for you affectionately" (AMPC).

All Creatures Great and Small

It happened when Lizbeth was sitting at the edge of a swimming pool somewhere in the South. It was far too early for people to be swimming, but to a person with white legs from the State of Maine, the sunshine felt warm, and she dangled her feet in the cool swimming pool. I found a spot under a palm tree and watched. As she sat there sipping bottled water, I noticed a wee small chameleon eying her. Of course, nobody but I knew that she had a pet chameleon in the fourth grade. He would take up residence on her long, brown, braided hair and entertain the kids.

I say nobody knew, but somehow this little creature wanted to make friends. I started to bark but changed my mind when I saw Lizbeth sprinkle a drop or two of water from the bottle onto the cement at the edge of the pool beside her. The wee small creature thought a moment, then scooted to the drop of water and lapped it with his tongue. He looked up again. She sprinkled another few drops, then another. He lapped them. Then he scurried away and turned and looked at her. She knew what he wanted, so did I. Sometimes, I look at her like that when I want something to eat. The wee small creature wanted her to catch some flies for him. Some very small flies were polluting the swimming pool, so Lizbeth picked one off the water and flicked it toward our friend. He made eye contact again, then made a dart for the fly, extending his tongue to grab it. Munch, munch! He made eye contact again and again! More flies. More and more until his little sides pooched out. Then what did he do, but come a little closer to her for a little nap in the warm sunshine. I closed my eyes, too. All was well.

Our Country

It was early morning, but the sand was warm. Lizbeth wiggled her toes in the sands of Daytona Beach, Florida. The foam of the surf was pink in the sunrise. Sandpipers scurried back and forth with the rhythm of the sea, searching for breakfast.

Spanish moss hung on the trees. I made a run for the sandpipers. But they were gone! So I just grabbed some water in my mouth and spat it out again when I found that it was salty! Lizbeth told me there was something familiar about this smell. It was a moment before she realized what it is. She was born here. She knows this smell. It was her first breath of air!

As the day began to warm, we watched a suntanned little girl in a green bathing suit building a sandcastle and trying to fortify it against the incoming tide. Lizbeth's mother played sandcastles here, too. I dug in the sand, looking for a dead fish, but up popped a crab and pinched my nose!

This is Lizbeth's home. It is woven into the fiber of her being. It's my home, too. It is our country! It's the heartbeat of America.

Strangers

It was at a truck stop at "Somewhere, USA," that Lizbeth noticed a young lady with tear-streaked face standing beside her as she paid for the gas. I knew Lizbeth's heart went out to her. She touched her arm lightly with her hand and spoke. "Has this been a bad day?"

At that, the tears gushed out, and the young lady buried her face in Lizbeth's shoulder and sobbed. "This is the worst day of my life! My mother hates me. She kicked me out. She wishes I were dead! I don't have anywhere to go, and my car is almost out of gas!" She sobbed again.

We pulled her aside, and Lizbeth spoke quietly, "Here, let's talk to God about it. He is your real Father, and He will never forsake You. He has promised to care for you affectionately."

When she finished a short prayer, the girl looked up and asked where she could find a church. Being a total stranger in the area, all Lizbeth could think of was directing her to drive down the street and let God impress her with which church to attend. I saw Lizbeth press some cash into her hand, and we drove away.

As we drove on down the highway, I heard Lizbeth praying for our God to make good on His promise and be a Father to one whose mother had forsaken her. It was a precious moment on the Journey of the Heart.

Lizbeth's Kids

A few days after we left home, we began to get warm. I wished I could leave my coat with someone and pick it up on the way back, but it is part of me!

I liked the campground. There were squirrels. Oh, if only I could climb trees! Lizbeth repacked the truck, so we could find things. I just lay on the green, green grass and thought how it might be to live in a place like this. My feet would never be cold again. Oh, but I would miss the snow! And my squirrels!

When Lizbeth saw her "kids" on the famous "Journey of the Heart," she knew it was worth it all! It was worth all the sleepless nights and arduous journeys. And when they are all together in the great hereafter, they'll weep for joy, and life will go on as God intended. Do "Very Fine Dogs" go to heaven? I'm planning to. I don't know what Lizbeth would do without me!

Linda

It was midafternoon, and the weather was warm. A gentle breeze was coming in over the ocean. All I could think of was how I would like to go swimming in the ocean. Lizbeth must have read my mind. When we arrived at Linda's, she let me take a dip in the warm water of the bay.

Linda is doing well at her first job after college, yet she is so alone now. Lizbeth's soul felt pulled to take the extra two days to visit her in South Florida. Sometimes, one must listen to the Holy Spirit and act. I knew Lizbeth's heart ached for her as we sat on the rug that night in Linda's condo by the sea. After the concert they talked for a long, long time. She shared her loneliness and her dreams.

"Linda, you have reached all the goals you set for yourself in the days when we sat with our friends with our feet under the green-striped comforter. Tell me, Linda, what are your dreams and goals now, little one?"

Linda debated whether she should say what she really wanted. Then, "I want to get married and have a baby," She smiled shyly.

"Is there someone special you are interested in right now?"

"Yes, he's so kind, so gentlemanly. He doesn't know God at all, though," she responded.

"Dear, dear Linda, I understand how you feel. I've been there, too. I had to make a hard decision. After crying all night, I knew I had to walk away," Lizbeth sighed.

Oh, I know how Lizbeth wants Linda connected to God in a way that will keep her from falling. It's hard when you are an "only" in a secular world. But Lizbeth believes in her. She believes she will make good decisions, even if there may be temporary heartache. Sometimes the Journey of the Heart makes the heart ache.

For breakfast we walked down the street to an outdoor cafe. I guess they did that so I could be with them. I crawled under the table. Maybe something would accidentally drop. The food smelled so good. They had waffles with fresh garden strawberries and whipped cream. Made my mouth water. But it's no use to beg. Somewhere, Lizbeth got the idea that you don't feed dogs at the table. Yet again, I realized that my place in life is to lie quietly under the table and pray they drop the whole thing!

I was hoping we could stay a long time. I like Linda. She was one of the prayer team that used to meet on Sabbath afternoon at our Old New England Farmhouse and pray and "juice" the Bible stories. But that was then. This is now. We waved goodbye and drove away.

"God," Lizbeth prayed as we traveled on down the road, "You know her. You are the great God, the only God. You see the future. I know You want both of them in heaven. Please, Father, please, press back the powers of darkness and glorify Your name. She belongs to You!"

We both felt the heartbeat of a friend.

It Will Be Worth It All

The younger ones we visited on this Journey of the Heart, were once Lizbeth's earliteen kids. They are still bonded to her heart because of their time together and with the Lord. It was the shared experiences again. I don't remember, but they tell me of the camping weekend in the front pasture at the Old New England Farmhouse. They tell me of the prayer time sprawled on the floor in the office under the green-striped comforter. They had a pretty little prayer book with pink roses on it. These intimate Sabbath afternoons were very tender moments. I guess you could say they were moments of the heart.

These intimate Sabbath afternoons were very tender moments. I guess you could say they were moments of the heart

One of their activities was the ministry trips where the kids put on the services at various small churches in New England. All these bound their hearts together and to God with the strong cords of love and devotion that are forged only in youth. Now they are grown.

We visit Debbie and Ryan and their son, Ben. He's such an active cradle roll child. But kids with lots of energy usually get things done! We're proud of his dad, too. He gets things done! The last time we were here was before Debbie was married. But she had a little apartment there in the Collegedale village.

When she heard that "Miss Elizabeth" was going to be there over Sabbath, she called all our youth in the Collegedale area to spend the whole day together at her apartment. Oh, I get all excited thinking about it! Out of the six from our prayer group, twenty-one showed up! We had the Green-striped Comforter with us, of course. The kids used to sit on the floor on the green rug and cover their feet with this Green-striped Comforter. This item went with them on all their mission trips.

So, of course, we sat on the floor in Debbie's apartment. There were forty-two feet all together under the Green-striped Comforter. I noticed that all of them knew the same songs! And the boys have grown, now, into men. They made such beautiful harmony. Oh, I wonder if the Pearly White City could be any more worshipful.

Now, lying under Ryan and Debbie's table on a Sabbath afternoon, I can tell that Lizbeth's heart feels warmed and comforted by the friendship that survived their teen years, and now is even stronger in adulthood. Whenever they are all together, they remember the shared experiences and remind each other of their appointment the second Sabbath after we get to heaven. We'll all be together there under the Fourteenth Palm Tree Down on the Silver Street right after church. It'll be a potluck. Yes, surely, Very Fine Dogs will be there too.

Lizbeth's kids will all be together. Lizbeth prays for them every night. Each class has its own special time and place to meet, but Lizbeth can imagine the whole group all together … and we'll never part again. Yes, as Lizbeth visits the youth of yesterday, she tells me it will be worth it all! She can feel their heartbeat.

Next of Kin—He Prayeth Best Who Loveth Best

DeWitte, our next of kin, is Lizbeth's baby brother! I know it gives Lizbeth heart to pray with him, to share the spiritual insights they have received that help them along their daily journey. I hear them on the phone several times a week.

Sometimes it's short. Sometimes they just open their hearts and share their souls. I guess you could call them soulmates.

Dee is a lover of the beautiful and has created a town of miniature castles and houses made of clay, crafted by his own fingers! The town is on the bank of a miniature river … people call it a stream. I waded in and sat in the cool water. I turned around and looked over my shoulder and smiled at Lizbeth. She was smiling, too. She winked at me, and I knew she wasn't mad.

Adding to the uniqueness of the miniature town is the superb landscaping. Vegetation flourishes all year there in Calhoun, Georgia. The local church owns the property, and they have given Dee permission to exercise his gifts of art, craftsmanship, horticulture, and friendship at the edge of the field about 100 yards from the church. "The Garden" is a place where people can come and commune with nature, with each other, and with God.

Occasionally, there will be a festival there. The castles and miniature homes come alive with candlelight at sunset, children squeal with delight, mothers bring snacks, fathers stand in little clumps and talk "man talk" around the food, and the old folks watch and smile from their lawn chairs, listening to the friendly chatter of the festivities. They hug their grandchildren. Their grandchildren hug ME! I like it here.

Lizbeth's baby brother is a man who has chosen to live life joyfully despite the broken dreams, the broken relationships, the losses. When they are together, they release their exuberance of soul and run together through the mountain meadow. And me? I laugh and look for squirrels!

Her brother has taught her how to release the perfume of her own alabaster box and live with exuberance. Maybe that's one reason she is so special to me. She smells of exuberance.

I think the quote from Coleridge's "Rime of the Ancient Mariner" sums up her brother: "He prayeth best, who loveth best All things both great and small."

I'm not sure how many grandchildren Dee has. He has eight children. "Every cat had seven kits ..." This could add up! Lizbeth and I park ourselves in the garden and let the children climb all over us. One falls asleep in her lap. Next-of-kin need hugs and a lap to nestle into! The older ones need their aunt Elizabeth to talk to about things like "what makes it night" and "tell me about when I was born," and "I miss my mommy."

I watch Dee and Lizbeth enjoying each other. They talk about what used to be. And about why they turned out the way they did. It's a comfortable time together. They cry. I think how lucky they are to have each other. There are almost thirteen years between them, but it doesn't matter! They are soulmates.

We get in the truck and drive away. He waves as long as he can see us. I give the Kleenex box a push with my nose. I think she'll be needing them.

A Soldier and a Gentleman

One of the more significant blessings of the "Journey of the Heart" was spending time with DeWitte's second son, Laramie. On Saturday night Laramie and wife, Laura, put together an auction. Laramie was the auctioneer and gave each participant an equal amount of Monopoly® money. The items to be auctioned were from Aunt Lizbeth's treasures and were treasures that needed to be passed on from her own father, who never lived to see these great-grandchildren.

I love grandchildren. I wish I could get a real job taking care of DeWitt's grandchildren. They are so much fun. You can lick their faces and help yourself to the food they try to hold up so you can't get it. They squeal, and I laugh! But I know Lizbeth can't get along without me.

At the auction I thought there would be a demonstration of greed and possessiveness but was heartened by the unselfishness and camaraderie of this family. Did I mention there are seven of them? The older kids helped the younger kids to bargain. Sometimes, two or more would pool their money and buy an item together!

Laramie even bartered for his grandfather's toy train, and then gave it to his older brother, Edward, because he knew how badly Ed wanted it. I could tell that almost made Lizbeth cry. There was a lump in my throat, too! Laramie is a "soldier and a gentleman."

When we went to bed that night, Lizbeth told me her own alabaster box had been refilled to overflowing by the unselfishness of her family. We were content.

Our Country

As I sat by Lizbeth on the grandstand at the fairground, I spotted a matched pair of black Tennessee Walking Horses prancing in a tight circle at the in-gate. Their black western saddles with silver trim reflected the morning sunshine. One rider carried the American flag, floating in the summer breeze. The other carried the Missouri state flag.

> *I looked at Lizbeth. Tears were streaming down her face. She always cries when they play the "Star-spangled Banner" at horse shows*

The gate opened, and the matched pair entered. The little Hammond organ on the platform outside the riding ring began to play. A strong, suntanned farmer stood beside the organ facing the grandstand. "Oh, say, can you see? ..." The crowd stood, and the words rang out. The matched pair of black Tennessee Walking Horses circled smoothly around the ring, flags flying.

"Oh, say does that star-spangled banner yet wave

O'er the land of the free and the home of the brave!"

I looked at Lizbeth. Tears were streaming down her face. She always cries when they play the "Star-spangled Banner" at horse shows. I get a lump in my throat, too. We love our country! It's our home, our native land.

We love the corner of the country where we live. But it's not just this little corner that we love… not just the rocky coast of Maine with the crying of the gulls and the lapping of the water and the hazy sunrise on an August morning. This little corner is only a part of the whole. That whole is a part of us, and we are a part of it. "This is my own, my native land." All of it.

I'm a Great American Cattle Dog! I'm an American! We felt the heartbeat of America!

Cousin Gwen

Cousin Gwen from Lizbeth's father's side is nearer to her than a sister. You see, they shared their earliest years together more like twins than cousins. But Gwen is older. She is three months older, and always will be the oldest. Gwen's mother and father shared the little house in Griffin, Georgia, with our granddaddy and our grandma, affectionately known as "Mama Frankie." Lizbeth came to stay with them when she was only a few weeks old. Her parents were doing medical school in California. Mama Frankie would dress Gwen and Lizbeth Ann alike and bathe and feed them together. They learned the same songs and Bible verses at Mama Frankie's knee. And while she sewed little things for them to wear, the girls would play with the pretty buttons in the button drawers on either side of the old treadle sewing machine.

Lizbeth Ann tells me that these dear ones have all passed on now. She and Gwen are the only ones that can remember.

When they are together, it is as if there has been no lapse in time. They take up right where they left off. Gwen is bound to Lizbeth Ann's heart and Lizbeth Ann to hers. Gwen is a safe person. She never scolds and never tells secrets.

Her life has been hard, really hard. But through it all, she has become gentle, meek, and unassuming. The two share their deepest thoughts and feelings because there is so much they don't have to explain—they just know.

The time together on the trip was a deep spiritual blessing. Every morning Gwen would do her hair in the bathroom while Lizbeth sat on the john and read from the Word as they shared insights from the Lord.

It's easy to let the alabaster box pour forth perfume with a person like that. They liked me there. Especially Gary. He knows I'm a Very Fine Dog. And Lizbeth? She felt the heartbeat of her own flesh and blood.

Blue Bonnets

I was listening to the folks there in the convenience store somewhere in the middle of Texas. They were telling Lizbeth about some flowers they call "Bluebonnets." "They are out now!" They said. It seemed like everybody in the store was smiling and saying, "The bluebonnets are out! The bluebonnets are out!" And sure enough, as we drove across the wide-open spaces, there were miles of the most beautiful color.

The bluebonnets reminded me of miniature lupine. They weren't very tall, but there they were amid the bright orange of the California poppies. Lizbeth stopped the truck, and we got out for a romp amid the flowers! Oh, I was hoping we could do that! I sleep most of the time in the back seat, but when she stops the car, I always hope it will be for a run and a potty break. Lizbeth stooped and petted the poppies and the bluebonnets. I like the way she pets things. She pets me that way, too. Bluebonnets—these are the heartbeat of America.

Dollie

Cousin Dollie and Lizbeth have a special bond. They are nearest in age of all the cousins on the Lucas side of the family. It was as if Dollie were Lizbeth's own "sister." You see, Dollie lived with "Daddy Talmadge" and "Mama Sue" while Dollie's dad finished medical school.

When Lizbeth and Dollie are singing harmony, it's like singing with the angels. I know—I curled up in the corner and listened. Oh, how I wish I could sing with them. But again, it seems that no one really appreciates my talents. They think I am howling!

Dollie can harmonize anything! But about twelve years ago, she presented with symptoms of Parkinson's disease. Dollie and her husband Harold, have no children and live far off the beaten path in central Tennessee. Funds are scarce, and they live a spartan life. Lizbeth felt it in her heart to reconnect with her precious cousin. They used to "walk into the house of the Lord in company" (see Ps. 54:14).

Lizbeth told me that Parkinson's patients almost always have tense necks, so she just asked Dollie if she could use her physical therapy hands to give her a neck massage. Giving back and neck rubs gives relaxed time to talk together. It was a peaceful time there on the mattress on the floor with Dollie and Harold and Lizbeth and me. Lizbeth shared with Dollie clips from her own life and some of the times when the Lord has carried her. The most significant moment of the visit came when Dollie looked up into Lizbeth's face and said wistfully, "You talk like you *know* Him."

I saw tears come into Lizbeth's eyes, and all she could say was, "Yes, Dollie, I do."

It was the time to feel the heartbeat of her own family.

Our Country's New Mexico

The vastness of New Mexico is what Lizbeth needs when life becomes cluttered. The buttes and the tablelands appeared. In this vast country, our country bares her soul. The bare bones of the earth expose themselves, and there is beauty.

Lizbeth has taken this trip over and over again, somehow resenting the desert. It has always seemed such a wasted land. Today, she looked more closely. Yes, she can name our country's vegetation, tumbleweed, sagebrush, yucca, ocotillo, saguaro. Today, I heard her apologize for her attitude toward New Mexico. "You, too, are my own, my native land. You show me yourself, your honest self. I've never been through this vast desertland in the springtime before. Last night it rained! You drank the water! I look more closely and see some of the dry bushes come alive! There's a pink tint to the dry desert bush. I've got to have a closer look." She parks alongside the road and gets out of the truck. There are tiny pink flowers up and down each stalk. They are individually so perfect. Should they be magnified, they would look something like a microscopic petunia. The entire stalk is covered as if it were a pussy willow. She picks one and takes it along to ponder. "What a delight! Yes, I owe you an apology; please accept."

Our Country's Great Divide

The motor purred on and on across our country. It was still early morning when we saw the hoary summits of the Great Rocky Mountains dead ahead. No, it wasn't clouds, it was the mighty summits, the summits of our country's Great Divide.

"Tip, we gotta do this! Let's go up there and listen to the heartbeat of our country! We gotta do this!" I felt the excitement. We left the main highway and took US Route 50 through Monarch Pass over the mountains to Montrose, Colorado. It was another one of those now-forsaken red roads on the map. I looked out the window. There was no traffic on this little two-lane highway. Up and up and up, we went, into the mountains toward the sky. The road was desolate. We were all alone. A small sign read, "Summit, 19,125 feet above sea level."

We stopped the car and got out. Lizbeth put my leash on my collar. We must be miles from the Old New England Farmhouse, and she was afraid I would get lost if I started to herd the antelope or spotted a squirrel! The wind swept down from the stately, snow-covered mountains. It was cold. I was thankful for my fur coat. There, on all sides, were the hoary-headed monarchs of the Rocky Mountains peering silently down at us. I pressed close to Lizbeth's leg. I felt so small. We both stood silent. Then the silence of these great snow-covered mountains began to speak. "We are the silent strength of this great nation. We are part of the whole. We are the heartbeat of America."

We stood silent again. We watched the wind blowing the snow across the summit. There was a stillness that filled both of us with awe. We were loath to leave. Etched in our memory were the silent monarchs with cords that bind us more strongly about our nation, our home. Our hearts beat together.

Our Country's Arizona

"Look at this, Tip!" Lizbeth said as the sun began to decline in the west. "Look at these shadows!" As the shadows lengthen, we see the purple desert. The sky even has a few puffy clouds far away. They turn purple, too, when the sun has set. And could it be that there, in the blue moonlight, even the spiny cactus are purple? Lizbeth puts down the window and lets the night air accompany us as we drive.

"There's a scent I never noticed before, Tip. It's the sagebrush, but this time, it's sagebrush in the rain!" Lizbeth smiles. "Do I have another apology to make?"

From the ranch on the west side of the mountain, overlooking Tucson, we watch the desert sunset. Lizbeth knows the silhouette of the mountains where Tucson does her best sunsets. Green light, flaming red and gold, and yellow and orange light … as we blink, the scene changes. Then, as the full moon rises behind us, we sit quietly and watch our city. "Tip, I have feelings about our cities. I see them teeming with lonely people. I want to tuck them all under the shadow of the wings of the Almighty.

"But tonight, Tip, they are celebrating the Fourth of July. The birthday of our own, our native land. My heart is full." There in the dusk of the desert city, a thousand fireworks begin. Each one trying to outdo the other. From all over the city's flat expanse, the skyrockets and whirligigs blaze! Lizbeth squeals and claps her hands as we watch! At last, the evening fades into night, and the city turns off the lights. We sit silently, watching the moon set across the same mountains that invited the sunset. There is the smell of night air and sagebrush and the sounds of the night. We sleep.

One Is Silver, the Other Gold

It was raining and windy here in Southern California when we stopped to spend the Sabbath with yet another life-long friend and prayer partner. Gerry is a couple of years younger than George and Ingrid. Lizbeth was telling me about Gerry. It was during Lizbeth's tumultuous early teen years that they became prayer partners. Lizbeth would flee for sanctuary to the little chapel just three doors away at the big hospital in Los Angeles. She and Gerry never discussed what was going on in her young life, but Gerry would meet her in the chapel, and together, they would pour out their conversational prayer into the ears of our prayer-hearing God.

Lizbeth told me about the time she and Gerry were stranded on the Los Angeles Freeway late at night. The little Morris Minor just quit. It died. It refused to start again. Gerry said, "Let's pray!" They did, but when Lizbeth tried the starter again, there was silence.

"Let's pray again!" Gerry said. And they did. Still, it refused to start. Lizbeth was trying to think of something else they could do, but all by themselves on the L. A. Freeway in the middle of the night, there were not any other options. I guess it was before the days of cell phones and Triple-A.

So Gerry said a third time, "Let's pray!" I wish I could have heard that prayer. I almost feel like I did because I listened to them pray all weekend.

Lizbeth tried again! This time, it kicked in, and the little car crept to the nearby exit! There was a Shell service station right there. The mechanic just shook his head and said, "Lady, you have thrown a rod, but I think you can make it back to Pasadena where you live. Go real slow."

It was the wee hours of the morning when they got to bed. When Lizbeth woke in the morning, Gerry wasn't to be seen. Lizbeth looked again, and there was Gerry on her knees by the bed. Praying!

Now, some years later, they are together again. I could tell it was heartening for them to kneel there together in the simple home in the shadow of Mt. San Jacinto that towered above the southern California valley. I got to listen to the "praise the Lord stories" and instances of closeness to our Maker. The perfume of God's own alabaster box mingled with theirs and brought joy to their hearts.

Gerry's dog didn't like me. He is a little stray chihuahua that followed Gerry home. Seems he should be a little more sociable. But I guess he didn't have a very good upbringing. I had to stay under the radar, but it didn't seem to bother Lizbeth or Gerry. Seemed Gerry smiled the whole time we were there. Lizbeth tells me that Gerry is eighty-eight years old. I gave her due obeisance and let her scratch me behind the ears. We got to sleep in Gerry's house because the wind and the rain were like a hurricane. I wanted to hide under the bed!

I'm expecting to see Gerry, and maybe even her sassy little chihuahua there in that "Pearly White City!"

Till We Meet at Jesus Feet

Lizbeth tells me that Aunt Ruthie is her own mother's baby sister, who used to wash Lizbeth's baby diapers. Auntie Ruthie reminds her of that every time she visits. This year is number ninety for Aunt Ruthie, too. It was only a few weeks from birth until Lizbeth went to live with her grandparents in Georgia.

Auntie Ruthie reminds Lizbeth no more because she is living only in the present moment. But her children come often.

They make her smile, they give her love and hugs—and so do Lizbeth and I. They pray together with Auntie Ruthie, Dwight, Jean, and Lizbeth. They pray for God to give Aunt Ruthie the comfort of His presence. Then, we left her in the care of others while we went for lunch.

Lizbeth's beautiful red-headed cousin Jeannie share a bond as cousins that is uniquely their own. Lizbeth prays that Jean and Dwight may be sustained in their care of this precious saint of God. May God give them courage, energy, and cheerfulness to do their God-given task. May He hold them near to His heart.

I smile because Lizbeth is the oldest cousin on the Lucas side of the family. They give her due respect as the historian. You see, Lizbeth understands. She understands how it is to be a caregiver and watch the one you love slip silently away farther and farther from reality.

Dwight went to do his business on his computer, while the girls sat on the grass there in the park and talked. They were thankful they have each other to share burdens. They have memories of being together on the farm in Missouri and of attending the neat little white church on the ridge across the valley. Their red-headed Uncle Felix would lead the singing in his strong tenor voice. "God be with you till we meet again …."

On this beautiful day of spring, the southern California hills were green with spring grass. Lizbeth tells me it is this way every year in March. She tells me chimes still ring on an Easter morning from Mt. Rubidoux— and she gets that faraway look in her eyes. She remembers. It was once home to her. She rode her horse away into the hills and away from people.

Sometimes she just needs to be alone and cry. Dogs understand. I pressed close to her leg and licked the back of her hand.

Almond Blossoms

We watch you, our country. You spread out before us as we come down off the Grapevine pass into the San Joaquin Valley. The valley is watered now. There are circles and squares of green and gold and brown, all watered by the irrigation ditches of the aqueduct. There are grapevines and white almond blossoms and pink peach blossoms. You feed America.

It's one of those warm spring noontides. I wish I could get out and romp through that green, green grass. It looks almost electric! The mountains rise off the valley to the right. There's an exit ramp! Lizbeth is thinking what I am thinking. We drive toward the mountains, but stop before we get there and get out of the car. Lizbeth takes off her shoes, and we run together through the grass toward the almond trees. The whole place smells like almond trees in blossom! Oh, what a glorious day. A little brown bunny sees me and tries to get away. I go full speed ahead and circle around in front. I think I can herd the little thing back to Lizbeth. I'm sure she wants to see what I brought her. Suddenly, as it came, the bunny is gone. Oh, no! I put my nose to the ground and catch the scent. There! There! He's in the boysenberry bushes. It's no use. Rabbit in the briar patch! I read about that in the Br'er Rabbit book. The rabbit always wins!

> *We drive toward the mountains, but stop before we get there and get out of the car. Lizbeth takes off her shoes, and we run together through the grass toward the almond trees*

The cool grass and moist sod feel good on our feet. I watch Lizbeth wiggle her toes and turn her face to the sunshine.

Then I heard a humming! It wasn't Lizbeth. No, it was honey bees. Lizbeth started to put her face in a clump of white almond blossoms but pulled back. Honey bees! They are doing their work, pollinating each little blossom. There'll be lots of almonds come October. We order them every year to be mailed to us in Maine while they are fresh. Lizbeth makes granola with them. Personally, I'd rather eat dog food, but her friends love granola and expect that for breakfast when they come to visit!

Bounding through the green, green grass is what makes this journey of the heart meaningful to Lizbeth. I feel her heart. It swells with love for all of nature! I know! I'm her dog!

Diane

She has been a life-long friend. She even worked with Lizbeth in starting the Traveling Medical Professionals registry. Lizbeth's heart was yearning for time to reconnect, to play together, pray together, sing together, to mutually support and encourage each other in their spiritual journey.

Diane called before we got there to tell us that the doctor had diagnosed her with tachy-brady syndrome. The heart would race at full speed, then slow to thirty to forty beats per minute. There were PVC's and PAC's and atrial fibrillation. There was a strong chance that soon, her heart would just stop—never to go again. Now, Diane is only two and a half years younger than Lizbeth, so this hit close to her heart.

The mood was somber when we arrived. Both son David and hubby Doug realized the seriousness of the condition. When we got there, they scheduled an implantation of a pacemaker to take care of the bradycardia. But they couldn't seem to do anything to keep the heart from running away with her in tachycardia. I was glad God let Lizbeth be there during this stressful time. She told me the most fulfilling part was the spiritual encouragements they experienced in the early mornings together. Lizbeth felt comfortable sitting on Diane's bed and reading to her out of *Desire of Ages*. I know all about it—I was under the bed with their dog, Trixie. The girls reviewed the promises. They prayed together intensely. They sang together while Doug played the organ. And they cried together. They humbled themselves before God and confessed their sins. They recommitted their lives all over again. The last morning we were there, Lizbeth, who is an elder in our local church, was impressed to take the anointing oil and anoint Diane for physical and spiritual healing. It was a peaceful, joyful time together with Jesus.

Lizbeth and I felt a real connection with her adult son, David, on this journey. He, too, loves the Lord and earnestly wants a deeper experience with Jesus. Then, as a bonus, David taught Lizbeth how to make oatmeal waffles! I wish they would let me have a whole one!

I knew Lizbeth especially hated to leave this family this time. Seems that on this journey, she dreaded parting more than usual! Maybe there is a reason. Not all the friends we saw on this trip will be there, should I make the trip again.

Mary

I liked Mary. Her dog is well-trained and smells right.

It was while Mary and "Lizzy" were at Pacific Union College that they became friends. They were amazed at how much they had in common as they sat on the gym floor in the sunshine with the coach, Ingrid.

Mary's dad was a doctor—Lizzy's, too. Mary was the oldest—Lizzy, too.

Mary had two brothers—Lizzy, too. One was much younger—Lizzy, too.

Their family spent a couple of years in the Far East for the U.S. Government—Lizzy's, too.

Mary took pre-nursing and switched to physical education—Lizzy, too.

They both transferred to Andrews University their junior year. Upon graduation, Mary taught in Lincoln, Nebraska—Lizzy taught in Washington, DC.

The list keeps going on and on. As with Cousin Gwen and Cousin Dollie, there were lots of things Mary and Lizzy didn't need to explain because they instinctively knew. Then many years ago, a rift came in their friendship. The dynamics changed. On the Journey we stopped there at the college where the girls first sat on the gym floor in the sunshine with Ingrid. The sacred school flower, Diogenes' lantern, was in bloom when Mary and Lizzy took a walk through the meadows in the hills with me.

Lizbeth told me she knew she needed to apologize for the rift created between them some years before. She swallowed hard, then began, "Mary, I want to ask you to forgive me for the things I did to you."

Mary just looked at her and smiled. "What things?" is all Mary said and smiled. Lizbeth knew she was forgiven. Like God, Mary remembered the sins no more and never made mention of them again!

Their hearts were lighter as they hiked along in the warm morning sunshine through the hills where they once hiked with the hiking club.

There was an unspoken peace that all was well. And me? All I could find were ground squirrels!

Arlene

She was there in the microbiology lab that first day of college. She has just always been there in Lizbeth's life ever since. She was a good student, but more than that, she was a good, wholesome young lady from Strawberry Valley, California, a few hours into the mountains outside Sacramento. Little did they know as they viewed slides of e-coli and b-subtilis that they would be lifelong friends. The next year, Arlene and roommate Heidi were suite-mates with Lizbeth and roommate, Hossie. There are fun dorm stories that won't be told here, but Arlene knows them, and Lizbeth knows them, and they told me!

Arlene married and moved to Korea, where husband Joe went to medical school. They came back to the States for internship.

Then tragedy struck. It was on a church picnic that Joe went for a swim with the rest of the group and never came back! Arlene was left with four young children and a declining mother.

When the family was on the way to Jamaica, the visas didn't clear. They had already moved out of their home, and they didn't know how long the wait would be before they could get to Jamaica. Well, Lizbeth invited them to stay with her. There were six of them and a one-bathroom, three-bedroom house. There were seven puppies, five horses, four cats, and a cow and four calves! It was a busy summer. Lizbeth loves pets and kids! There was plenty of room out of doors, and the kids could walk to the shore if there were an adult.

Now time has fled. I could see the peace in Lizbeth's face as we camped there on Arlene and Bob's little farm. There was a peacefulness about Bob and Arlene's place in the mountains of northern California that made one seem far away from the struggle and strife of life. There was a huge fenced yard so I could look for squirrels.

Arlene is a comforting person. She often sings around the house, and when she and Lizbeth are together, there is two-part harmony! When Diane is there with them, there is three-part harmony! They tell me that once upon a time, cousin Dollie was there to make it four-part harmony! And since they all sort of grew up together, they taught each other their repertoire of songs. On Sunday they sat together beside the river with the church folks while the Pathfinders did their fifty-mile bike ride. The baby blue eyes were blooming and mixed in with the orange of the California poppies. The riverbank was covered with stunning color. Baby blue eyes have always been special to Lizbeth. I noticed that Mary's eyes are the same color as the baby blue eyes!

But Lizbeth's favorite moment of the time with Arlene on the Journey of the Heart was first thing in the morning. The air was still and fresh. There was the smell of pine and cedar. She opened the door of the little camper to let me out to do my chores, and there was Arlene just coming out of the house with Bible in hand. The girls just sat together on the bed in the camper and spent an hour or so in worship together. They sang, they prayed, they shared, yes, and cried a little. It was safe.

Debbie and Dan

Doug and Diane's daughter, Debbie lives in southeast Washington State, a two days' journey north of her parents. I liked it there. I got to round up the horses. Dan and Debbie have about twenty of them! I got into the burdocks again. I just don't know how to stay out of them. But Lizbeth and Debbie spent some time pulling burdocks out of my coat. I was a bit embarrassed!

Lizbeth felt impressed that she should spend time alone with Debbie and give her a chance to connect on a deeper level as an adult. After dinner with Debbie and Dan, the girls talked for a long time while Dan did his computer work. I pretended to be asleep. I don't tell secrets, and neither does Lizbeth.

Debbie had a chance to ask questions and get answers from someone who had known the whole family since Debbie's mother was seventeen. It was that first year at Berrien Springs that they met. Debbie and Lizbeth talked about some of the experiences, and though they cried together, they felt encouraged as they prayed for each other and for the family.

Lizbeth told me that she is pained deeply that a road trip is only a temporary band-aid for lonely lives. Yes, we came home like we always do, missing the ones we had become reconnected with. I found Lizbeth crying inside because, like us herd dogs, she feels uneasy and unsettled when we can't get all our flock together. Lizbeth told me about Jesus and how His heart yearns for the companionship of His people's presence more than they yearn for His. Imagine how they will feel when they are all herded together again! Maybe they will sing, "Never Part Again!" Will there be tears of joy when it finally hits us that this is for real! We'll feel at home there because it really IS home!

Our Country's Washington State

A part of our country is the Yakima Valley along the Yakima River in Washington State. Lizbeth tells me they lived here when she was only nine. They let her climb the cherry tree and pick cherries with the rest of the family. "One for me and one for the bucket, one for me and one for the bucket!" The sun was warm and made playful shadows through the leaves of the cherry tree. The big, dark red cherries almost glowed in the sunshine.

We find ourselves in the Yakima Valley again. There should be a river here. Yes, we park the truck and walk across the grass to the edge of the river. Lizbeth takes off her shoes and steps in. The water is cool, the Washington summer air warm. Ah, it feels so good to wade in and sit in the cool water. I soak a bit, then stand up and shake. Lizbeth squeals and laughs.

This is our country, our home, and we are bound by strong cords to this part of the whole. We felt the heartbeat of America!

Marguerite

Lizbeth had lost track of Marguerite. They were colleagues at Columbia Union College in Washington, DC, during those years of teaching. She told me about one bright winter day just after a major snowstorm. The city was shut down. All was quiet.

A very tall Being in a long white garment fell into step with her and was walking beside her. She didn't see His face, but she felt a peace and confidence that all would be well, no matter what the outcome

Snow sparkled on the branches of the oak trees as the two of them tramped, ran, skidded, and laughed along the winter wonderland of the deserted Sligo Creek Parkway.

Interestingly, they both talked about death that day. Both of them had a dream that they were dying. Lizbeth's dream was of a hospital where someone had put electrodes on her head and was getting ready to throw the switch. But she felt no fear. Someone who loved her was there with her. She couldn't identify who it was, but still knew it was someone who loved her.

Marguerite's dream was of dying also, and the thing that stood out in her mind was also the fact that there was someone there beside her that loved her. She was not afraid either. I'm glad Marguerite shared that with Lizbeth because it has been important to her since that time to "be there" at critical times in the lives of her friends. It has been so rewarding to her!

Lizbeth and Marguerite changed jobs and went their separate ways. Now, some fifty years later, Lizbeth got word through the grapevine that Marguerite was in grave physical crisis. Lizbeth called. It was then that she told Lizbeth that she was facing open-heart surgery and that they didn't hold out a lot of hope for a full recovery. She had been concerned. She was thinking of the situation as she was walking into Walmart. A very tall Being in a long white garment fell into step with her and was walking beside her. She didn't see His face, but she felt a peace and confidence that all would be well, no matter what the outcome.

Lizbeth and Marguerite and I spent Sabbath together drinking in the beauty of the western mountains that are Marguerite's home in northeastern Oregon. Then, in the evening, they sat on the floor in front of the fireplace and shared their spiritual history. They were strengthened in the Lord even as David and Jonathan were able to strengthen each other in the Lord on their last visit together before Jonathan's death. Their faith was encouraged.

The next morning at breakfast, Marguerite told us that during the night, God had impressed her with her own selfishness. She hadn't seen things in quite that light before. She realized that everything she did was tinged with self. She came to God for His forgiveness. All was well. A few weeks later, God impressed Lizbeth of the same thing!

Our Country's Nighttime in Nevada

How is it that the stars are so big and bright at night on the lonely road, Route 50, across the middle of Nevada somewhere between Ely and Reno? We stopped in the vastness of the desert, got out of the car, and looked up at the heavens. They were bright with stars so close together you couldn't crowd another star into the space. The desert night was quiet except for the stirring of the wind in the sagebrush and yucca. The stars in the black dome of the heavens seemed to roll on forever. Wave after wave of galaxies that, from the desert of Nevada, seemed like only stars in the black night. They seemed to wink at me. The night air felt cool on my black nose after the day's travel. There was the smell of sagebrush and the howl of a coyote. I wonder where they live. I wonder if we could romp together on the desert hills? But Lizbeth tells me they run in packs, and that they would grab my hamstrings and bring me down, and I wouldn't have a prayer of a chance. We drove on through the night, yet there were a quiet peace and assurance of the presence of our God. This, too, is our home, our native land.

Alexander

No, it's not as though Lizbeth didn't know Alex. They worked at the hospital together off and on. He was the on, and she was the off. Lizbeth's heart always felt tender toward him because of the love they shared for God.

Then suddenly, Alex lost his soulmate in a tragedy.

Next thing Lizbeth knew, he was planning to move to out West all alone, leaving his friends, his grown kids, and all the memories. Her heart went out to him because what he was planning was something she had done a few years before when life got brittle. She knew the pangs of loneliness, the tears, the strangeness, the sense of just being all alone. Lizbeth decided to risk opening up to him. He didn't reject her, so she decided to write notes of encouragement to him every week and send Safari Survival Stories. These stories are about what it was like traveling all alone, far from home when her own life fell apart.

I tell her she should put all those stories together and make another book. But what about me? I only know the stories by hearsay!

On the Journey of the Heart, Lizbeth was drawn out West in hopes of maybe being of some encouragement. When her heart says, "Go," she has learned that she'd better "Go"! I knew she was afraid, afraid of rejection. But when she saw him, her heart skipped. His eyes lighted, he opened his arms, hugged her to himself, and planted a little kiss on her forehead.

Next day, we took a picnic and went exploring in the canyon. Even if I had to stay on the leash, it was OK. Lizbeth appreciated the time to relax and enjoy his company. She felt accepted and secure. They shared on a deep level that I thought was only open to her dog. "It's safe, Liz, it's safe," he reassured her. It was a very vulnerable time for them both.

Sometimes, I could see Lizbeth's eyes glisten with tears. They talked a lot about his wife, Andrea. Lizbeth's heart was moved. Lizbeth and I felt as if we knew her.

At the canyon vista point, we stood on the rock together and looked over the vastness of the Flaming Gorge. Alex put his arm around Lizbeth's waist and pulled her to his side. They sang. They sang, "God Bless America." It's one of my favorites. Our spirits seemed to expand with the vastness. The hoary summits of the Great Divide reared their heads again. They seemed to roll on and on and on until they finally faded from view. I loved the vastness!

As we were driving on through the tablelands, I spied something that made my heart leap. There was just something in me that felt the urge to herd. They didn't look like horses; they didn't look like deer. They had horns and stripes, but didn't look at all like zebra! About that time, Alex spoke. "Don't blink, or you'll miss them! There is a herd of antelope right over there! You really have to watch out for them when you are driving. If they decide to rush across the road, they just don't stop. They look so much like the landscape and blend in with the colors, you can miss them, and they are upon you before you know it."

So that's what they are! We must be in the land "where the deer and the antelope play!" I thought how fun it would be to go on a trail ride with Lizbeth and Alex and have a chance to circle and herd the antelope! Oh, if only!

Alex loves to talk about God. People like to talk about what they love. He seemed to want to go deeper. So does Lizbeth. It is as if he is a mentor to her yet a colleague.

The visit was short, and when we parted, I found Lizbeth feeling abandoned again. We cried together. I licked the back of her hand. There was something about Alex that I haven't found in anyone else. I came to him and put my head on his knee. He reached down and took my head in both his hands and looked deep into my soul. I knew I could trust him to have veto power over all my decisions for the rest of my life, too.

Lizbeth and I had to have a talk.

Our Country's Heartland

We drive down out of the snowcapped mountains and into the city of Denver, then on beyond into the breadbasket of our country. Lizbeth's heart is bound by loving memories to America's Heartland. She looks across the freshly-mown hayfields of north-central Missouri and feels again the sweat running down her face and into her eyes as she helped our uncle in the hayfield. Meadowlarks sing their silver-throated songs from the fence posts in the noonday heat. A herd of black Angus cattle is under the shade of the oak trees chewing slowly with their mouths open.

Later, the lightning bugs blink in the twilight. In her memory she rides bareback down the dirt road east of the farmhouse in the moonlight. A coyote howls far away. Big green bullfrogs croak in the pond that rests quietly at the foot of the hills. Her heart is bound to these people who sing, "The Sweet By and By" in the little white church that sits on the ridge overlooking the rolling hills that go on forever. This, too, is our home. This is our own, our native land. Yet it's the people we love that make our country our own.

Alyssa

We had to get a motel before we got to Chicago. Lizbeth didn't want to take a chance navigating Chicago traffic and trying to find Alyssa at Wheaton College. So Alyssa kindly took a whole day off to come to Berrien Springs to spend time with Lizbeth. She still calls her "Miss Elizabeth," and Lizbeth calls her "Miss Alyssa." They laugh a lot.

This place had a heated pool. I didn't even ask if I could go in. I'm only a dog, and it's OK because I know I'm a Very Fine Dog. I waited.

It was really the walk that I want to tell you about. A walk through the woods is a good time to sniff around and maybe find a squirrel! I could hear them talking, though. Lizbeth asked Alyssa what she was really excited about. Now you gotta know that Alyssa and Lizbeth enjoy being excited! Especially when they are together. Well, that question really turned Alyssa on! I thought she'd never stop talking about it! You see, she is working on her master's degree and wants to move on to the doctorate. Lizbeth is proud of her.

In answer to the question about what she's excited about, Alyssa's eyes sparkled, and she said that she's been doing some research on women's studies.

"You know, Miss Elizabeth," she said, "I could jump out of bed every morning and get busy working on this project and never quit till bedtime every day of my life!"

They giggled and whirled each other around. Well, I have never seen such excitement from a student talking about a research project! The Extreme Teens have a song they sing. Maybe it's just a chant, but it goes like this:

Journey of the Heart | 273

I'm excited, I'm excited, I'm excited in the Lord.
I'm excited, I'm excited, I'm excited in the Lord.
I'm excited, I'm excited, I'm excited in the Lord!
When you walk with the Lord, you don't get bored.
Sing hallelujah! ! AMEN! (Clap clap!) (Yeah!)

They were talking about the first road trip Alyssa went on. It was to Cape Cod, Massachusetts. The vanload of young women (age –twelve to seventeen) sang most of the way. It was a good four-hour trip to the church where they were to put on the weekend services on prayer. Alyssa had never been on the road with the group before. In fact, I'm not sure that she had ever traveled without her parents. You see, she had been home-schooled all her life. Home was her world. But when she finally got to go on a road trip with other teens, she was so excited. I mean *so* excited. This was the time when they could use all the Scripture they had been studying. They talked about the blind man. He had been blind from birth. Then Jesus came along and blew people out of the water by creating eyes in a man who had never had them before! From this story the youth juiced the text. I went to sleep under the table while they were bringing out their insights, and when I woke, it was time to eat.

The time of their life for these kids was staying in the old New England bed and breakfast. Oh, there were so many rooms! I tried to herd them, but it was worse than herding squirrels! So I just stayed at Lizbeth's feet and watched.

Now, Debbie knows that Lizbeth gets up early in the morning to visit with God, so she said, "Miss Elizabeth, when you get up in the morning, will you wake me. I want to have my worship while you are."

About that time, I heard Alyssa say, "Well, don't wake me! I want to sleep in." I remember Lizbeth and I tiptoed down the dark hallway to the girls' room the next morning about the time the stars started to get drowsy. She whispered for Debbie and went on down to the eastern sitting room carrying the green-striped comforter.

Soon blurry-eyed Debbie came quietly with her Bible and stuck her feet under the comforter with Lizbeth. They didn't turn on any lights. They just sat silently and watched the sky brighten in the east.

It wasn't long till Alyssa groped her way into the dark sitting room. I thought it would be too brazen for a dog to ask to join them under the green-striped comforter, so I just stayed out of sight under the table. I could see the girls were wrapped in thought. Gradually, the sun rose above the water and began to waken the birds. Debbie drew a sharp breath, smiled, and looked at Miss Lizbeth. The three of them knew they had been in the presence of God!

But that was then. Now we are back on the highway again. Lizbeth is praying. "God, I know You love these kids more than I do. Keep them strong; keep them true to You. I'm asking that You fill their hearts with Your love and Your peace and guide their young lives safely into Your kingdom. Oh, God, I do so yearn for us all to be together on that second Sabbath under the fourteenth palm tree down on Silver Street! Do everything to make it happen!"

Summer Come-Softly

The lightning bugs were blinking over the summer hayfield when we pulled in for the night. It was warm, and we felt content.

You see, Summer Come-Softly is brother DeWitte's youngest daughter. Lizbeth hadn't seen her since she was age seven. There was a painful divorce … then silence. But Summer turned twenty-one this year. She wanted to know more about the other side of herself. Lizbeth knew we needed to take that extra day to visit her on her first job. They had corresponded for some time, but really they were strangers. I can imagine she wondered what to do with this aunt from the strange side of her family. But Lizbeth found her easy to laugh with, and even open up herself to her niece and let her know who she really is. I think Summer was relieved. We took a long walk along the country road so I could chase squirrels. I got into the burdocks, though, and Summer and Lizbeth took a long while, helping me get them out of my coat. I still wish I could take this coat off.

The visit was just overnight, but Lizbeth told me it contained one of the most precious moments. You see, Summer's aunt on her mother's side of the family was standing in front of us, telling her to be sure and get "all the family medical history," as if it were the only contact she would ever have with her father's side of the family! Lizbeth stopped her in mid-sentence—"No need to worry about all that. I'm not going to abandon her. She *belongs* to me! Summer is bone of my bone and flesh of my flesh." I was proud of Lizbeth for putting things in perspective!

Yes, the look on Summer's face, the look of belonging, of acceptance, significance, and security was what made the Journey of the Heart fulfilling to Lizbeth and me. And it was fulfilling to Summer Come-Softly, too!

Our Country's Michigan

As we neared Lizbeth's alma mater in Michigan, Andrews University, she began to talk to me about the long ago and far away. It was winter in

Michigan, almost Christmas. All was quiet in the women's residence hall. Lizbeth's shift on the night watch was from 1:00 a.m. to 4:00 a.m. The kids are all asleep. She stood in the semi-dark of the quiet lobby of the women's residence hall looking out the big picture window as the snow fell softly on the tall blue spruce adorned with Christmas lights. It stood tall there in front of the big brick building. It had been there for generations. She watched the snow rest quietly on each finger of the blue-green branches.

Snow falls silently. She held the memory in her heart. Memories like these bind her to the whole. ... Her country, my country, our home.

Cousin Martin

He is so alone now. His mom and dad are the Uncle Felix and Aunt Mary Lizbeth talks about so much. They have passed on now. The wife is estranged, the son is a grown man, the farm was auctioned off a few years ago. I know Lizbeth's heart is tender toward him. It wasn't till we got home that Martin came by to see Lizbeth and Brother DeWitte. Martin was on his own road trip alone across the country, and so was Dee and his friend. It was a heart-warming Sabbath. We had cornbread in memory of Aunt Mary and Uncle Felix, and then the next meal we had what they call "Mama Lu Roast" in memory of their mutual grandparents.

Martin was sick, though. Lizbeth put him to bed in the big puffy recliner, and then took some oil and rubbed his feet. I love her cousin Martin. He's the son of a Midwestern farmer, and I felt a kinship to him. When it was time to leave, I watched from under the table. They had a family hug. It's sort of like they are the only family Martin has now who love the God of his fathers.

Did they cry when they left? Well, from under the table, it looked like it.

Cousin Jana

It was a rainy Sabbath. Cousin Jana and Lizbeth lay on the bed there in Jana and Steve's home near where Lizbeth would come to work in the hayfield during the summer. Lizbeth read to her like she did when Jana was little. She read to her about the wonders of nature and human nature on the rocky coast of Maine —"Watching Spring Come."

Jana's motto is, "Joy is the reason of life." But when the winter storms hit, Lizbeth wants Jana to have a shelter under the wings of the Creator. However, on this rainy Sabbath afternoon at Steve and Jana's home in Missouri, they just relaxed together. It was a time of openness and a time when God surrounded them with the fragrance of His love from His own alabaster box.

Early in the morning, Lizbeth and I walked up the gravel road to the "old place" where Aunt Mary and Uncle Felix used to live. I ducked under the fence and found a squirrel to chase. What glee to run through the field. It felt good to be chasing something! I've been on that back seat a long time! As we walked east in the morning sunshine, Lizbeth told me about when she used to come to the farm in the summertime and work with Uncle Felix in the hayfield. She told me that after a day's work, she would jump on old "Doc" bareback and ride through the cooling evening amid the whippoorwills down the east road. Nobody but me knows about that. There, where nobody could see or hear her, she told me she would cry. She said it felt safe there, not like being cooped up in Los Angeles where there was no place was ever safe for a teenaged girl!

I liked it with Jana. She has a cat. He just looks at me like he would some foreign body! I laugh!

Follow Your Heart

We follow the interstate highway east again, through the busy cities, past the Adirondacks, and on into New England.

Springtime comes quietly to the little plot of earth near the shore of the great Atlantic Ocean. Lizbeth and I know where the spring beauties grow, and the lady slippers and the trillium. The earth is warm in the rays of the spring sunshine. Neighbors smile and wave.

Somehow, the Journey of the Heart seemed to pull things together again. You see, I am a Very Fine Dog, I am a herd dog. Lizbeth is like me. We want us all to be together. We felt the heartbeat of the people. We felt the heartbeat of America. Our hearts beat all together again. May all our journeys be a Journey of the Heart.

"Tip," Lizbeth spoke, "You're a herd dog. Surely, you must know the answer to the question that haunts me now. What's the action? What's my responsibility to these people who have touched my life once again? God has blessed me with such a precious flock, and the trip renewed our souls, but now what? I tend to be overwhelmed when I get on overload then I can't do *anything*! Then I remember, 'The safest path is to follow the heart.' That's what the whole trip was about this time, following the heart. I am at peace."

I put my head on her lap and looked up. She reached for the Kleenex.

Lizbeth spoke again, "It's time to go home, Tip. We'll go back to the Old New England Farmhouse now. We'll walk to the shore, and you can chase squirrels to your heart's content.

Linda-Lee will be there working with the apple trees. I'll bake some whole-wheat bread and take some to her. We'll sit in the spring sunshine and watch the tide come in, and the tide go out. We'll slather butter on the hot whole-wheat bread and eat Cortland applesauce from last fall. Tina and Katie will come by, and we'll walk along with them and tell them all about the Journey of the Heart.

"You know, Tip, I'm in love again. I'm in love with life. I'm not the same person anymore. I feel refreshed, renewed, and connected again." Our journey was truly a Journey of the Heart!

Lizbeth wraps her arms around Our Country, Our Own, Our Native Land, and falls asleep in her own bed as she listens to the honk of the geese through the open window of the Old New England Farmhouse. Home.

We invite you to view the complete
selection of titles we publish at:
www.TEACHServices.com

We encourage you to write us
with your thoughts about this,
or any other book we publish at:
info@TEACHServices.com

TEACH Services' titles may be purchased in
bulk quantities for educational, fund-raising,
business, or promotional use.
bulksales@TEACHServices.com

Finally, if you are interested in seeing
your own book in print, please contact us at:
publishing@TEACHServices.com

We are happy to review your manuscript at no charge.

www.ingramcontent.com/pod-product-compliance
Lightning Source LLC
Chambersburg PA
CBHW071146160426
43196CB00011B/2025